ENTERPRISE IRELAND

A Directory for Entrepreneurs and Small Business Owners

Oak Tree Press

Dublin

in association with

Dublin Business
Innovation Centre

Oak Tree Press
Merrion Building
Lower Merrion Street
Dublin 2, Ireland

© 1995 Oak Tree Press
Cover Design by Aileen Caffrey

A catalogue record of this book is
available from the British Library.

ISBN 1-872853-97-8

First edition published 1994
This revised and updated edition, 1995

Printed in Ireland by Colour Books Ltd.

CONTENTS

Subject Index xi

Foreword xxi

Introduction xxiii

How to Use this Book xxv

ACTION TALLAGHT 1

AIB BANK ENTERPRISE DEVELOPMENT BUREAU 3

AREA PARTNERSHIP COMPANIES 5

THE ARTS COUNCIL 9

BALLYMUN PARTNERSHIP 10

BANK OF IRELAND ENTERPRISE SUPPORT UNIT 12

BICs (BUSINESS INNOVATION CENTRES) 14

BOARDROOM CENTRE 17

BORD FÁILTE 18

BORD IASCAIGH MHARA 28

AN BORD TRÁCHTÁLA 31

BUREAU DE RAPPROCHEMENT DES ENTREPRISES 35

BUSINESS EXPANSION SCHEME 38

BUSINESS INCUBATION CENTRES 43

BUSINESS INFORMATION CENTRE 46

BUSINESS INNOVATION FUND 47

BUSINESS RESULTS LTD. 49

CATHAL BRUGHA RESEARCH AND DEVELOPMENT UNIT 50

CENTRAL STATISTICS OFFICE 52

CENTRE FOR CO-OPERATIVE STUDIES 54

CHAMBERS OF COMMERCE OF IRELAND 56

CHAPMAN FLOOD 57

CITY OF DUBLIN VOCATIONAL EDUCATION COMMITTEE 58

COMERFORD TECHNOLOGY MANAGEMENT LTD. 60

COMMUNITY ENTERPRISE PROGRAMME 62

COMMUNITY ENTERPRISE SOCIETY LTD. 65

CO-OPERATION NORTH 67

COOPERS & LYBRAND 68

COUNTY ENTERPRISE BOARDS 69

CRAFTS COUNCIL OF IRELAND 78

CREG ASSOCIATES 81

DEPARTMENT OF ENTERPRISE AND EMPLOYMENT 83

DESIGN DESK 88

DUBLIN CITY ENTERPRISE BOARD 90

DUBLIN INSTITUTE OF TECHNOLOGY 92

DUNDALK EMPLOYMENT PARTNERSHIP..95

EAMON DUNDON & ASSOCIATES 97

ENTERPRISE LINK 98

THE ENTERPRISE TRUST 99

ENVISION MARKETING CONSULTANTS..101

EOLAS, THE IRISH SCIENCE AND TECHNOLOGY AGENCY 103

ERNST & YOUNG 104

EUROPEAN COMMISSION 105

EUROPEAN INFORMATION CENTRES..113

EUROTECH CAPITAL 115

FARRELL GRANT SPARKS 118

FÁS, THE TRAINING AND EMPLOYMENT AUTHORITY 120

FÁS CO-OPERATIVE   DEVELOPMENT UNIT......................................136

FINGLAS BUSINESS INITIATIVE...142

FIONTAR..145

FIRST STEP...146

FOOD PRODUCT DEVELOPMENT CENTRE..149

FORBAIRT...150

FRIEL STAFFORD...168

GERMAN-IRISH CHAMBER OF INDUSTRY AND COMMERCE..............................169

GET TALLAGHT WORKING CO-OPERATIVE SOCIETY LTD...............................171

GREENFIELD CO-ORDINATORS LTD...175

GUARANTEED IRISH LTD...178

GUINNESS WORKERS EMPLOYMENT FUND LTD.......................................180

HACKETT & ASSOCIATES...181

HAYDEN BROWN...183

HOOD ASSOCIATES..184

ICC BANK...185

IDEAS FORUM..187

INDUSTRIAL DEVELOPMENT AUTHORITY...188

INDUSTRIAL LIAISON CO-ORDINATION GROUP.....................................189

THE INNOVATION CENTRE..190

INSTITUTE OF CERTIFIED PUBLIC ACCOUNTANTS IN IRELAND.......................192

INSTITUTE OF CHARTERED ACCOUNTANTS IN IRELAND..............................193

INTEGRATED RESOURCES DEVELOPMENT DUHALLOW..................................194

INTERNATIONAL FUND FOR IRELAND...198

IRISH BUSINESS AND EMPLOYERS' CONFEDERATION................................202

IRISH CRAFT AND GIFT EXHIBITORS..203

IRISH LEAGUE OF CREDIT UNIONS..204

IRISH MANAGEMENT INSTITUTE...206

IRISH PRODUCTIVITY CENTRE 208

IRISH QUALITY ASSOCIATION..211

IRISH SMALL AND MEDIUM ENTERPRISES ASSOCIATION....................213

IRISH TRADE UNION TRUST..215

KPMG STOKES KENNEDY CROWLEY 216

LEADER PROGRAMME 218

LIFFEY TRUST 219

LIMERICK CHAMBER OF COMMERCE 221

LIMERICK FOOD CENTRE...222

LOUTH COUNTY ENTERPRISE FUND 223

MADDEN CONSULTANTS LTD. 224

MARKETING CENTRE FOR SMALL BUSINESS 225

THE MARKETING INSTITUTE...227

MEITHEAL MHAIGH EO 228

MGM CONSULTANTS 230

MONAGHAN COUNTY ENTERPRISE FUND......................232

THE NATIONAL FOOD CENTRE 233

NATIONAL IRISH BANK LTD. 235

NATIONAL MICROELECTRONICS APPLICATION CENTRE 236

NATIONAL MICROELECTRONICS RESEARCH CENTRE 238

NATIONAL REHABILITATION BOARD..............................239

NEW OPPORTUNITIES FOR WOMEN 240

NORTHERN IRELAND BUSINESS CLUB 242

O'CONNOR, LEDDY & HOLMES 243

PEMBROKE CONSULTANTS 244

PLASSEY MANAGEMENT & TECHNOLOGY CENTRE 245

PLATO 247

POWERHOUSE 249

PRICE WATERHOUSE..250

PROJECT DEVELOPMENT CENTRE.......................................252

QUALITY ASSURANCE RESEARCH UNIT 254

REGIONAL TECHNICAL COLLEGE, GALWAY.......................255

REGISTRAR OF FRIENDLY SOCIETIES.................................257

REGISTRY OF BUSINESS NAMES 259

REVENUE COMMISSIONERS 261

SAINT PAUL'S AREA DEVELOPMENT ENTERPRISE LTD. 265

SHANNON DEVELOPMENT 266

SIMPSON XAVIER..281

SMALL FIRMS ASSOCIATION...283

SMURFIT JOB CREATION ENTERPRISE FUND 285

SOCIETY OF SAINT VINCENT DE PAUL...............................287

SOUTHSIDE UNION OF CARING COMMUNITY ENTERPRISE SOCIETY...288

STRATEGIC PROGRAMME FOR INNOVATION AND TECHNOLOGY
    TRANSFER (SPRINT) 289

TEAGASC...291

TIPPERARY SOUTH RIDING COUNTY ENTERPRISE BOARD 293

ÚDARÁS NA GAELTACHTA..296

ULSTER BANK..299

UNIVERSITY COLLEGE DUBLIN MARKETING DEVELOPMENT
    PROGRAMME 302

WATERFORD CITY ENTERPRISE BOARD 305

WATERFORD REGIONAL TECHNICAL COLLEGE....................306

WERKSAÂM IRELAND LTD. 308

WESTERN MANAGEMENT CENTRE 309

WEXFORD ORGANISATION FOR RURAL DEVELOPMENT.....................310

WOMEN'S LOCAL EMPLOYMENT INITIATIVES (LEI)............312

SUBJECT INDEX

Accounting/Tax/Financial Advice

Action Tallaght 1
AIB Bank Enterprise Development Bureau 3
Area Partnership Companies 5
Ballymun Partnership 10
Bank of Ireland Enterprise Support Unit 12
Business Incubation Centres 43
Business Results Ltd. 49
Chapman Flood 57
Comerford Technology Management Ltd. 60
Community Enterprise Programme 62
Community Enterprise Society Ltd. 65
Coopers & Lybrand 68
Crafts Council of Ireland 78
Dundalk Employment Partnership 95
Ernst & Young 104
European Commission 105
European Information Centres 113
Eurotech Capital 115
Farrell Grant Sparks 118
FÁS Co-operative Development Unit 136
Finglas Business Initiative 142
Friel Stafford 168

Get Tallaght Working Co-operative Society Ltd. .. 171
Greenfield Co-ordinators Ltd. 175
Hayden Brown 183
Institute of Certified Public Accountants in Ireland 192
Institute of Chartered Accountants in Ireland 193
Irish Small and Medium Enterprises Association 213
Irish Trade Union Trust 215
KPMG Stokes Kennedy Crowley 216
Liffey Trust 219
New Opportunities for Women 240
O'Connor, Leddy & Holmes . 243
Pembroke Consultants 244
Price Waterhouse 250
Project Development Centre 252
Revenue Commissioners 261
Shannon Development 266
Simpson Xavier 281
Small Firms Association 283
Western Management Centre 309

Business Planning/Consultancy

Action Tallaght 1
AIB Bank Enterprise
    Development Bureau 3
Area Partnership Companies 5
Ballymun Partnership 10
BICs (Business Innovation
    Centres) 14
Business Results Ltd. 49
Chapman Flood 57
City of Dublin Vocational
    Education Committee 58
Comerford Technology
    Management Ltd. 60
Community Enterprise
    Programme 62
Community Enterprise Society
    Ltd. 65
Coopers & Lybrand 68
County Enterprise Boards 69
Dublin City Enterprise Board
    90
Eamon Dundon & Associates
    97
Ernst & Young 104
Farrell Grant Sparks 118
FÁS Co-operative
    Development Unit 136
Finglas Business Initiative 142
Forbairt 150
Friel Stafford 168
Get Tallaght Working
    Co-operative Society Ltd.. 171

Greenfield Co-ordinators Ltd.
    175
Hackett & Associates 181
Hayden Brown 183
Innovation Centre, The 190
Institute of Certified Public
    Accountants in Ireland 192
Irish Productivity Centre 208
Irish Small and Medium
    Enterprises Association 213
Irish Trade Union Trust 215
Liffey Trust 219
Madden Consultants Ltd. 224
Marketing Centre for Small
    Business 225
Meitheal Mhaigh Eo 228
MGM Consultants 230
O'Connor, Leddy & Holmes
    243
Pembroke Consultants 244
Shannon Development 266
Simpson Xavier 281
Small Firms Association 283
Údarás na Gaeltachta 296
University College Dublin
    Marketing Development
    Programme 302
WerkSaâm Ireland Ltd. 308
Western Management Centre
    309
Women's Local Employment
    Initiatives (LEI) 312

Business Representation/Networking

Bureau de Rapprochement des
    Entreprises 35
Chambers of Commerce of
    Ireland 56
Co-operation North 67

German-Irish Chamber of
    Industry and Commerce ... 169
Irish Business and Employers'
    Confederation 202

Irish Craft and Gift Exhibitors
....203
Irish Small and Medium
    Enterprises Association 213
Limerick Chamber of
    Commerce 221
Northern Ireland Business Club
....242

Plato 247
Price Waterhouse 250
Small Firms Association 283
Women's Local Employment
    Initiatives (LEI) 312

Capital Grants

Arts Council, The 9
Bord Fáilte 18
Bord Iascaigh Mhara 28
Bord Tráchtála, An 31
Community Enterprise
    Programme 62
County Enterprise Boards 69
Dublin City Enterprise Board
....90
Dublin Institute of Technology
....92
European Commission 105
Eurotech Capital 115
FÁS, The Training and Employ-
    ment Authority 120
FÁS Co-operative
    Development Unit 136
First Step 146

Forbairt 150
International Fund for Ireland
....198
Irish League of Credit Unions
....204
Irish Productivity Centre 208
LEADER Programme 218
National Rehabilitation Board
....239
Shannon Development 266
Society of Saint Vincent
    de Paul 287
Údarás na Gaeltachta 296
Waterford City Enterprise
    Board 305
Women's Local Employment
    Initiatives (LEI) 312

Co-operatives

Centre for Co-operative Studies
....54
FÁS, The Training and Employ-
    ment Authority 120
FÁS Co-operative
    Development Unit 136
Get Tallaght Working
    Co-operative Society Ltd..171

Irish League of Credit Unions
....204
Irish Trade Union Trust 215
Registrar of Friendly Societies
....257
Registry of Business Names
....259

Employment Grants

County Enterprise Boards........69
Dublin City Enterprise Board
....90
FÁS, The Training and Employ-
    ment Authority 120
FÁS Co-operative
    Development Unit 136
Forbairt 150
Irish Productivity Centre........208

National Rehabilitation Board
   239
Shannon Development...........266
Tipperary South Riding
    County Enterprise Board ..293
Údarás na Gaeltachta.............296
Waterford City Enterprise
    Board 305

EU-Related Funding/Information on EU Funding

BICs (Business Innovation
    Centres) 14
Bord Fáilte 18
Bord Iascaigh Mhara 28
Bureau de Rapprochement des
    Entreprises..........................35
Central Statistics Office...........52
City of Dublin Vocational
    Education Committee.........58
Co-operation North..................67
County Enterprise Boards........69
Crafts Council of Ireland 78
Department of Enterprise and
    Employment 83
European Commission...........105
European Information Centres
   113
Eurotech Capital 115

Integrated Resources Develop-
    ment Duhallow 194
KPMG Stokes Kennedy
    Crowley 216
LEADER Programme.............218
New Opportunities for Women
   240
Project Development Centre
   252
Shannon Development...........266
Strategic Programme for
    Innovation and Technology
    Transfer (SPRINT)...........289
Údarás na Gaeltachta 296
Wexford Organisation for Rural
    Development 310
Women's Local Employment
    Initiatives (LEI) 312

Exporting

Bank of Ireland Enterprise
    Support Unit.......................12
Bord Tráchtála, An 31
German-Irish Chamber of
    Industry and Commerce ...169
Get Tallaght Working
    Co-operative Society Ltd..171

Irish Business and Employers'
    Confederation 202
Irish Craft and Gift Exhibitors
   203
Madden Consultants Ltd........224
Shannon Development...........266
Small Firms Association........283

Feasibility-Study Grants

Comerford Technology
  Management Ltd. 60
Community Enterprise
  Programme 62
County Enterprise Boards........69
Dublin City Enterprise Board
 90
FÁS, The Training and Employ-
  ment Authority 120

FÁS Co-operative
  Development Unit 136
Forbairt 150
Liffey Trust 219
Shannon Development..........266
Tipperary South Riding
  County Enterprise Board..293
Údarás na Gaeltachta.............296
Waterford City Enterprise Board
 305

Legal Advice/Advice on Legislation

Ballymun Partnership 10
Bord Tráchtála, An 31
Department of Enterprise and
  Employment 83
European Information Centres113

German-Irish Chamber of
  Industry and Commerce ...169
Irish Trade Union Trust 215
Small Firms Association........283
Údarás na Gaeltachta.............296

Loans/Finance/Information on Raising Finance

AIB Bank Enterprise
  Development Bureau.............3
Area Partnership Companies 5
Arts Council, The 9
Ballymun Partnership 10
Bank of Ireland Enterprise
  Support Unit 12
BICs (Business Innovation
  Centres) 14
Bord Fáilte.............................18
Bord Iascaigh Mhara 28
Bord Tráchtála, An 31
Business Expansion Scheme ...38
Business Innovation Fund........47
Chambers of Commerce of
  Ireland 56
Comerford Technology
  Management Ltd. 60
Coopers & Lybrand.................68

County Enterprise Boards........69
Dundalk Employment
  Partnership.........................95
Enterprise Link 98
Enterprise Trust, The 99
Ernst & Young 104
European Commission...........105
Eurotech Capital 115
FÁS, The Training and Employ-
  ment Authority 120
FÁS Co-operative
  Development Unit 136
Finglas Business Initiative.....142
First Step...............................146
Forbairt 150
Friel Stafford..........................168
Get Tallaght Working
  Co-operative Society Ltd..171

Guinness Workers Employment
  Fund Ltd. 180
Hayden Brown......................183
ICC Bank..............................185
Industrial Liaison Co-ordination
  Group 189
Innovation Centre, The 190
Institute of Certified Public
  Accountants in Ireland 192
Institute of Chartered
  Accountants in Ireland 193
International Fund for Ireland
 198
Irish League of Credit Unions
 204
Irish Productivity Centre........208
Irish Trade Union Trust 215
KPMG Stokes Kennedy
  Crowley...........................216

LEADER Programme............218
Liffey Trust 219
Louth County Enterprise Fund
 223
Meitheal Mhaigh Eo 228
Monaghan County Enterprise
  Fund..................................232
National Irish Bank Ltd. 235
Price Waterhouse 250
Shannon Development...........266
Small Firms Association........283
Smurfit Job Creation Enterprise
  Fund..................................285
Southside Union of Caring
  Community Enterprise
  Society..............................288
Ulster Bank 299
Women's Local Employment
  Initiatives (LEI) 312

Local Enterprise/Community Development

Action Tallaght 1
Ballymun Partnership 10
Business Results Ltd...............49
Community Enterprise
  Programme.........................62
Community Enterprise Society
  Ltd. 65
County Enterprise Boards........69
Dublin City Enterprise Board
 90
Dundalk Employment
  Partnership.........................95
FÁS, The Training and Employ-
  ment Authority 120
FÁS Co-operative
  Development Unit.............136
Finglas Business Initiative.....142
Forbairt 150
Get Tallaght Working
  Co-operative Society Ltd..171

Greenfield Co-ordinators Ltd.
 175
Integrated Resources Develop-
  ment Duhallow 194
Louth County Enterprise Fund
 223
Meitheal Mhaigh Eo 228
Monaghan County Enterprise
  Fund..................................232
Saint Paul's Area Development
  Enterprise Ltd. 265
Shannon Development...........266
Society of Saint Vincent de Paul
 287
Southside Union of Caring
  Community Enterprise
  Society..............................288
Tipperary South Riding County
  Enterprise Board...............293
Údarás na Gaeltachta 296

Waterford City Enterprise
  Board 305
Western Management Centre
  309

Wexford Organisation for
  Rural Development 310

Marketing/Selling Advice/Assistance

Action Tallaght 1
AIB Bank Enterprise Develop-
  ment Bureau 3
Area Partnership Companies 5
BICs (Business Innovation
  Centres) 14
Bord Tráchtála, An 31
Business Results Ltd. 49
Cathal Brugha Research and
  Development Unit 50
Co-operation North 67
Creg Associates 81
Design Desk 88
Eamon Dundon & Associates
  97
Envision Marketing
  Consultants 101
European Commission 105
Friel Stafford 168
German-Irish Chamber of
  Industry and Commerce ... 169
Get Tallaght Working
  Co-operative Society Ltd.. 171
Greenfield Co-ordinators Ltd.
  175
Guaranteed Irish Ltd. 178
Hackett & Associates 181

Integrated Resources Develop-
  ment Duhallow 194
International Fund for Ireland
  198
Irish Business and Employers'
  Confederation 202
Irish Craft and Gift Exhibitors
  203
Irish Management Institute 206
Limerick Chamber of
  Commerce 221
Madden Consultants Ltd. 224
Marketing Centre for Small
  Business 225
Marketing Institute, The 227
MGM Consultants 230
National Food Centre, The 233
Project Development Centre
  252
Shannon Development 266
Simpson Xavier 281
University College Dublin
  Marketing Development
  Programme 302
Western Management Centre
  309

Mentor Programmes

AIB Bank Enterprise Develop-
  ment Bureau 3
Area Partnership Companies 5
Finglas Business Initiative 142
First Step 146
Forbairt 150

Greenfield Co-ordinators Ltd.
  175
Project Development Centre
  252
Shannon Development 266

Premises/Administration

Action Tallaght..........................1

Area Partnership Companies.....5

Ballymun Partnership..............10

BICs (Business Innovation
    Centres)..............................14

Bord Tráchtála, An..................31

Business Incubation Centres....43

Chambers of Commerce of
    Ireland.................................56

Community Enterprise Society
    Ltd. 65

Forbairt...................................150

Get Tallaght Working
    Co-operative Society Ltd..171

Innovation Centre, The..........190

International Fund for Ireland
   198

Liffey Trust............................219

Limerick Food Centre...........222

Monaghan County Enterprise
    Fund..................................232

Powerhouse............................249

Saint Paul's Area Development
    Enterprise Ltd...................265

Shannon Development...........266

Society of Saint Vincent
    de Paul..............................287

Quality Programmes/Advice on Quality Standards

Cathal Brugha Research and
    Development Unit...............50

Department of Enterprise and
    Employment........................83

Eamon Dundon & Associates
   97

Ernst & Young.......................104

FÁS, The Training and Employ-
    ment Authority.................120

Food Product Development
    Centre...............................149

Irish Quality Association.......211

National Food Centre, The 233

National Irish Bank Ltd. 235

Quality Assurance Research
    Unit..................................254

Teagasc 291

Rent-Subsidy Grants

Area Partnership Companies.....5

Shannon Development...........266

Údarás na Gaeltachta.............296

Research and Development

Bord Tráchtála, An..................31

Business Expansion Scheme ...38

Cathal Brugha Research and
    Development Unit...............50

Centre for Co-operative Studies
   54

Comerford Technology
    Management Ltd. 60

Creg Associates.......................81

Department of Enterprise and
    Employment........................83

Dublin Institute of Technology
   92

Food Product Development
Centre 149
Forbairt 150
Hood Associates 184
Ideas Forum 187
Industrial Liaison Co-ordination
Group 189
Innovation Centre, The 190
International Fund for Ireland
....198
Limerick Food Centre 222
National Food Centre, The 233

National Microelectronics
Application Centre 236
National Microelectronics
Research Centre 238
Plassey Management &
Technology Centre 245
Regional Technical College,
Galway 255
Shannon Development 266
Teagasc 291
Údarás na Gaeltachta 296

Start Your Own Business / Enterprise Development Courses

Ballymun Partnership 10
Business Information Centre
....46
City of Dublin Vocational
Education Committee 58
FÁS, The Training and Employ-
ment Authority 120
Forbairt 150

Plassey Management &
Technology Centre 245
Project Development Centre
....252
Regional Technical College,
Galway 255
Shannon Development 266
Waterford Regional Technical
College 306

State Bodies

Bord Fáilte 18
Bord Iascaigh Mhara 28
Bord Tráchtála, An 31
County Enterprise Boards 69
Department of Enterprise and
Employment 83

FÁS, The Training and Employ-
ment Authority 120
FÁS Co-operative
Development Unit 136
Forbairt 150
Shannon Development 266

Training

Area Partnership Companies 5
BICs (Business Innovation
Centres) 14
Cathal Brugha Research and
Development Unit 50
Centre for Co-operative
Studies 54

City of Dublin Vocational
Education Committee 58
Community Enterprise
Programme 62
Crafts Council of Ireland 78
Creg Associates 81

Enterprise Ireland

Department of Enterprise and
Employment 83
Dublin Institute of Technology
....92
FÁS, The Training and Employ-
ment Authority 120
FÁS Co-operative
Development Unit.............136
Finglas Business Initiative.....142
Fiontar.....................................145
Get Tallaght Working
Co-operative Society Ltd..171
Greenfield Co-ordinators Ltd.
....175
Innovation Centre, The..........190
Integrated Resources Develop-
ment Duhallow..................194
Irish Business and Employers'
Confederation...................202
Irish Management Institute....206
KPMG Stokes Kennedy
Crowley.............................216
Madden Consultants Ltd........224
Marketing Centre for Small
Business.............................225

National Food Centre, The 233
National Microelectronics
Research Centre................238
New Opportunities for Women
....240
Plassey Management &
Technology Centre...........245
Plato.......................................247
Project Development Centre
....252
Regional Technical College,
Galway 255
Shannon Development...........266
Small Firms Association........283
Teagasc 291
Údarás na Gaeltachta.............296
Waterford Regional Technical
College 306
WerkSaâm Ireland Ltd. 308
Western Management Centre
....309
Women's Local Employment
Initiatives (LEI) 312

Women in Business

FÁS, The Training and
Employment Authority.....120
New Opportunities for Women
....240

Women's Local Employment
Initiatives (LEI) 312

FOREWORD

The Board of the Dublin Business Innovation Centre (Dublin BIC) is delighted to be associated with the publication and sponsorship of the second edition of *Enterprise Ireland* and has no hesitation in recommending it to all involved in enterprise development — whether directly as small business owners or would-be entrepreneurs, or indirectly as advisers and consultants.

Accurate, timely and relevant information is increasingly the distinguishing characteristic of successful start-ups. *Enterprise Ireland* contains a wealth of information about the many agencies — both public and private — that assist, advise and nurture the small business owner through to ultimate viability. It is hard to see how any business can operate without recourse to *Enterprise Ireland*. The inclusion of case studies in some of the entries is particularly valuable in guiding the entrepreneur in targeting his or her approach for assistance.

Dublin BIC is part of a network of Business Innovation Centres, operating not just in Ireland, but also throughout Europe. Indeed, Dublin BIC's Chief Executive, Desmond Fahey, is currently Chairman of EBN, the network co-ordinator for the 100 EU-approved Business Innovation Centres spread across Europe. Dublin BIC provides counselling and assistance and access to seed capital for selected start-up enterprises. Dublin BIC also provides business development counselling and assistance to SME support agencies and organisations.

I congratulate Oak Tree Press on its commitment to enterprise publishing in Ireland and, on behalf of the Board, I wish *Enterprise Ireland* and you, the reader, every success.

Anthony M. Prendergast
Chairman, Dublin BIC

INTRODUCTION

My first book, *Starting a Business in Ireland* (Oak Tree Press, 2nd edition, 1995), was born out of the frustration I experienced in the early stages of setting up my own business. It covers, step-by-step, what the would-be entrepreneur needs to do to develop his or her idea into a viable business. One chapter — by coincidence, the longest in the book — provides an introduction to the sources of assistance available to the entrepreneur. In researching the chapter, I found (i) that there were many more organisations able and willing to help entrepreneurs and small business owners than I had expected (and too many to include all of them in *Starting a Business in Ireland*), and (ii) that few entrepreneurs or small business owners were aware of even a fraction of the range of assistance available. *Starting a Business* went to the printers with an outline of the major sources of assistance and some examples of specific, less well-known, sources. But more information was clearly needed.

Karen McGrath, whose research provided the basis for Chapter 3 of *Starting a Business in Ireland*, undertook further research and collected data on over 140 organisations, both in the state and private sector, that provided assistance of one kind or another — by way of grants, loans, advice or whatever — to entrepreneurs and small business owners. That research was published in directory form as *Enterprise Ireland* in 1994.

This second edition of *Enterprise Ireland* updates and expands on Karen's original research. It now includes some 128 organisations, all of which have something to offer the entrepreneur.

Though it is gratifying to see the upsurge in enterprise and increasing recognition of the importance of enterprise development in Ireland in recent years, many entrepreneurs still find it difficult to navigate their way through the maze of agencies, organisations, schemes and initiatives that are launched, relaunched, revised, renamed or amended. The Department of Enterprise and Employment's initiative, Enterprise Link, operated by Forbairt, which provides a referral service to other agencies and organisations, is thus to be welcomed as a step that was long overdue.

The Enterprise series of books is Oak Tree Press's contribution to enterprise development in Ireland — one that has been positively received, judging by both press comment and sales figures. *Enterprise Ireland*, as a comprehensive directory of sources of assistance, is central to the series. We are grateful therefore for financial assistance from the Dublin Business Innovation Centre for this second edition of *Enterprise Ireland*, which has allowed us both to update the directory and to reduce the price — to £9.99, to bring it within reach of a wider audience.

I hope that you find *Enterprise Ireland* of use to you, whether in sourcing advice or assistance for your own business or for your clients. Please feel free to contact Oak Tree Press with your comments for improvements in the directory.

Brian O'Kane
June 1995

HOW TO USE THIS BOOK

The primary aim of this directory is to highlight the many sources of assistance available to start-up and small/medium-sized enterprises in Ireland.

For convenience, the directory is arranged alphabetically by organisation, with a contact name, address, telephone and fax number for each, where possible. Each entry summarises the assistance provided by the organisation, describes how entrepreneurs can avail of the assistance, details the conditions that must be met and, where they have been made available to us, includes a case study. Where an organisation has links with other organisations listed in the directory, these are shown under the heading "See Also". The information has been checked before publication with the organisations listed but, of course, is subject to change. Contact the organisations direct for the most up-to-date position.

A Subject Index appears at the start of the directory, so that readers searching for a specific form of assistance — Rent Subsidies or Employment Grants, for example — can quickly identify the providers.

ACTION TALLAGHT

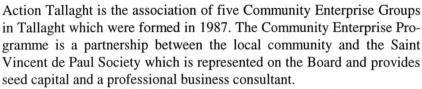

West Tallaght Enterprise Centre
Old Church, Killinarden, Tallaght, Dublin 24
Tel: (01) 459 6110, Fax: (01) 459 6114
Contact: Willie Rigney

Action Tallaght is the association of five Community Enterprise Groups in Tallaght which were formed in 1987. The Community Enterprise Programme is a partnership between the local community and the Saint Vincent de Paul Society which is represented on the Board and provides seed capital and a professional business consultant.

Action Tallaght provides integrated support services for people from Tallaght who intend to establish a business or enter self-employment — including sales and marketing advice, business consultancy/counselling, accountancy, financial management, feasibility studies, business plans and funding applications. Action Tallaght also provides workspace units and central secretarial services for start-up businesses.

Other programmes operated by Action Tallaght include:

- A community/worker co-operative development programme

- Home-ownership co-operatives

- A targeted job-placement programme (including CV preparation, career guidance, etc.)

- Community-employment schemes

- Environmental-improvement schemes.

Future developments envisaged by Action Tallaght include:

- Establishing links with similar community groups in the UK, Europe and the USA and creating a network for innovative venture and technology transfer

- An innovations/inventions development unit

- Programmes to develop an enterprise culture amongst communities.

Action Tallaght directs four community enterprise centres and one business technology centre.

OTHER ADDRESSES

Brookfield Enterprise Group
Enterprise Centre
30 Glenshane Grove
Brookfield, Tallaght, Dublin 24
Tel: (01) 452 3288
Contact: Tony Brennan

Jobstown Enterprise Group
Enterprise Centre
127 Drumcarra Avenue
Jobstown, Tallaght, Dublin 24
Tel: (01) 452 3447
Contact: Susan Deegan

Killinarden Enterprise Group
Enterprise Centre
80 Killinarden Heights
Tallaght, Dublin 24
Tel: (01) 452 6098, Fax: 452 6441
Contact: Olive Whelan

Kilnamanagh Enterprise Groups
Enterprise Centre, The Presbytery
Kilnamanagh, Tallaght, Dublin 24
Tel: (01) 459 9341
Contact: Michael O'Flaherty

Tymon Enterprise Group
St Engus Presbytery
Tymon, Tallaght, Dublin 24
Tel: (01) 451 5370/459 9341
Contact: Deirdre Sweeney

SEE ALSO: SOCIETY OF SAINT VINCENT DE PAUL

AIB BANK ENTERPRISE DEVELOPMENT BUREAU

Bankcentre, Ballsbridge, Dublin 4
Tel: (01) 660 0311, Fax: (01) 668 2009
Contact: John Kelly/Tom Branigan/Dave Roberts

The AIB Bank Enterprise Development Bureau is AIB Bank's focal point for start-up and expanding businesses, both in manufacturing and service industries. It administers AIB Bank's Enterprise Loan Scheme which was increased from IR£20 million to IR£40 million in 1994. The scheme is aimed at export-oriented and import substitution businesses with significant job-retention or creation prospects. The AIB fund does not exclude service-sector industries and welcomes tourism-related projects.

The Bureau meets with members of the business community and provides help and assistance on a wide range of issues pertaining to small businesses. It can also assist business development by providing advice and counselling on business matters and through arranging interviews with local AIB branch management to discuss lending proposals. However, AIB's approach to small business is decentralised to the branch management teams, hence the branch manager has the key input into all crucial decisions.

In 1992 AIB Bank announced the creation of an Enterprise Loan Scheme as a supplemental form of finance for small businesses. The details of the scheme are as follows:

- Any entrepreneur engaged in manufacturing or service industries may apply

- The amount lent ranges from £10,000 upwards

- The loan requirement remains flexible for up to 10 years and includes a moratorium on capital repayment up to two years

- Interest rates are standard "AA" rates

- For security, mortgages are accepted on business or non-personal assets only.

Applications for the Enterprise Loan Scheme are welcome from all forms of trading entities including sole traders, limited companies, partnerships and individuals. For a loan to be considered for the scheme, projects submitted must have job creation prospects and must be export-oriented or facilitate import substitution. This form of assistance is available to new and existing AIB customers.

Interested individuals should contact their local branch for an initial consultation or call the Enterprise Development Bureau directly. AIB Bank insists on the availability of a well-structured business plan as part of the overall submission. To assist in the preparation of the business plan, AIB will make available a free copy of "Services for Small Business" which contains helpful information on business planning.

AIB has also introduced the Business Credit Line, an additional working capital facility to supplement the existing product range for business and farming customers. The working capital is provided at a discount of 2 per cent on standard AA interest rates.

AIB initiated a series of workshops entitled "Essentials for Success" for groups of local entrepreneurs throughout the country. The workshops are run with the aim of improving core management skills in owner-driven enterprises. The workshops provide essential guidelines on finance, human resource management, marketing and key business success factors. Practical ideas are exchanged between participants on all aspects of starting and running a small business. The seminar includes hand-out material for future reference. Another 40 seminars are planned for 1995 at various national locations. (For details, contact your Local AIB Branch or Enterprise Development Bureau, AIB Bankcentre, Ballsbridge, Dublin 4.)

Through the Enterprise Development Bureau, AIB Bank sponsors the Forbairt Mentor Programme. AIB assistance is specifically for the mentor "start-up panel", which enables AIB customers to access the Forbairt Programme without having to undergo additional Forbairt screening. Further details of the scheme may be obtained from any AIB branch, or direct from the Enterprise Development Bureau.

If assistance is required in relation to any banking matter the Bureau provides a "Help Desk" which may be contacted for guidance. For telephone and fax details, see above.

AREA PARTNERSHIP COMPANIES

Area Development Management Ltd.
Hollbrook House, Holles Street, Dublin 2
Tel: (01) 661 3611, Fax: (01) 661 0411
Contact: Dr Tony Crooks

The Area Partnership Companies (APCs) were set up under the Programme for Economic and Social Progress (PESP). In 1991, 12 areas of high unemployment were selected as the locations for pilot partnerships as an area-based response to long-term unemployment. In 1994 the Government designated a further 21 disadvantaged areas for the establishment of Area Partnership Companies. The APCs are funded under the Operational Programme for Local Urban and Rural Development 1994–1999, through a global grant managed by an intermediary company, Area Development Management Ltd.

One of the main aims of the Area Partnership Companies is to work at local level to generate more jobs through sustainable enterprises and through the promotion of local economic projects and initiatives. Each Partnership, is autonomous and agrees different work practices. Each Partnership Company works on a Land Development Plan for its own region. Practical measures are taken to discriminate in favour of the long-term unemployed and those who are socially excluded. Each company provides support for unemployed people who are setting up their own business. This is done mainly through the following enterprise activities:

- Financial support for enterprise creation including non-repayable grants, interest subsidies, loan guarantees, small-scale investment and joint ventures

- Support for the development of business plans and business ideas

- Mentoring system, including the provision of sources of advice

- Provision of workspace, including help in obtaining enterprise incubation units

- Rent subsidies

- Marketing, including the identification of gaps in the market

- Training and education in enterprise with the support of FÁS.

Note: Partnerships are open for all activities which will encourage enterprise. There is variety in what each Partnership offers, and entrepreneurs should contact the relevant Partnership Company in their area.

Area Allowance (Enterprise)

The Area Allowance (Enterprise) is paid to people who live in the Partnership area, have been unemployed for 6 months or more and have been signing the Live Register, and who have a suitable enterprise/business project within the Partnership area. The project must be one that does not displace existing enterprises/businesses, and must be approved by the APC. When approved, applicants will receive an allowance equivalent to their full unemployment payment, and will receive any secondary benefits to which they were entitled while in receipt of the unemployment payment. This will continue for 12 months after which the applicant may be entitled for a further two years to the Back to Work Allowance operated by the Department of Social Welfare. Application is made directly to the local APC.

Enterprise Officers

Many Partnerships have a number of staff whose role is to provide a range of back-up, advisory and support services to small start-up businesses. The emphasis in such support is on the following:

- Tying the entrepreneur into a mentoring network

- Financial assistance

- Advising on business plans etc.

The addresses of the existing 12 APCs are given below.

AREA PARTNERSHIP COMPANIES:

Ballymun Partnership
43 Sillogue Road, Ballymun, Dublin 11
Tel: (01) 842 3612, Fax: (01) 842 7004
Contact: Michael Cowman

Cresp-Southwest Kerry Partnership
Community Office
Forbairt Industrial Estate
Caherciveen, Co. Kerry
Tel: (066) 72724, Fax: (066) 72725
Contact: Bill Thorne

Dublin Inner City Partnership
Equity House
Upper Ormond Quay, Dublin 7
Tel: (01) 872 1321, Fax: (01) 872 1330
Contact: David Connolly

Dundalk Employment Partnership Ltd.
Carlton House, Dublin Street, Dundalk
Tel: (042) 30288, Fax: (042) 30552
Contact: John Butler

Finglas Partnership
Rosehill House, Finglas, Dublin 11
Tel: (01) 836 1111, Fax: (01) 836 2104
Contact: Michael P. Bowe

Meitheal Mhaigh Eo
Lower Main Street, Foxford, Co. Mayo
Tel: (094) 56745, Fax: (094) 56749
Contact: Justin Sammon

North Lee Development Ltd.
Sunbeam Industries, Mallow Road, Cork
Tel: (021) 302 310, Fax: (021) 302 081
Contact: Tim O'Flynn, The Northside Partnership

Bonnybrook Activity Centre
Bunratty Drive, Coolock, Dublin 17
Tel: (01) 848 5630, Fax: (01) 848 5661
Contact: Marian Vickers

PAUL Partnership Limerick
Unit 25, The Tait Centre
Dominic Street, Limerick
Tel: (061) 419 388, Fax: (061) 418 098
Contact: Neil Walker

South West Wexford Partnership Ltd.
Campile, Wexford
Tel: (051) 88348, Fax: (051) 88347
Contact: Mary Lou O'Kennedy

Tallaght Partnership
Unit 312, Level 3, The Square
Tallaght, Dublin 24
Tel: (01) 459 7990, Fax: (01) 459 7991
Contact: Anna Lee

West Waterford Development Partnership Ltd.
c/o Teagasc Office, Lismore, Co. Waterford
Tel: (058) 54646, Fax: (058) 54126
Contact: James Taaffe

SEE ALSO: BALLYMUN PARTNERSHIP
               DUNDALK EMPLOYMENT PARTNERSHIP
               THE ENTERPRISE TRUST
               FÁS, THE TRAINING AND EMPLOYMENT
                   AUTHORITY
               FINGLAS BUSINESS INITIATIVE
               GET TALLAGHT WORKING CO-OPERATIVE
                   SOCIETY LTD.
               MEITHEAL MHAIGH EO
               PLATO

THE ARTS COUNCIL

70 Merrion Square, Dublin 2
Tel: (01) 661 1840, Fax: (01) 676 1302
Contact: Laurence Cassidy

The Arts Council assists publishing houses with block grants, where part or all of the production of the individual publishing house is concerned with contemporary literary work. Approximately 15 publishers are assisted in this way. The Arts Council offers grants of up to £50,000 and loans of up to £30,000 in the cases of its largest recipients. Some publishing houses may receive grants and loans simultaneously.

In so far as one can consider arts organisations as being small enterprises, the Arts Council grant-aids over 200 such client-partners per annum. Arts organisations or publishing houses applying to the Arts Council for funding must supply an income and expenditure budget with detailed breakdown of 100 per cent of their financial plans and a clear demonstration of the cultural aspect of the enterprise. It is essential that applicants give a verbal explanation of their projects or their company's business plan.

BALLYMUN PARTNERSHIP

North Mall
Ballymun Town Centre
Ballymun, Dublin 11
Tel: (01) 842 3612 / 842 3277, Fax: (01) 842 7004
Contact: Terence Kavanagh

The Ballymun Partnership Ltd. works closely with the Ballymun Job Centre to provide a range of services to small businesses. It provides the entrepreneur with free business consultancy on all aspects of business start-up: sources of finance and grants; assistance with projections and business plans; advice on taxation and legal aspects of business; advice on setting up management accounts, budgets and cash flows and assessment of business ideas. It will organise ongoing business support for those who have started in business. It also runs free "Start Your Own Business" courses, on a user-demand basis — depending on numbers. (Details of these courses can be obtained from the Job Centre and the Ballymun Partnership at the above address.)

These services are provided through an informal business-advisory clinic. Consultancy services are also provided for projects that require them. The only precondition for support is a commitment on the part of the Ballymun individual(s) to starting their business.

Also offered to entrepreneurs are:

- Area Allowance Enterprise. This scheme allows a person to keep their Social Welfare payments plus their secondary benefits for at least the first year's trading.

- Loans — and in some special cases, grants — for the following:

  — Market research and training

  — Business registration and start-up costs.

- A monitoring and consultancy service.

- It is planned to provide workspace/incubator units this year.

SEE ALSO: AREA PARTNERSHIP COMPANIES
DUNDALK EMPLOYMENT PARTNERSHIP
THE ENTERPRISE TRUST
FÁS, THE TRAINING AND EMPLOYMENT
    AUTHORITY
FINGLAS BUSINESS INITIATIVE
GET TALLAGHT WORKING CO-OPERATIVE
    SOCIETY LTD.
MEITHEAL MHAIGH EO
PLATO

BANK OF IRELAND ENTERPRISE SUPPORT UNIT

Head Office, Lower Baggot Street, Dublin 2
Tel: (01) 661 5933, Fax: (01) 676 3493
Contact: Barry McNamara, Michael Gannon, Tom Meally,
Larry Burke or Clare Shine.

Enterprise Support Unit was established in 1989 to provide finance and support to new and developing businesses. It has a £50 million fund available to support projects throughout the country. To date 265 Irish companies have benefited from their support. These businesses have been allocated £16 million which helped to create over 3,200 jobs.

Who Can Apply?

Enterprise Support Unit supports projects across the productive commercial sectors including:

- Import substitution

- Export potential

- Internationally-traded services

- Value-added tourism

- Food and agricultural projects

- Service projects with new or niche markets.

The objective of the Unit is to identify start-up or developing businesses with a distinct competitive advantage which can demonstrate viability and have the capacity to create new jobs.

Features of the Fund

- Hands-on support

- No personal guarantees required

- Full range of lending products

- Experienced business specialists

- AA lending rate

- Information and advice on starting your own business

- Normal lending range £20,000–£150,000.

What the Enterprise Support Unit Provides

The Enterprise Support Unit provides short- and medium-term working capital and works closely with the business to assist in providing the right financial package to allow the company to develop and grow. The new business will also receive advice and help from staff who understand small businesses. All loans are accompanied by a comprehensive free financial advisory service. The staff of the Enterprise Support Unit will familiarise themselves with every aspect of the business and will remain in close contact.

The Enterprise Support Unit Commitment

Bank of Ireland's Enterprise Support Unit is committed to addressing the specific and sometimes complicated needs of small- and medium-sized businesses in the most professional and personal manner.

SEE ALSO: FIRST STEP

BICs
BUSINESS INNOVATION CENTRES

The Tower, IDA Enterprise Centre
Pearse Street, Dublin 2
Tel: (01) 671 3111, Fax: (01) 671 3330
Contact: John McInerney/Desmond Ryan

There are five BICs (Business Innovation Centres) in Ireland (including one in Northern Ireland) which have been partly funded by the EU. They are in Dublin, Cork, Galway, Limerick and Derry.

BICs are private limited not-for-profit companies with their own boards of directors, nominated by the private and public sectors. They operate as autonomous entities, receiving part of their funding through the government and the EU, under the EU-co-financed Operational Programme for Industry. Specific help on market research, access to funding and seed capital is provided by BICs for business start-ups.

They will evaluate and select entrepreneurs and projects in order to identify those that are viable. Guidance is provided in the drawing-up of a business plan. A BIC will assist in the search for or will provide offices or incubation premises and shared services (secretariat, tele-communication, audiovisual equipment, etc.) for SMEs. It will also provide access to sources of seed and early-stage venture capital. The Irish BICs formed and launched the first ever Seed Capital Fund in Ireland which opened for business in January 1992 as the Business Innovation Fund (BIF). This Business Innovation Fund operates as an independent organisation. The BICs hold a seat on the BIF Board to reflect their equity interest in this Business Innovation Fund (see also Business Innovation Fund p. 47,). Ongoing assistance is given to projects during their early development phases. There may be a small charge for these services, including a percentage fee where a BIC finds equity capital for a business.

BIC services include the provision of advice and consultancy assistance, as well as practical support for entrepreneurs wishing to start a business or to develop the potential of their existing small business.

Each of the Irish BICs is an independent institution specialising in a different area, yet together they form part of the 200 European Business

Network (EBN) specialising in entrepreneurial development and training. The EBN is used as a cost-effective mechanism, particularly for sourcing, valuable market/product information, technology and buyers in other European regions. The sectors in which BICs specialise are typical of those within their operating regions and include agriculture, aquaculture, tourism, manufacturing, international services including TV and film production, multi-media, animation and the food sector. BICs make business development services available to those with emerging innovative ideas within their regions. These services include:

- Promotion of entrepreneurship and detection of innovative projects

- Evaluation and selection of viable entrepreneurs and projects through feasibility studies

- Development of entrepreneurial and managerial skills through the Entrepreneurial Skills Development Programme

- Formulation of business plans

- Innovation and technology assistance

- Marketing assistance

- Access to finance (the four Irish BICs were instrumental in establishing the National Seed Capital Fund)

- Provision of avenues to a network of regional, national and international experts

- Assistance in the establishment of new SMEs

- Project monitoring in post-launch stage.

ADDRESSES

Dublin Business Innovation Centre
The Tower, IDA Enterprise Centre
Pearse Street, Dublin 2
Tel: (01) 671 3111, Fax: (01) 671 3330
Contact: John McInerney/Desmond Ryan

Business Innovation Centre
South West Business and Technology Centre
Enterprise Centre, North Mall, Cork
Tel: (021) 397 711, Fax: (021) 395 393
Contact: Michael O'Connor

Galway Business Innovation Centre
Hardiman House, 5 Eyre Square, Galway
Tel: (091) 567 974/5/6, Fax: (091) 567 980
Contact: Mary Ryan/Joe Greaney

Business Innovation Centre
Shannon Development
The Innovation Centre, Enterprise House
Plassey Technological Park, Limerick
Tel: (061) 338177, Fax: (061) 338065
Contact: Alice Morgan

Business Innovation Centre
Innovation Centre Noribic
Springgrowth House, Balliniska Road
Springtown Industrial Estate, Derry
Tel: (08) (01504) 264 242, Fax: (08) (01504) 269 025

SEE ALSO: BUSINESS INNOVATION FUND
                 EUROPEAN INFORMATION CENTRES

BOARDROOM CENTRE

National Management Centre
Sandyford Road, Dublin 16
Tel: (01) 295 6911, Fax: (01) 295 5150
Contact: Pat Mullally

The Boardroom Centre was set up to make companies aware of the benefits that independent non-executive directors can bring to both large and small company boards. The Centre, which is sponsored by a number of major institutions, both public and private, is a non-profit-making organisation. It also maintains an updated register of people suitable to act as prospective non-executive directors.

Companies can avail of the Boardroom Centre's services by phoning or by writing to the above address. No preconditions need to be met prior to the setting up of an interview.

BORD FÁILTE

Baggot Street Bridge, Dublin 2
Tel: (01) 676 5871, Fax: (01) 676 4764
Contact: Jim McGuigan

Tourism Development Incentives

Bord Fáilte is responsible for administering a range of incentives for the development of tourism. Full details and application forms can be obtained from the Investment and Product Development Department of Bord Fáilte, or at any of the head offices of the regional tourism organisations.

Operational Programme for Tourism 1994–1999

The £652 million Operational Programme for Tourism 1994–1999, launched in September 1994 by the Minister for Tourism and Trade, is the latest phase in the strategic development of this vital sector by the Irish government and the industry itself. It has the support of the European Union under the aegis of its European Regional Development Fund and the European Social Fund.

The programme represents an unprecedented commitment to the future of the industry and is geared to meet the following targets:

- 35,000 new jobs by the end of the decade

- £2,250,000 in Foreign Exchange earnings by 1999

- Achieving growth in off-peak periods

- Expanding, developing and marketing the range of Irish Tourism products

- Increasing training to improve quality of service.

The launch of the 1994–1999 Operational Programme offers tremendous business opportunities for those involved in tourism product development. These opportunities can now be realised and the industry is invited to participate in the wide-ranging programme.

Funding will be channelled through five sub programmes:

- *Product Development* — this will be administered by Bord Fáilte, Shannon Development and the Central Fisheries Board. Total available funds are £139,000,000.

- *Marketing* — this will be administered by Bord Fáilte. Total available funds are £51,000,000.

- *Natural/Cultural Tourism* — this will be administered by the Department of Arts Culture and the Gaeltacht and the Office of Public Works. Total available funds are £94,000,000.

- *Training* — this will be administered by Cert and the Department of Education. Total available funds are £82,000,000.

- *Technical Assistance* — this will be administered by the Department of Tourism. Total available funds £3,000,000

Product Development

Five measures will be supported under this sub-programme:

1. Large Tourism Projects
   This measure will encourage:

   - The provision of 4–6 large-scale national projects to add a new dimension to the Irish tourism product — typically, such projects will cost more than £12 million and each will be capable of delivering new tourism business to Ireland. Examples of projects include:
     — The proposed National conference Centre for Dublin
     — An integrated, dedicated holiday park for families
     — A health tourism centre
     — A large-scale integrated holiday complex featuring high-quality accommodation, conference facilities and a mix of activity features.

   - Development/improvement of stand-alone, high-profile weather-independent regional tourist attractions — typically, each new project will cost at least £2 million and will be part of an overall regional action programme designed to upgrade the ambience and quality of an area. Particular attention will be given to delivering a wide variety of distinctive attractions in both traditional and developing tourist centres.

- Provision of small complementary projects or improvements to existing projects of regional scale.

2. Tourist Information and Heritage Projects
   Under this measure, it is anticipated that:

   - New and improved Tourist Information Offices will be provided at a number of locations, namely: Dublin, Boyne Valley, Waterford, Galway, Clifden, Salthill, Dingle and Killarney.

   - Additional touring routes will be developed, supported by guide books and appropriate signposting.

   - Support for the development of the designated Heritage Towns will be continued.

   - Public and private-sector heritage projects of scale will be supported where they are capable of generating 75,000 visitors in their third year.

   - The improvement and presentation of visitor facilities at Great Houses, Historical Buildings and Stately Homes, which complement the range of tourist attractions in established or developing tourist areas, will also be eligible for ERDF aid.

3. Tourism Angling
   The purpose of this measure is to upgrade Ireland's coarse and game angling resources to the best international standards. Works supported under the measure must:

   - Qualify as Bord Fáilte branded fisheries

   - Attract additional foreign visitors

   - Be readily available for tourist use

   - Be in harmony with the environment

   - Generate economic benefit and additional jobs

   - Conform to the EU's common Fisheries Policy.

   Assistance will go towards:

   - Physical in-stream and bank development

   - Removal of physical obstructions to fish migrations

   - Stock management and predator/competitor control

- Improved water-quality monitoring systems

- Establishment of new stocked coarse/game fisheries

- Rehabilitation of depleted sea trout fisheries

- Establishment of title to certain fisheries

- Acquisition of certain strategic sport fisheries to ensure their use by tourist anglers

- Measures to ensure the rational use and management of sports fish stocks

- Signposting, educational and informational material.

This measure, involving ERDF funds of £13 million, will be implemented by the Department of the Marine/Central Fisheries Board.

4. Special-Interest Holiday Facilities
   This measure will encourage the further development of activity and other special-interest holiday facilities. Areas to be assisted include:

- Improved adventure-holiday facilities

- Development of "themed" cycling routes and the provision of cycle hire and associated equipment directly related to the generation of overseas tourism business

- Development and upgrading, in association with Cospóir, of branded walking routes

- Creation of a major centre for international equestrian events of all types and the improvement of operational linkages, together with trail development, between existing equestrian operators

- Development of a limited number of new championship golf courses in remote areas, where they can serve as a catalyst for tourism development. Provision or improvement of visitor/learner facilities in Bord Fáilte branded courses that have not already received assistance will also be supported.

- Purchase of new lake- and sea-angling boats, the provision of access to angling waters, the development of angling centres, including bait rooms, tackle rooms, visitor changing- and drying-room facilities. Conversion/upgrading of boats of less than 15 years old and suitable for sea angling will be eligible for aid.

- Development of new cruising bases in selected inland waterways, additional to the cruising fleet, and the upgrading of cruisers of less than 10 years old. The purchase of water-buses or passenger ferries for use in certain environments will also be considered

- Restoration of up to 30 Irish gardens, including the provision/ upgrading of visitor facilities at gardens of tourism merit

- Improvement/development of language-learning facilities

- Further development of the genealogy product

- Provision of other activity/special-interest holiday facilities, where a real contribution to generating additional employment and overseas revenue can be demonstrated.

5. Specialist Accommodation-Related Developments
   Assistance will be available for the development of certain specialist accommodation needs for overseas visitors, including:

- Weather-independent leisure facilities attached to hotels and other approved establishments offering a minimum of 20 bedrooms or equivalent, subject to a minimum overall investment of £100,000

- Conference facilities attached to hotels and other approved establishments offering a minimum of 30 bedrooms, subject to a minimum overall investment of £100,000

- Modern simultaneous translation and audio-visual equipment at existing conference facilities, subject to a minimum investment of £50,000.

The building of touring caravan and camping facilities near the major sea access points at Dublin, Rosslare and Cork will be supported. Grants will also be available to existing touring caravan and camping sites around the country to upgrade to the highest international standards. Funding will be subject to the parks having over 50 touring pitches and being active in international marketing. A minimum investment of £100,000 will be necessary.
This measure will also help:

- To upgrade and improve existing buildings for hostel or other specialist accommodation and associated facilities on branded walking routes currently without appropriate provision

- To provide new and improved outdoor pursuits centres in remote areas currently with appropriate accommodation where the centre co-operate in trail development

- To improve existing accommodation at approved residential equestrian centres

- To support horse-drawn caravan and motor-home investments

- To alleviate the additional costs of providing, in existing hotels, suitable access-friendly accommodation for people with disabilities, where it is planned to develop the premises for international business in this area

- To improve access for people with disabilities at hotels and major visitor centres, where this can be done cost-effectively.

Minimum investments of £100,000 will be required in these cases.

A scheme of very selective assistance will be introduced to upgrade small and medium-sized hotels with a current capacity of up to 100 bedrooms and graded up to and including three star. Assistance will only be considered in exceptional cases where all of the following conditions apply:

- Improvements are necessary to bring promises up to modern international standards in a new or developing tourist area

- Accommodation needs cannot otherwise be met

- Proprietors can provide satisfactory evidence that they will cater for new tourist business to Ireland.

Exclusions from this provision include the main metropolitan areas. A minimum investment of £250,000 on eligible works will be required, in all cases.

Aid Rates — Product Development

In general, the maximum aid rates for eligible public and private sector activity under the Programme are 75 per cent and 50 per cent respectively. However, lower maximum aid rates will apply in certain cases:

Public Sector:
Improved Caravan/Camping Parks	50 per cent
Disabled Access	

Private Sector:
Equestrian Facilities	33 per cent

Sailing Facilities (excluding marinas/moorings)   33 per cent
New Lake and Sea Angling Boats
Bait/Drying Rooms etc.
Cycling Equipment
Golf Courses
Golf Clubhouses
Upgraded Sea-Angling Boats
Additional Cruising Craft
Language-Learning Facilities
Improved Hotel Conference Facilities

Accommodation-Related Leisure Facilities   25 per cent
Improved Caravan/Camping Parks
Horse-Drawn Caravans
Motor-Homes
Improved Accommodation at Equestrian Centres
Disabled Access/Hotel Conversion
Selective Accommodation Improvement Scheme

Upgraded Cruisers   20 per cent

Product Development Sub-Programme Contact Points

Information on the Tourism Angling measure may be obtained from:

EU Projects Manager
Central Fisheries Board
Mobhi Boreen, Dublin 9
Tel: (01) 837 9206, Fax: (01) 836 0060

Details of other measures in the Product Development Sub-Programme, are available on a regional basis from the Regional Tourism Managers. Persons in the Clare, Limerick, North Tipperary, North Kerry and South West Offaly area should contact:

Tourism Investments Manager
Shannon Development, Shannon, Co. Clare
Tel: (061) 361 555

Alternatively, information on these measures can be obtained from:

The Manager
Investment and Product Development Department
Bord Fáilte Éireann, Baggot Street Bridge, Dublin 2
Tel: (01) 676 5871, Fax: (01) 662 0263

International Fund for Ireland

Bord Fáilte administers a product-development grant scheme on behalf of the International Fund for Ireland. This scheme provides financial support for quality improvements in hotels and guesthouses and for the development of tourism amenities by the private sector and community groups.

Purpose

• To improve the range of tourism facilities and amenities in order to attract increased tourism revenue to Ireland

• To assist the lower grade hotels and guesthouses in improving the physical standard of accommodation and guest facilities

• To assist community-based groups in improving and developing amenities aimed at attracting foreign revenue to Ireland.

Scope

The schemes apply to projects in the border counties of Donegal, Leitrim, Louth, Cavan, Monaghan and Sligo.

Eligible Developments

• Angling, waterways development, sailing, marine development, water sports, outdoor-pursuits centres, recreational facilities in resorts, education/language schools, cultural/folk entertainment for tourists, historic/cultural interpretative centres, development studies

• Provision to approved standards of *en suite* facilities in hotels and guesthouses

• Structural improvements to hotels'/guesthouses' recreation, dining-room and kitchen areas

• Provision at hotels and guesthouses of suitable scale, all-weather leisure facilities and amenities for guests — tennis, pitch and putt, games room, snooker room and gymnasium

• Essential exterior redevelopment to enhance the external appearance of the hotels/guesthouses to meet consumer perceptions of a typical Irish village/country hotel, or family guesthouse.

Level of Assistance

Grants of up to 50 per cent are available in respect of private sector development except in the hotel and guesthouse improvement scheme, where 33 per cent maximum grants apply.

For community-sponsored projects, there is a maximum of 75 per cent, with a development threshold of £10,000 and a maximum grant of £100,000.

Acquisition costs are not eligible.

Applications should be submitted on the appropriate form to:

International Fund for Ireland
Tourism Programme
Bord Fáilte
Baggot Street Bridge, Dublin 2

The Agri-Tourism Scheme

This scheme is administered by the Regional Tourism Organisations and Shannon Development on behalf of the Department of Agriculture and co-ordinated by Bord Fáilte.

Purpose

The objective of the scheme is to provide incentives to farmers and other rural dwellers towards the cost of providing facilities that will enhance the attractiveness of an area for tourists and will meet clearly-identified tourist demands.

Scope

At the time of going to press this grant scheme was closed to applications. A new agri-tourism scheme under the aegis of an Operational Programme for Rural Development was anticipated.

The INTERREG Scheme

Purpose

The objectives of the Interreg scheme, which is EU-funded, is to develop and promote cross-border projects for the purpose of increasing visitor numbers and extending the tourist season.

Scope

The scheme applies to projects in the border counties of Donegal, Leitrim, Louth, Cavan, Monaghan and Sligo. At the time of going to press the grant scheme under the Interreg programme was closed to applications, the agreed total of £6 million for tourism projects having been committed. A new Interreg programme negotiated between the Irish Government and the European Commission was anticipated.

Tax Schemes

A number of tax-based schemes are available. These include, the Business Expansion Scheme, the Seed Capital Scheme, and Provision for Urban Renewal Relief. As these schemes can be intricate it is recommended that a tax adviser or accountant be consulted.

SEE ALSO: BUSINESS EXPANSION SCHEME
             INTERNATIONAL FUND FOR IRELAND

BORD IASCAIGH MHARA/
IRISH SEA FISHERIES BOARD

Crofton Road, Dún Laoghaire, Co. Dublin
Tel: (01) 284 1544, Fax: (01) 284 1123

Bord Iascaigh Mhara (BIM) is the statutory authority responsible for the development of the commercial seafish industry, including aquaculture.

Vessel Construction and Vessel Improvement Grants

Under the Operational Programme for Fisheries 1994–1999, grants can be considered for fleet-renewal (construction) and fleet-modernisation (improvement) projects carried out by those involved in commercial fishing. The grants are first considered at national level, under the BIM Marine Credit Plan (present rate is 5 per cent), and then, if approved, are submitted to the Department of the Marine under the EU FIFG scheme (present rate is 25 per cent).

Modernisation of vessels includes such items as shelterdecks, new engines, new electronics, new net drums and winches, new haulers, new wheelhouses and general improvement items. Work deemed as repairs and maintenance is excluded from the Scheme.

To qualify for a modernisation grant, work must not commence until such time as a formal application has been lodged with BIM.

For full discussion of the above information, contact The Fleet Development Division, BIM.

Grant Scheme for Aquaculture

Fish Handling and Upgrading

The Aquaculture Grant Scheme is the main vehicle by which BIM promotes the development of the aquaculture industry.

Commercial Aquaculture Projects

The Scheme provides the mechanism for accessing EU financial support from the Operational Programme for Fisheries 1994–1999 under which an amount of approximately IR£11.039 million in EU aid has been set aside for an investment programme of IR£36.038 million in aquaculture over this period. The objective is to stimulate the expansion of aquaculture output and employment by promoting the establishment of new projects, modernising and expanding existing projects and developing new cost-efficient and environment-friendly production techniques.

BIM grant-aid under the Aquaculture Grant Scheme is available at a rate of 5 per cent for all new commercial projects, with the exception of projects concerned with the development of novel species and those involving the introduction of new techniques for finfish and shellfish culture, where the BIM grant is provided at a rate of 10 per cent.

EU intervention rates are provided at a rate of 35 per cent for all projects.

Pilot Aquaculture Projects

Pilot projects, namely those with an investment below ECU 50,000, including those projects concerned with developing new species and production techniques, will continue to be supported by BIM in 1995. These projects will not be submitted for EU grant-aid, but this situation will be reviewed depending on the evolving demand for, and availability of, EU funding from the Operational Programme 1994–1999.

BIM grant-aid for Pilot Projects is provided at a rate of 40 per cent. Pilot projects concerned with new species development and technology transfer will, however, be supported at a rate of 45 per cent.

Fish-Handling Grant Scheme

The Fish-Handling Grant Scheme is the mechanism by which BIM promotes the quality handling of fish and shellfish up to the point of first sale. BIM grant-assistance to EU co-funded fish-handling projects is provided at a rate of 5 per cent and, on this basis, projects can qualify for EU grant-aid under the Operational Programme for Fisheries, at a rate of 35 per cent

BIM grant rates for small fish-handling projects, namely those with an investment below ECU 50,000, are 40 per cent. Eligible investments include auction halls, fish-handling/packing facilities and chill/cold rooms, hygiene equipment and shellfish depuration and packing facilities. Financial assistance for fish-processing development is provided by Forbairt or Údarás na Gaeltachta and not by BIM.

Upgrading Grant Scheme

Companies involved in the processing and marketing of fishery and aquaculture products that are required to upgrade their premises to comply with the requirements of EU Directives 492/91 and 493/91 on Health and Hygiene can qualify for grant assistance towards the cost of these works. The grant is provided at a rate of 50 per cent of the qualifying expenditure on the project, comprising a BIM grant of 5 per cent and an EU grant of 45 per cent. Eligible expenditure is that which is identified by the Department of the Marine Fishery Officer as necessary to bring the premises up to the required standard. The latest date for receipt of applications under this scheme is 31 March and all works must be completed by 31 December of the same year.

Market Incentive Grant Scheme

Under the Market Incentive Grant Scheme, financial assistance may be available to processors/exporters to cover:

- Promotional travel overseas — up to 50 per cent of air fares

- Participation in overseas trade fairs and exhibitions — up to 30 per cent of costs

- Overseas in-store advertising and promotion — up to 30 per cent of costs for selected products.

- Packaging and sales-literature design — up to 30 per cent of costs.

AN BORD TRÁCHTÁLA/ THE IRISH TRADE BOARD

Merrion Hall, Sandymount, Dublin 4
Tel: (01) 269 5011, Fax: (01) 269 5820

An Bord Tráchtála (ABT)/The Irish Trade Board is the successor to Córas Tráchtála Teo. (CTT) and the Irish Goods Council. It is the state organisation responsible for the promotion and development of sales in Ireland and abroad. It provides a range of market-development services to make winning new business easier, quicker and cheaper for Irish firms — manufacturers and providers of certain internationally-tradable services.

Bord Tráchtála's expertise is in:

1. Identifying market opportunities for indigenous companies — being their eyes and ears in the marketplace

2. Working with companies to turn these opportunities into sales through its network of 23 overseas offices, head office in Dublin and regional offices in Cork, Waterford, Limerick, Galway and Sligo

3. Providing services and incentives to companies to undertake market development activities.

Bord Tráchtála works with existing industry. And while it generally does not help in start-up situations, new businesses will not be turned away. Bord Tráchtála works closely with Forbairt, and small industries must have completed a Forbairt/Bord Tráchtála feasibility study before Bord Tráchtála starts to work with them.

The main services provided by Bord Tráchtála include:

- *A Promotional Programme* of trade exhibitions, trade missions, inward buyer missions and in-store promotions.

- *Marketplace Services* such as: providing office facilities overseas; carrying out market research; identifying and setting up appointments with potential customers, agents and distributors; providing inter-preters; assessing the potential for products or services; helping with direct marketing; helping in organising product launches and receptions; monitoring developments that affect companies and reviewing the progress of companies on a regular basis.

- *Design and Product Development* assistance to help companies to create a competitive edge through product development. Bord Tráchtála's design and product development assistance is available to exporters under a range of specialist programmes:

  - *Design Audit Programme* provides an expert impartial assessment of existing design activity.

  - *Individual Company Counselling Programme* offers confidential and impartial advice on the improvement of existing products, packaging or promotional literature.

  - *Group Development Programme* brings together groups of firms with common marketing objectives or needs to gather design and market information on a shared cost basis.

  - *Advanced Products Programme* enables concepts to be developed by qualified specialist consultants for market research and testing.

  - *Design Intelligence Programme* gathers design intelligence and forecast information in a number of product areas.

- Bord Tráchtála's Information Centre (located in Head Office, Dublin) has the largest collection of *market information* in Ireland. Staffed by information specialists and designed specifically for the needs of Irish companies selling in both Ireland and overseas markets, the Centre's market-information service may be accessed through any of Bord Tráchtála's regional offices or by telephone, post or personal visit. Up-to-date information is available on domestic and foreign manufacturers, importers and distributors. Data on markets, commodities, political developments and economic statistics is also available.

- Bord Tráchtála's *Trade Information Service* has details of government regulations, legislation and conditions of trading around the world which enable companies selling abroad to get the paperwork right the first time. A special service is also provided to expedite the legalisation of documents at embassies overseas, and to obtain visas and passports.

- *Graduate Recruitment*: Bord Tráchtála assists small and medium enterprises in expanding their marketing resources by facilitating recruitment and training of business graduates.

- *Ireland Market Services*: Bord Tráchtála's Ireland Market Department works with trade buyers, North and South, to assist Irish companies in winning increased sales locally as a stepping stone to international trade. Ireland Market Development addresses three main professional buyer audiences — buyers in manufacturing industry, buyers in retailer groups and buyers in the public sector.

- *Services to Buyers*: Bord Tráchtála works closely with professional buyers worldwide, matching their requirements to products and services from Ireland. It answers questions about Irish goods and services, including listings of companies with their export capabilities; making initial contacts simple and trouble-free; and organising buying trips to Ireland.

- Bord Tráchtála operates two incentive schemes:

  - *Market Activities Grant*: Small and medium-sized exporters of goods and services may be eligible for grants to help to develop their international marketing capacity. Grants of up to 50 per cent, to a maximum of eligible costs of research, market visits, sales personnel recruitment, trade fairs and exhibitions, advertising and promotion, tender costs, overseas customer visits, product design, sales literature and product testing may be available in any one year.

    - *Targeted Marketing Consultancy (TMC)*: This Bord Tráchtála programme was devised to assist companies in preparing and implementing a plan for *major* marketing initiatives. The TMC is reserved for companies with a strong commitment to developing their overseas markets and which can demonstrate that they have potential to increase export sales substantially. The TMC operates in two phases: 1) it supports an independent consultant who works with the company to develop a marketing strategy; and (2) it supports the company in implementing the plan. The maximum expenditure eligible for assistance is £750,000 — which includes a maximum grant of £250,000 and a maximum repayable incentive of £250,000 which will be repayable in the form of sales royalties. The minimum expenditure required by a company over a two-year period is £60,000.

OTHER ADDRESSES

Bord Tráchtála
67–69 South Mall, Cork
Tel: (021) 271 251/252, Fax: (021) 271 347

Bord Tráchtála
Mervue Industrial Estate, Galway
Tel: (091) 756 600/1/2, Fax: (091) 756 606

Bord Tráchtála
The Granary, Michael Street, Limerick
Tel: (061) 419 811 / 419 908, Fax: (061) 413 683

Bord Tráchtála
Finisklin Industrial Estate, Sligo
Tel: (071) 69477/69478, Fax: (071) 69479

Bord Tráchtála
Industrial Estate, Cork Road, Waterford
Tel: (051) 78577, Fax: (051) 79220

SEE ALSO: EUROPEAN INFORMATION CENTRES
              FORBAIRT

BUREAU DE RAPPROCHEMENT DES ENTREPRISES

80 rue d'Arlon, B-1040 Brussels
Tel: (00) (322) 295 9117, Fax: (00) (322) 296 4271
Contact: Paola Tardioli-Schiavo

The BRE aims to help small and medium-sized enterprises (SMEs) in the EU member states and certain non-member countries to find partners with a view to boosting their competitiveness. It is run by the Commission of the European Union, Directorate-General XXIII (Enterprise Policy, Distributive Trades, Tourism and Co-operatives), Unit B/2. The BRE's main task is to assist SMEs in their search for partners in the commercial, financial or technical fields. It offers SMEs an easily accessible service for publicising their co-operation offers or requests.

How the BRE Operates

The BRE handles non-confidential co-operation opportunities and relies on a network of correspondents located in all the member states and certain non-member countries. The search process involves the exchange of documents between enterprises, correspondents and the BRE central.

If an SME wants to co-operate with other SMEs beyond its national frontiers, an application form for a co-operation search must be filled in, which is then sent to the Commission Directorate-General in Brussels. The form, which is called the Co-operation Profile, can be obtained from the BRE and seeks general information about the company, a description of the proposed business co-operation, and a list of countries where partners are sought.

Co-operation Profile

The BRE acknowledges receipt of the Co-operation Profile and gives it an identification number. It feeds details of the search into a database and draws up an advertisement which quotes the identification number and describes the proposed co-operation. The advertisement and the company profile are then circulated among the network of BRE correspondents located in the target countries.

Advertisement

The correspondents then disseminate the advertisement through the channels open to them — namely, press, magazines, newsletters, on-line databases or other means — in order to publicise the business opportunity. At this stage the opportunity is anonymous, since the advertisement has either to quote the BRE identification number or to refer to the BRE otherwise, but may not divulge the name or address of the company offering the co-operation.

Company Profile

Businesses interested in the proposed co-operation should contact either the correspondent who disseminated the advertisement or the BRE, for further information. The correspondent or the BRE will then send the participating company a Company Profile containing:

- The name and address of the business, name of individual to contact, and relevant telephone, fax and telex numbers.

- General information provided by the company concerning its activities and size, bank references, etc.

There is no restriction on the number of co-operation opportunities that can be proposed by a company but the life span of an opportunity is limited to six months. At the end of this period, the company may ask the BRE Central Unit to extend the co-operation profile for a further six months.

Who Can Use the BRE?

The service is open to all small and medium-sized enterprises established in EU member states or in non-member countries. If a company contacts the BRE Central Unit in Brussels directly, the service is available free of charge but the company must follow up its own research. The BRE service is available through the six European Information Centres (EICs). The cost varies from centre to centre but will be approximately £75 per company. This includes assistance with research.
    The official BRE correspondents for Ireland are:

Chambers of Commerce of Ireland
22 Merrion Square, Dublin 2
Tel: (01) 661 2888, Fax: (01) 661 2811
Contact: Simon Nugent

European Commission
Jean Monnet Centre, 39 Molesworth Street, Dublin 2
Tel: (01) 671 2244, Fax: (01) 671 2657
Contact: Tim Kelly

An Bord Tráchtála
Merrion Hall, Sandymount, Dublin 4
Tel: (01) 269 5011, Fax: (01) 269 5820
Contact: Margaret Hogan

Shannon Development
Town Centre, Shannon, Co. Clare
Tel: (061) 361 555, Fax: (061) 361 903
Contact: Jim Harmon

EIC Cork
67 South Mall, Cork
Tel: (021) 509 044, Fax: (021) 271 347
Contact: Tara Dennehy

International Management Consulting Systems
Strand Road, Bray, Co. Wicklow
Tel: (01) 286 2969, Fax: (01) 286 4541
Contact: Michael Phelan

BUSINESS EXPANSION SCHEME

Direct Taxes Administration Branch
Office of the Revenue Commissioners
Dublin Castle, Dublin 2
Tel: (01) 679 2777, Fax: (01) 679 9287
Contact: Catherine Tierney

Anyone who owns a business and is looking for outside investors, or alternatively, anyone who is an investor looking for a suitable unquoted company in which to invest, may be able to take advantage of a tax incentive scheme known as the Relief for Investment in Corporate Trades (RICT) or the Business Expansion Scheme (BES). In order to qualify, investments must be in companies engaged in manufacturing, certain tourist projects, or in rendering certain services. The BES is a form of venture capital introduced by the Finance Act, 1984, which will continue until 5 April 1996. The scheme is intended to help small businesses which are established as limited companies to obtain additional capital. It allows an individual investor to obtain tax relief on investments — up to a maximum of £25,000 per annum — in each tax year for the duration of the scheme.

The following conditions apply:

1. The company must be incorporated and resident in Ireland.

2. The company must not be quoted on the Stock Exchange.

3. Seventy-five per cent of the income of the company must be earned from a qualifying trade within the state.

4. The company must be a bona fide new (to obtain tax refund for new enterprises) venture with the potential to create sustainable employment. This condition will be satisfied if the company obtains a certificate from the IDA, Údarás na Gaeltachta, Shannon Development, Bord Fáilte, Bord Iascaigh Mhara or An Bord Tráchtála, stating that the company may be eligible to be grant-aided.

5. The company must not be involved in a partnership with an individual or with another company.

6. Investors must purchase new ordinary share capital in the company. Shares must carry no preferential rights. Normally the minimum investment in any one company which qualifies is £200.

7. Relief can be claimed immediately in the case of established companies or after four months' trading in the case of new companies.

8. Shares must be held and certain conditions satisfied in relation to the investor for a period of five years. Other conditions in relation to the company need only be satisfied for three years.

BES has subsequently been amended several times. The Finance Act, 1993, lifted a restriction that prevented promoters owning more than 30 per cent of the share capital in a company from getting BES relief on investments in their own company. BES relief was made available to such persons where the share capital of the company was less than £150,000. This amount was increased to £250,000 in the 1994 Finance Bill.

It is up to the business to find potential investors and, when it does so, to obtain approval of the arrangement from the Revenue Commissioners. Usually, businesses that want to raise finance in this way go through a broker or accountant who sponsors the share issue. Most BES investors invest through funds set up for this purpose.

Tax Refunds for New Enterprises

The main period of BES issues tends to be towards the end of the income tax year (5 April), when potential investors see the scheme as a way of reducing immediate tax liabilities. The following scheme is an extension of BES called Tax Refunds for New Enterprises, introduced by the Finance Act, 1993.

To claim a refund under the Tax Refunds for New Enterprises scheme certain steps must be followed:

1. The appropriate agency should be identified and a completed application form for a certificate submitted to that agency.

2. The agency will also issue tax refund application Forms RINE C and RINE 1. When the company has been incorporated, all the shares have been issued (including those which the entrepreneur will

purchase) and the company has commenced trading, Forms RINE C and RINE 1 should be completed and submitted.

3. The tax years should be selected for which the applicant claims a refund. These can be any three of the previous five years. They do not have to be consecutive years.

4. The completed forms, together with the certificates, should be sent to the above address.

Seed Capital Scheme

An employee who leaves employment and invests in a new business (incorporated after 17 June 1993) may claim a refund of income tax paid in the previous years. An unemployed person may also avail of this facility. The refund may be claimed immediately the company starts to trade. An investor may claim a refund in this manner only once. Finally, an investor must, as an employee, enter into a full-time employment contract with the new company for one year, starting in the tax year in which the investment is made.

The refund of tax can be claimed as soon as the company commences trading and has obtained the appropriate certificate from the relevant agency. A refund will normally be made within four weeks of receipt of an adequately completed claim.

The RICT form for application for the Business Expansion Scheme requires the company to produce satisfactory evidence that the money raised by issue of the shares was used, is being used or is intended to be used for the purposes of:

- Enlarging the capacity of the company to undertake qualifying trading operations

- Research and development

- Identifying new markets and developing new products

- Increasing sales or provision of services.

All the above must be with a view to the creation or maintenance of employment in the community.

Details of all subsidiary companies, shareholders and proposed subscribers must be listed.

Designated Investment Fund

Investors looking to invest in a business can put their money in a special investment fund designated by the Revenue Commissioners under the scheme. A Designated Investment Fund comprises the subscriptions of a number of investors. The fund will be likely to invest in a number of companies. Broadly, each investor will get a share in each company in proportion to the value their subscription bears to the total size of the fund.

Investing in a Designated Investment Fund allows investors to spread their investments over a number of ventures. A fee will normally be payable by the investor to the fund manager. Entrepreneurs who seek equity from the fund can concentrate on their own venture rather than devoting time to persuading a number of investors to invest in the company.

Entrepreneurs Seeking Investors for their Company

The same procedures apply for designated funds, only in reverse. Entrepreneurs can find someone with funds to invest, consult a professional adviser, approach a Designated Investment Fund or employ a combination of these methods.

Business Expansion Scheme Changes in the Finance Act, 1993

- Extension of BES relief for a further period of three years until the end of the 1995–96 income tax year

- Removal of the lifetime ceiling of £75,000 on the amount in respect of which an individual can obtain BES relief

- Increase in the amount that a company can raise in BES funds from £500,000 to £1,000,000

- Research and development to qualify for BES funding subject to certification by an industrial development agency that it is satisfied that the research and development project is undertaken with a view to the ultimate establishment of new business

- In a situation where the capital of the company does not exceed £250,000 (Finance Act 1994) individuals are now entitled to relief where more than 30 per cent of the capital of the company is held or there is a right to more than 30 per cent of the assets on a winding-up.

- The production for a film (within the meaning of section 35 of the Finance Act, 1987) shall not — as regards a subscription for eligible shares made on or after 6 May 1993 — be regarded as qualifying trading operations.

> SEE ALSO: BORD FÁILTE
>   REVENUE COMMISSIONERS

BUSINESS INCUBATION CENTRES

Ossory Road, North Strand, Dublin 3
Tel: (01) 836 3994, Fax: (01) 836 3997
Contact: Rory O'Meara

Richmond Business Campus
North Brunswick Street, Dublin 7
Tel: (01) 872 7190, Fax: (01) 872 6252
Contact: Rory O'Meara

The Business Incubation Centres are ideally situated close to Dublin's City Centre. Though a relatively new concept in Ireland, Business Incubator Centres in the US have proven very successful in combating unemployment and encouraging enterprise. There are now over 800 such centres across the world. Some are as large as 450,000 square feet, with as many as 6,000 small businesses operating their own companies. Start-up companies are offered low-cost factory and/or office space, as well as financial, legal and business advice. Small businesses have access to equipment and services, without having large capital expenditure.

The Dublin Business Incubation Centres charge from £39 to £69 a week for a unit ranging in space from 140 to 200 square feet. When the business becomes established and starts to grow, it can move to a bigger premises within the Incubation Centres or may choose a premises within the Richmond Business Campus or Ossory Business Park.

Other advantages include:

- Fully serviced offices and workshops. The Incubation Centre comprises self-contained units, each with its own power, water, telephone and fax plus a shared communal kitchen for clients' use (applicable to both Ossory and Richmond Centres)

- Choice of premises — small; medium or large (if available) (applicable to both Ossory and Richmond Centres)

- Top security — 24-hour manned security, backed up by a Chubb electronic surveillance system (applicable to both Ossory and Richmond Centres)

- Remote 24-hour manned closed circuit camera surveillance (applies only to Richmond)

- Designated tax status (applies only to Richmond)

- 24-hour access (applicable to both Ossory and Richmond Centres)

- Indoor supervised car parking (applies only to Ossory)

- Management advice service — including financial, marketing and legal aspects of business (applicable to both Ossory and Richmond Centres)

- Private enterprise — no bureaucratic hitches or hold-ups in starting (applicable to both Ossory and Richmond Centres)

- Prime location (applicable to both Ossory and Richmond Centres)

- Full secretarial support — typing, photocopying, message-taking, word processing, use of fax and telephone numbers as well as prestigious business address etc. (applicable to both Ossory and Richmond Centres)

- Use of boardrooms (applicable to both Ossory and Richmond Centres)

- Conference centre — for product launches or training sessions (applicable to both Ossory and Richmond Centres)

- Café/dining room (applicable to both Ossory and Richmond Centres).

There are no preconditions to setting up a business in the Business Incubation Centres but a payment is required in advance, and this is based on what the enterprise can afford. In certain cases, space is given free of charge, on a scholarship basis, whereby if the project succeeds, the entrepreneur will pay for the service at a later stage. If, on the other hand, the business does not succeed, the centre is prepared to write off the rents due, but it is expected that services such as ESB and telephone be paid for. To qualify for this scholarship certain conditions must be agreed beforehand.

The Richmond Business Incubation Centre is unique in that it has laboratory space, facilities for art and catering, and includes a research and development unit. It will also have a clinic for outside consultants, including experts in export, research and development, manufacturing, marketing, and other technical matters.

Case Study

T.R. Control Systems

Proprietor: Tom Rourke

T.R. Control Systems was started in 1986 to service Heating and Air-Conditioning Control Systems, associated with commercial and industrial buildings. The service was operated from home, and then moved to the Finglas Enterprise Centre prior to relocating at Ossory Business Park Business Incubation Centre.

The reason for the move to Ossory was the opportunity for a workshop/office facility which was preferable to merely an office-type facility. This type of facility is ideal for small start-up businesses as all the facilities are provided at a reasonable cost.

From a purely maintenance-type of business, T.R. Control Systems gradually changed to provide a supply and installation service with emphasis on building management systems. This is a computerised system, capable of monitoring and controlling all aspects of a building's environment.

To cope with the extra work load and the technology changes it was necessary to employ a graduate engineer. Now all the design work is carried out in house at the Business Incubation Centre.

BUSINESS INFORMATION CENTRE

Central Library, ILAC Centre, Henry Street, Dublin 1
Tel: (01) 873 4333, Fax: (01) 872 1451
Contact: Deirdre Ní Raghallaigh/Betty Boardman

Each winter the ILAC Library hosts a series of business lectures aimed at those with an entrepreneurial spirit who want practical advice and information on starting and maintaining a business in Ireland. The lectures take place on a monthly basis on Tuesday evenings. Talks in the past have included information on turning a hobby — such as crafts — into a business, and how a business incubation centre can help. A further series of talks is held in the libraries in the Dublin PESP areas.

The business information service is also available in the Cork and Belfast city libraries, where Business Reference Sections contain sample business plans, etc.

BUSINESS INNOVATION FUND

Molyneux House
67–69 Bride Street, Dublin 8
Tel: (01) 475 3305, Fax: (01) 475 2044
Contact: Karl Schutte

The Business Innovation Fund is an independent seed capital fund operated on a national basis and funded by a number of institutional and private investors. It provides seed capital in the region of £25,000–£75,000 for start-up and early-stage businesses. In return for the high-risk investment, the fund seeks a minority share, typically between 25 and 35 per cent of the equity in the investee company.

The majority portion of the first round of financing for the Business Innovation Fund has come from the private sector and at no cost to the Irish taxpayer.

The objectives of the fund include:

- To foster Enterprise Creation which will facilitate the development of sustainable employment

- To provide an effective means of investing seed and early-stage venture capital and to minimise risks by extending the duties of the Fund manager to include responsibility for nurturing the new business — combining capital and management support

- To achieve capital appreciation which will facilitate further investments and provide investors with a return on their capital

- To create a balanced portfolio of investments to spread the risk

- To stimulate additional private-sector funding.

To maintain the Fund's focus on start-up/early-stage companies, the current criteria for investment by the Fund are:

- A need for start-up/early-stage capital

- Reasonable prospects for growth in output, employment and exports

- Fewer than ten people employed

- An annual turnover of less than £75,000 (ECU 100,000) but with potential to grow significantly in the future

- Pre-investment issued fully paid-up share capital of less than £1,150,000 (ECU 1,500,000). If previous risk capital of more than £40,000 (ECU 50,000) has already been invested in a start-up business, the Fund will not invest further in that company

- Projects should meet the commercial criteria of the Board of Investors.

The reason for these criteria is to concentrate investment on the small start-up/early-stage businesses with prospects for growth, employment and export.

Investment Procedure

The promoter of a project must develop the business concept, assess its feasibility and prepare a detailed business plan demonstrating that the concept has a future that will attract an investment. On receipt of a business plan, the Fund manager carries out an initial screening process followed by a close "due diligence" process. Once the Fund manager is satisfied with the results of this screening process and a suitable deal is negotiated with the promoters, the Fund manager will put a board paper to the Board of Investors. Prior to the Board's decision on the project, the promoters are given an opportunity to present themselves and their project to the Board at one of the Fund's Enterprise Evenings.

Enterprise Evenings are open only to entrepreneurs who have got through the Business Innovation Fund initial screening of projects. This has been found to be very beneficial for both the promoters and the members of the Board of the Business Innovation Fund.

The Business Innovation Fund was established on the basis of having a 10-year fixed-term life. A voluntary exit may include one of the following mechanisms:

- Sales to other shareholders including the original promoters

- Sale to a "third party". This may involve selling to a trade investor who would facilitate the continued development of the company

- Under the 1990 Company Legislation, it is possible, in certain circumstances, for a company to buy back its own ordinary shares.

- Company flotation.

BUSINESS RESULTS LTD.

80–82 Rainey Street, Magherafelt BT45 5AJ
Tel: (08) (01648) 31032, Fax: (08) (01648) 31033
Contact: Maria Conaghan

Business Results Ltd. is the consultancy division of Workspace Ltd., a community-based and community-owned development organisation. Business Results sells economic development expertise gained by Workspace, to government agencies and local groups within Ireland and abroad.

Services provided by the firm include:

- Business Planning

- Marketing

- Enterprise and Economic Development

- Personnel and Recruitment Services

- Community Economic Development

- Event Management.

For a local community group wishing to set up a community-owned business, Business Results can help on a consultancy basis. Generally, the firm will assist such a group in developing a local area plan, identifying projects and in the preparation of business plans. It will assist companies with administration and budgeting, as well as in feasibility testing.

Case Study

Business Results recently completed a project in Raphoe, Co. Donegal, which involved helping the local development group to create a food technology centre for the town. The project will provide training and support for new food businesses, will make use of a deteriorating building in the village and will involve cross-border co-operation.

CATHAL BRUGHA RESEARCH AND DEVELOPMENT UNIT

Dublin Institute of Technology
Cathal Brugha Street, Dublin 1
Tel: (01) 874 6058, Fax: (01) 874 8572
Contact: Bernadette McLaughlin

The Unit provides research and consultancy in Hotel and Catering, Tourism, Quality Management, Environmental Health, Social Care and Child Development.

In the hotel, restaurant and catering area, research is carried out on new products and services. Advice and information are provided on the design and development of food and drink products and the types of facilities and service systems. The Unit assists in enterprise development with regard to design, development, quality control, marketing, cost control, production management and personnel training.

Commissions in the tourism area are undertaken for both public and private organisations. The work includes development plans, feasibility studies, operational audits, marketing, new product research, language training and management-information systems.

The Unit advises on quality systems and quality audits for the food and pharmaceutical industries. In addition, development work is carried out on product and processing techniques.

The Centre for Environmental Health undertakes research in food science and technology, environmental science and technology, environmental health, management and administration. It provides a service to industry in quality assurance, hygiene auditing, air and water quality management and environmental health promotion.

For social sciences, research and consultancy activities encompass early childhood care and education, child and adolescent development, residential and day-care services, staff development, social and psychological assessment.

The Cathal Brugha Research and Development Unit is supported by the complete range of college facilities: food production units, science and technology laboratories, library and computer laboratory.

Companies which contribute to the college to enable them to undertake research in certain subjects may qualify for tax relief under section 21 of the Finance Act, 1973, as amended. Alternatively, companies covenanting income to the college for research for a period of three years or longer may qualify for tax relief under section 439 of the Income Tax Act, 1967.

CENTRAL STATISTICS OFFICE

Skehard Road, Mahon, Cork
Tel: (021) 359 000, (021) 359 090
Contact: Áine De Baróid

Ardee Road, Rathmines, Dublin 6
Tel: (01) 497 7144, Fax: (01) 497 2360

The Central Statistics Office is the government agency responsible for the collection and publication of most Irish official statistics. General queries are dealt with by the Information Section while CSO Libraries in Cork and Dublin and the Trade Information Service, Dublin, are open to the public for consultation.

CSO information includes:

- Agriculture

- National Accounts

- Balance of Payments

- Economic and Financial Statistics

- Foreign Trade

- Prices, Agricultural Prices, Import and Export Price Indices

- Tourism and Travel

- Transport

- Building and Construction

- Census of Population

- Vital Statistics

- Household Budget Survey

- Industry

- Labour Force Survey

- Live Register, Consumer Price Index, Wholesale Price Index

- Services including Distribution Data Bank.

The principal results of the CSO statistical inquiries are published in special statistical releases, *Consumer Price Indices to Live Register Statements,* and are reproduced in the monthly *Economic Series* publication. The full details are subsequently published in the quarterly *Statistical Bulletin.* The main features are also included in the annual *Statistical Abstract.*

Current statistical information is posted weekly to the worldwide Reuters terminal and to Minitel. Regular EU bulletins are published on a monthly basis on matters such as the consumer price index, energy and industrial trends. The publications of international organisations such as the EU statistical office EUROSTAT, the UN, FAO, ILO and the OECD may be consulted in the CSO library.

To meet specialist requirements of some users, the CSO provides on a fee basis to individual users a large number of special series and analyses tailored to their particular needs. Arrangements also exist whereby the CSO will run on its computer data files — in a manner that preserves the confidentiality of the individual records — computer programs written by specialist users. These services are charged on a user fee basis.

All CSO publications are available from the Government Publications Sales Office or can be ordered through any bookseller.

CENTRE FOR CO-OPERATIVE STUDIES

University College Cork, Cork
Tel: (021) 276 871 Ext. 2570/2719, Fax: (021) 276 929
Contact: Siobhán O'Neill

The Centre for Co-operative Studies has over 12 years' experience and practical links with all sections of the co-operative movement in Ireland, as well as links with co-operative organisations internationally.

The Centre has been involved in applied research, practical support to start-up worker co-ops, provision of training courses and the development of training and promotional material for co-operatives. It is also involved in teaching a postgraduate course in Co-operative Organisation, Food Marketing and Rural Development.

The resource room in the Centre has the largest supply of co-operative material in the country, with over 2,000 books, reports and videos on the co-operative theme. It also provides an information service for groups and individuals wishing to access information for their own particular co-operative needs. There is no charge for co-operative information and the Centre is open to the public by appointment.

A set of 12 co-op guide booklets is published by the Centre. The pack costs £6 and covers the following areas:

- *Where Do We Start?*

- *Why Keep Books?*

- *Co-op Selling*

- *Planning for Survival*

- *Co-op Rules OK!*

- *Co-op Meetings*

- *Who Needs Professionals?*

- *Getting Information*

- *Co-op Workers' Rights*

- *Market Research*

- *Raising Money*

- *Dealing with the Media.*

SEE ALSO: FÁS CO-OPERATIVE DEVELOPMENT UNIT
                 IRISH LEAGUE OF CREDIT UNIONS
                 REGISTRAR OF FRIENDLY SOCIETIES

CHAMBERS OF COMMERCE OF IRELAND

22 Merrion Square, Dublin 2
Tel: (01) 661 2888, Fax: (01) 661 2811
Contact: Paul Skehan

The Chambers of Commerce of Ireland (CCI) represents 7,500 businesses in Ireland, from 62 affiliated chambers of commerce, and 40 direct corporate members. The aim of the CCI is to promote, develop, and act in the interests of Irish business, industry, services, commerce and tourism.

Chambers in cities and towns throughout Ireland are in a position to assist new entrepreneurs and to point them in the right direction. Some chambers run incubator units and enterprise centres, operate mentoring schemes, and can help new firms to find investors. All chambers provide an opportunity for business people to meet each other and do business. CCI can provide a list of chambers throughout Ireland, with contact addresses and phone numbers. For this detailed listing of chambers of commerce, contact the national office.

SEE ALSO: FIRST STEP
LIMERICK CHAMBER OF COMMERCE

CHAPMAN FLOOD

Chartered Accountants
Mount Herbert Court, 34 Upper Mount Street, Dublin 2
Tel: (01) 676 1116, Fax: (01) 676 6640
Contact: David L. Chapman

Chapman Flood is a firm of chartered accountants which can assist a small business by compiling business plans and cash-flow forecasts, and in the installation of management and financial information systems. The company prepares, submits and negotiates grant assistance proposals, as well as preparing submissions to government and financial agencies.

Chapman Flood introduces clients to sources of venture capital and equity funding and assists with negotiation of bank facilities.

Tax Consultancy Services

Tax services supplied by Chapman Flood include:

- Corporate Tax Planning

- Corporate Finance Support Services

- VAT Services

- Revenue Audits

- PAYE Services

- Personal Tax Planning

- Company Directory Services

- Capital Acquisitions Tax (Inheritance/Gift Tax)

- Capital Gains Tax.

Chapman Flood also offers advice on management structures and personnel recruitment and will take part in investigating the market and business opportunities for a small business, including acquisitions, management buyouts, joint ventures, and licensing opportunities.

CITY OF DUBLIN VOCATIONAL EDUCATION COMMITTEE

Town Hall, Merrion Road
Ballsbridge, Dublin 4
Tel: (01) 668 4394, Fax: (01) 668 0710
Contact: W.J. Arundel

The City of Dublin Vocational Educational Committee (CDVEC), which is responsible for the city's 21 vocational schools and colleges, offers a wide range of courses including "Start Your Own Business".

Rathmines Senior College has successfully run this course over the past number of years. It is also offered in several other colleges, but has been withdrawn because of insufficient numbers. Commencing in September, the courses are held in the evening, one night per week over a 10-week period and the fee is approximately £35.

Whitehall Language and Commercial College (address below) runs a night-time and a full-time day course in "Entrepreneurial Skills". The course is aimed at school-leavers, graduates and unemployed professionals. The emphasis is divided between theory and practice, with particular emphasis on individual projects which are assessed by successful entrepreneurs. The day course, beginning in September, is funded by the European Social Fund, and students need only pay approximately £65 for CDVEC certification and class materials. Students must supply their own books and pay for external examinations. Application forms are available from the College.

The CDVEC has an annual *Guide To Courses* which costs £1 and gives more details regarding day and evening programmes.

USEFUL ADDRESSES

Entrepreneurial Skills Course
Whitehall House Language and Commercial Centre
Swords Road, Whitehall, Dublin 9
Tel: (01) 837 6011, Fax: (01) 837 5031

Start Your Own Business Course
Rathmines Senior College
Town Hall, Rathmines
Dublin 6
Tel: (01) 497 5334/5336

COMERFORD TECHNOLOGY MANAGEMENT LTD.

50 Wilson Road
Mount Merrion, Co. Dublin
Tel/Fax: (01) 288 9877
Contact: Kieran Comerford

Comerford Technology Management Ltd. provides services in the commercial exploitation of new technology, specialising in all the management-related aspects. The consultancy company provides entrepreneurs with specialist assistance for projects based on a patentable product or process. It specialises in raising finance through the tax incentive for inventions, which gives tax exemption for patent income. By setting up a patent holding company and selling shares to an outside investor, it is possible to raise funds to carry out the development, patenting and continuing commercial exploitation of the invention by manufacturing it in Ireland. In some cases it is possible to obtain extra revenue in the project by arranging to have the product manufactured under licence abroad.

Comerford Technology Management Ltd. charges a fee for an initial assessment of projects. On the basis of this assessment, entrepreneurs are advised on the best method of commercial exploitation, and the likely investment needed to carry this out. Entrepreneurs can then choose to proceed to the next stage, which involves engaging the firm to carry out any or all of the following activities:

- Providing advice on patent tax structures

- Raising funds using the patent tax incentive

- Seeking other sources of finance, arranging joint ventures

- Research and development, technology acquisition and feasibility grants

- Management of R&D programmes

- Providing advice on commercial exploitation

- Licensing in and licensing out

- Searching for new products and technologies

- Intellectual property valuation and management.

- Patent insurance services.

COMMUNITY ENTERPRISE PROGRAMME

FÁS External Training Division
Tel: (021) 544 377
Contact: Jim St Leger

in conjunction with

City of Cork Vocational Education Committee
Emmet Place, Cork
Tel: (021) 273 377 / 313 945, Fax: (021) 275 680
Contact: Enterprise Development Officer

The Community Enterprise Programme provides a package of advice, training and financial assistance to community groups who want to become involved in the creation of economically viable jobs.

The programme concentrates its assistance and support on supplementing the skill and expertise of local groups. Its thrust is to assist groups through the development stages of a business, from the initial idea, through trading.

Any community group with the energy and commitment to turn an idea into a viable business is eligible. Assistance and support are provided by FÁS at each stage of development of the idea. First, a business development plan is developed by the group. Here, FÁS can provide grant-aid for feasibility studies to quantify the market and the feasibility of the idea. In the case of there being a number of project ideas identified which have passed initial feasibility stage, and which show some viable potential, the group may apply to FÁS for grant-aid for the recruitment of an Enterprise Worker.

The Enterprise Worker

The role of this person is to assess the initial feasibility of ideas, including market research, estimating initial costs and capital requirements. During this start-up stage, the community group can apply to FÁS for recruitment of a project manager and worker wage subsidies, depending on the stage of development of the project. At various stages, further grant-aid may be made available for diversification and development of products or services.

Grant-Aid Package

- Up to £2,000 development grant is available for product investigation and group development.

- Up to £17,500 is available towards the employment of an enterprise worker for a period of 52 weeks to develop the specific business ideas to the point of start-up. Alternatively, this grant, pro rata, can be used toward consultancy costs for development of specific business ideas.

Assistance towards the cost of development and management of the new project is also available through the following means:

- A Commercial Aid Grant of £14,000 towards the management and administration of the new commercial enterprise for a period of one year

- On a minimum salary of £5,000 per worker, a Commercial Aid Grant in the form of wage subsidies for commercially viable projects in manufacturing (up to £3,750 per worker) and selected services sectors (up to £2,500 per worker)

FÁS will also assist in the delivery of training modules to help and manage the particular enterprise project.

Case Studies

Bantry French Armada Exhibition Centre

In 1988, the Bantry 1796 French Armada Trust Ltd. was established to develop local awareness and tourism potential in the area. One of the initial objectives of the group was the establishment of an exhibition centre in the courtyard of Bantry House.

The exhibition centre was officially opened in 1991. FÁS is currently funding a manager for the centre, and is also supplying development and wage subsidy grants for the two full-time and six part-time workers on this innovative project.

Corabbey Crafts, Midleton

A community-based business, Corabbey Crafts manufactures and supplies specialised high-quality linen and crochet products to markets at home and abroad. The linen is spun from the finest flax, which is grown, harvested and bleached by a totally natural process dating from the 1840s. The majority of overseas trade to date has been in the US, but the company is currently designing a new product range, aimed primarily at European markets.

Having had an initial employment of six workers, the company now employs eight people, operating from a premises provided rent-free by the Presentation Sisters. FÁS provided assistance to the project in the form of training and commercial development grants to help the business in getting started, and is currently supporting export effort through marketing grants to help promote its products in Italy.

SEE ALSO: FÁS, THE TRAINING AND EMPLOYMENT AUTHORITY

COMMUNITY ENTERPRISE SOCIETY LTD.

17 Rathfarnham Road
Terenure, Dublin 6W
Tel/Fax: (01) 490 3237
Contact: Pauline Doyle

The Community Enterprise Society Ltd., also called the Terenure Enterprise Centre, has 28 fully serviced business units available to prospective tenants, including 3 food processing units, which have Health-Board approval, operating on a monthly licence basis. Each business remains independent while sharing the basic running costs incurred.

Terenure Enterprise provides:

- Incubator-unit space

- Reception, secretarial and office facilities

- Business-address facility

- Free business consultancy — advice on all aspects of business start-up; sources of finance and grants; assistance with business plans and projections; hands-on business advice and support.

Each project is evaluated by the manager and the Venture Analysis Committee, who assess its viability and make constructive suggestions regarding the proposed venture. The preconditions are:

- A sound, well-researched business idea

- Evidence of commitment

- A basic business plan

- Completion of a one-page application form.

Within a period of approximately three years, tenants should have a viable business established and are expected to relocate their enterprise.

Case Study

Thermo Dial Ltd.

This company took a small unit in Terenure Enterprise Centre early in 1987. The Directors were three mechanical engineers who established the company to provide heating, ventilation and air-conditioning services to the industrial and commercial sector.

The Enterprise Centre provided the day-to-day back-up for the business, including telephone-answering, reception, fax and secretarial services. This support allowed the proprietors of the business to concentrate on developing the client base and on extending the range and quality of services offered.

The business grew from strength the strength and the company is now successfully operating from its own premises at Clanbrassil Street, Dublin 8. It currently employs 14 people.

CO-OPERATION NORTH

37 Upper Fitzwilliam Street, Dublin 2
Tel: (01) 661 0588 / 676 3608, Fax: (01) 661 8456
Contact: Maurice Inglis

7 Botanic Avenue, Belfast BT7 1JG
Tel: (08) (01232) 321 462, Fax: (08) (01232) 247 522
Contact: Deirdre McKervey

Co-operation North, through its Economic Co-operation Programme, works towards facilitating co-operation between and within the business community, North and South. To this end, two or three business training seminars for small enterprises are held every year to provide networking and marketing opportunities for entrepreneurs, particularly those who wish to develop cross-border trade.

Co-operation North also has several publications helpful to small enterprises, and which provide useful data on an all-Ireland basis. Recent publications include:

- *Marketing Practice in Northern Ireland and the Republic of Ireland*

- *North South Directory*

- *Public Sector Purchasing Directory*

- *People and Population Change* (Demography Study).

COOPERS & LYBRAND

Chartered Accountants
Business Services Division, PO Box 1283
Fitzwilton House, Wilton Place, Dublin 2
Tel: (01) 661 0333, Fax: (01) 660 1782
Contact: John Tuffy

Coopers & Lybrand is a firm of chartered accountants which offers a wide range of financial, accounting and business-advisory services to entrepreneurs, start-up companies and owner-managed companies.

The firm offers:

- Assistance in the preparation of business plans and financial projections

- Advice on sources of finance

- Introductions to and liaison with banks and other organisations.

It also takes part in investigating and researching the feasibility of new projects, including market research and sectoral studies.

A series of half-day development workshops is run by Coopers & Lybrand, aimed at formulating a clear set of objectives and strategies through which success for small businesses can be achieved (contact Coopers & Lybrand for exact dates).

Negotiation

Using international networks and databases, Coopers & Lybrand takes part in negotiations concerning technology transfer, licensing, distribution and franchising agreements on behalf of clients.

Financial Services

Financial services supplied by Coopers & Lybrand include accounts preparation, and audit and taxation compliance. The firm also offers advice on company formations and strategic tax planning, and assists in the selection and implementation of appropriate accounting systems.

Coopers & Lybrand has branches throughout the Republic of Ireland and in Northern Ireland (contact Coopers & Lybrand in Dublin for a full list of branch addresses).

COUNTY ENTERPRISE BOARDS

Department of Enterprise and Employment
Kildare Street, Dublin 2
Tel: (01) 661 4444, Fax: (01) 676 2654
Contact: John Rutledge

The establishment of the County Enterprise Boards is one of the main priorities of the 1993–97 Programme for a Partnership Government, which proposes to encourage local initiative by the establishment of these Boards, empowering local communities to obtain local funding to develop their own areas.

Thirty-five City and County Enterprise Boards have been set up. Each has an executive staff, headed by an Acting Chief Executive Officer who also acts as a facilitator, directing individual projects or local community-enterprise initiatives to the existing state agencies. The Boards receive administrative support from the local authorities, but are at present being incorporated as companies limited by guarantee, a process which was expected to be completed by the end of June 1995.

City/County Enterprise Boards have 14 members drawn from elected members of the local authority, the social partners, state agencies and community/other representatives. There are currently only two female acting Chief Executive Officers on the County Enterprise Boards. However, the Boards have been formed on an ad hoc basis and have not yet been given formal status. "When this happens and the County Enterprise Boards are established as companies limited by guarantee, Chief Executive Officer positions will be filled from open competition and more women may be recruited to the posts" (Spokesperson, Department of Enterprise and Employment).

The intention is for the Boards to assume responsibility in business areas not already covered by the state industrial development agencies. The Boards will, for the first time, provide direct support for services employment. They have prepared three-year County Enterprise plans through the following means:

- Identifying and commercially developing local resources

- Creating and strengthening networks between the local community and state agencies in the interest of mobilising and co-ordinating their energies and knowledge in pursuit of employment opportunities

- Promoting the creation and development of enterprises from within the local economy, particularly through support for local enterprise

- Influencing the allocation of resources for small enterprises from European-Union, private and public funding sources.

The Boards will have responsibility for supporting existing and new small and micro enterprises. Where applications for funding and advice are more appropriate to the remit of existing agencies — Forbairt, for example — they are directed to such bodies. Projects in manufacturing and in the internationally traded sector which exceed a threshold of 10 people in terms of employment potential are reserved to Forbairt, IDA Ireland and Shannon Development. Areas of enterprise where the County Enterprise Plan has indicated that there is already a sufficient number of firms participating will not be eligible, neither will areas of enterprise on the EU and national sensitive-sectors list, nor enterprises coming under other schemes or Operational Programmes.

The activities of the Boards will be co-ordinated at national level in respect of:

- Allocation of funds to the County Enterprise Boards

- Criteria for the evaluation of project applications to Boards.

Each Board has access to the County Enterprise Fund which has been established to assist small projects. Except where the Minister for Enterprise and Employment has given consent, County Enterprise Boards will not consider proposals involving grant support in excess of £50,000 or projects with investment costs in excess of £100,000.

Criteria for Assistance

Project promoters should be able to demonstrate that:

- There is a market for the proposed product or service.

- Adequate overall finance will be available to fund the project.

- They possess the management and technical capacity to implement the proposed project.

- Projects to be assisted will add value so as to generate income or supplement income for those involved, and will have the capacity to create new direct employment whether full-time, part-time or seasonal, or will, as a minimum, contribute directly to the main-tenance of employment in existing small enterprises.

- They will comply with existing policies on tax clearance, the certification of subcontractors, and related matters.

The Boards do not support projects which are contrary to public policy. Nor do they duplicate support for projects which are eligible for assis-tance from any existing sectoral or grant structure. Projects involving primary agricultural production are ineligible for assistance.

Limited assistance may be provided, for certain county-level economic promotional activities.

Grant Levels

The following grant levels will apply:

- A maximum of 50 per cent of the cost of capital and other invest-ment, or £50,000 — whichever is the lesser
- A maximum of 75 per cent of the cost of preparing a feasibility study/business plan, subject to an overall limit of £5,000 in the case of a single project.

Following the incorporation of the Boards, assistance will not be con-fined to grant supports. Other supports will include the provision of loans and loan guarantees and the taking of equity stakes.

Applications for Assistance

Promoters of projects should contact the relevant County Enterprise Officer (see list of addresses for names), who will advise as to whether the project is suitable, in the first instance, for consideration by the Evaluation Committee of the County Enterprise Board.

Certain projects may qualify for tax relief under the Business Expansion Scheme. Boards and potential investors in projects should consult with the Revenue Commissioners to determine whether any such investments proposed qualify for relief under the scheme.

Co-ordination of Activities

Each Board will operate in harmony with, and maintain close liaison with all state agencies and local authorities within the area. The purpose of this is:

- To ensure maximum benefit and contribution to the local community through co-ordination of local development efforts

- To monitor the progress of enterprise-project activities undertaken under the promoter's business plan, including any necessary follow-up visits to ensure completion of work, confirmation of private investment, etc.

A list of contact points and the addresses for the County Enterprise Boards follows. This list may be subject to change as the Boards secure accommodation outside local authority offices.

COUNTY ENTERPRISE BOARDS:

Carlow County Enterprise Board
c/o Carlow County Council
County Offices, Carlow
Tel: (0503) 31126, Fax: (0503) 41503
Contact: Pat O'Meara

Cavan County Enterprise Board
c/o Cavan County Council, Courthouse, Cavan
Tel: (049) 31799, Fax: (049) 31384
Contact: Vincent Reynolds

Clare County Enterprise Board
Enterprise House, Mill Road, Ennis, Co. Clare
Tel: (065) 41922, Fax: (065) 41887
Contact: Eamonn Kelly

Cork:

Cork City Enterprise Board
Albert House, Albert Quay, Cork
Tel: (021) 961 828, Fax: (021) 961 869
Contact: Dave Cody

North Cork County Enterprise Board
26 Bank Place, Mallow, Co. Cork
Tel: (022) 43235, Fax: (022) 43247
Contact: Rochie Holohan

South Cork County Enterprise Board
Exham House, Douglas, Cork
Tel: (021) 895977, Fax: (021) 895979
Contact: Jim Brennan

West Cork County Enterprise Board
County Offices (West), 8 Kent Street
Clonakilty, Co. Cork
Tel: (023) 34700, Fax: (023) 34702
Contact: Michael Hanley

Donegal County Enterprise Board
Donegal County Council
County House, Lifford, Co. Donegal
Tel: (074) 41066, Fax: (074) 41205
Contact: Leonard Roarty

Dublin City Enterprise Board
Liffey House, Tara Street, Dublin 2
Tel: (01) 677 3066, Fax: (01) 677 0497
Contact: Tom Gibney

Fingal (Dublin North) County Enterprise Board
c/o Fingal County Council
46–49 Upper O'Connell Street, Dublin 1
Tel: (01) 872 7777, Fax: (01) 872 7247
Contact: Anita Morris

Dublin South County Enterprise Board
PO Box 4122, Tallaght Town Centre
Tallaght, Dublin 24
Tel: (01) 462 0000, Fax: (01) 462 0111
Contact: Ciaran Murray

Dún Laoghaire/Rathdown County Enterprise Board
Ballygowan House, 4 Marine Road
Dún Laoghaire, Co. Dublin
Tel: (01) 280 6961, Fax: (01) 280 6969
Contact: John Byrne

Galway County and City Enterprise Partnership Board
Woodquay Court, Woodquay, Galway
Tel: (091) 65269, Fax: (091) 65384
Contact: Charles Lynch

Kerry County Enterprise Board
c/o Kerry County Council
Áras an Chontae, Tralee, Co. Kerry
Tel: (066) 21111, Fax: (066) 26712
Contact: Eamon O'Mahony

Kildare County Enterprise Board
Kildare County Council
St Mary's, Naas, Co. Kildare
Tel: (045) 897 071, Fax: (045) 871 011
Contact: Brendan McGrath

Kilkenny County Enterprise Board
c/o County Hall, John Street, Kilkenny
Tel: (056) 52699, Fax: (056) 63384
Contact: Anthony Walsh

Laois County Enterprise Board
Laois County Council
County Hall, Portlaoise, Co. Laois
Tel: (0502) 22044, Fax: (0502) 22313
Contact: Declan Byrne

Leitrim County Enterprise Board
Parklane House
Carrick-on-Shannon, Co. Leitrim
Tel: (078) 20450, Fax: (078) 21491
Contact: Michael Tunney

Limerick City Enterprise Boards
The Granary, Michael Street, Limerick
Tel: (061) 312611, Fax: (061) 311 889
Contact: Eamon Ryan

Limerick County Enterprise Board
c/o Limerick County Council
79–84 O'Connell Street, Limerick
Tel: (061) 318477, Fax: (061) 318 478
Contact: Gerard Behan

Longford County Enterprise Board
Longford County Council
Great Water Street, Longford
Tel: (043) 46231, Fax: (043) 41233
Contact: Frank Sheridan

Louth County Enterprise Board
Jocelyn House, Jocelyn Street, Dundalk, Co. Louth
Tel: (042) 27099, Fax: (042) 27101
Contact: Jerry Duffy

Mayo County Enterprise Board
Spencer Street, Castlebar, Co. Mayo
Tel: (094) 24444, Fax: (094) 24416
Contact: Frank Fullard

Meath County Enterprise Board
c/o Meath County Council
County Hall, Navan, Co. Meath
Tel: (046) 21581, (046) 21463
Contact: Hugh Reilly

Monaghan County Enterprise Board
c/o Monaghan County Council
Court House, Monaghan
Tel: (047) 82211, Fax: (047) 84786
Contact: Aidan Golden

Offaly County Enterprise Board
c/o Offaly County Council
Cormac Street, Tullamore, Co. Offaly
Tel: (0506) 52971, Fax: (0506) 52973
Contact: Seán Ryan

Roscommon County Enterprise Board
c/o Roscommon County Council
Court House, Roscommon
Tel: (0903) 26100, Fax: (0903) 25474
Contact: Jerry Finn

Sligo County Enterprise Board
Courthouse, Teeling Street, Sligo
Tel: (071) 43221, Fax: (071) 44779
Contact: Frank Dawson

Tipperary North County Enterprise Board
Summerhill, Nenagh, Co. Tipperary
Tel: (067) 33086, Fax: (067) 33605
Contact: Peggy Roche

Tipperary SR County Enterprise Board
c/o Tipperary South Riding County Council
County Hall, Clonmel, Co. Tipperary
Tel: (052) 25399, Fax: (052) 24355
Contact: Ciaran O'Brien

Waterford City Enterprise Board
c/o Waterford Corporation
7 Lombard Street, Waterford
Tel: (051) 73501, Fax: (051) 79124
Contact: Fergus Galvin

Waterford County Enterprise Board
Cross Bridge Street, Dungarvan, Co. Waterford
Tel: (058) 44811, Fax: (058) 44817
Contact: Gerard Enright

Westmeath County Enterprise Board
c/o Westmeath County Council
County Buildings, Mullingar, Co. Westmeath
Tel: (044) 40861/5, Fax: (044) 42330
Contact: Christy Kiernan

Wexford County Enterprise Board
c/o Wexford County Council
County Hall, Spawell Road, Wexford
Tel: (053) 42211, Fax: (053) 43406
Contact: Sean Mythen

Wicklow County Enterprise Board
Wicklow County Council
County Buildings, Wicklow
Tel: (0404) 67324, Fax: (0404) 67792
Contact: Thomas Broderick

SEE ALSO: DEPARTMENT OF ENTERPRISE AND
EMPLOYMENT
DUBLIN CITY ENTERPRISE BOARD
LOUTH COUNTY ENTERPRISE FUND
MONAGHAN COUNTY ENTERPRISE FUND
TIPPERARY SOUTH RIDING COUNTY
ENTERPRISE BOARD
WATERFORD CITY ENTERPRISE BOARD

CRAFTS COUNCIL OF IRELAND

Crafts Council HQ, Powerscourt Townhouse
South William Street, Dublin 2
Tel: (01) 679 7368, Fax: (01) 679 9197

Crescent Workshop, Castle Yard, Kilkenny
Tel: (056) 61804/62734
Contact: Leslie Reed

The Crafts Council of Ireland is the national design and economic development agency for the crafts in Ireland, with funding from government and the European Commission. The Council itself, which is not a funding organisation, acts in an advisory and promotional capacity to other state agencies and the craft sector, and has a wide range of activities:

- "Showcase Dublin" Trade Fair

- Gallery exhibitions and Gallery Shop in Dublin

- Business advisory services

- Training courses in Co. Kilkenny:

    1) Craft and Design Business Development Course, Crescent Workshop

    2) Pottery Skills Course, Thomastown

    3) Jewellery Skills Course, Crescent Workshop

    4) CAD/CAM Knitting Course, Limerick

- Information Services to retailers, buyers and the general public

- Bi-monthly *Newsletter*

- Database register of craftworkers in Ireland.

In addition, for eleven years, the Crafts Council of Ireland has been running the Business/Design Skills Course, initially in Kilworth, Co. Cork, and for the past five years at the Crescent Workshop in Kilkenny.

The course has been successful in aiding craft entrepreneurs in setting up and developing in business in both batch craft production and designing for industry. Seventy per cent of the graduates now run their own businesses and many have become employers.

Business/Design Skills Course

The fundamental objective of this course is to produce qualified crafts-people with the necessary skills to set up in business as craft entre-preneurs providing employment. This programme facilitates the imple-mentation of solid plans to set up in a wide range of craft businesses.

There is no course fee for EU residents. Participants can apply for a Crafts Council one-year interest-free loan to purchase materials. They will also receive a training allowance for the course duration, depending on punctuality and attendance.

Applicants should be qualified in a crafts discipline with either a third-level qualification or having served an apprenticeship. Each person should have a coherent plan to set up in business. Possible applicants might be:

- Those wishing to establish a business where they design and produce their own work themselves, either in individual or batch production

- Those wishing to design, prototype and test market work which they will eventually commission an industrial manufacturer to produce in batch or volume runs

- Those wishing to develop their design skills and portfolio (particu-larly in the use of the computer for textile or graphic design) to make it easier to find employment as designers in industry.

Every year a special residency is awarded to a graphic designer. The work they cover includes corporate identities for other course partici-pants and promotional material for the Crafts Council. This often in-volves full-colour processing and the complete supervision of print production. The experience and the business studies enable graphic designers to establish their own studio or to advance their career in the graphics industry. The project is co-funded by the EU through the European Social Fund, the Crafts Council of Ireland and SERtec (South East Region of (former) Eolas Technology Support).

Pottery Skills Course

The main objective of this course is to provide Ireland's commercial potteries with skilled staff who will be able to assist in the expansion of production, while also helping to maintain quality. The course has enabled the long-term unemployed to gain the necessary experience and skills to find work in the pottery industry. Individuals who would like to work with clay, but who have been unable to gain employment because they lack previous experience, are offered a chance to gain a place within the industry. Twelve trainees are accepted on each session.

Acceptance for the course is determined by interview. It is helpful, though not essential, to show some evidence of manual skills at this stage. In some cases an aptitude test may be offered to candidates to see how appropriate the course would be for their personal development.

The course consists of one 40-week session, commencing in September and ending in June. It runs from 9 a.m. to 5 p.m., Monday to Friday.

This project is funded by the EU through the European Social Fund and by Ireland through SERtec funding. The course, which is now in its fourth year, has had a 95 per cent success rate in trainees gaining full-time employment in potteries all around Ireland (for further information about this course, write to the above address).

Jewellery Design and Production Skills Course

The main aim of this course is to provide Ireland with a generation of craftspeople capable of producing jewellery of high technical and creative standard and to give applicants accepted on the course the technical fluency in jewellery fabrication which creative design demands. Specifically, the course aims:

- To develop 2-D skills so that design ideas can be easily sourced and rendered on paper for creative research and for presentation drawings to employers or clients

- To provide training that will enable participants to contribute to commercial production in established jewellery workshops

- To take further business studies to assist them in establishing their own independent studios/workshops.

CREG ASSOCIATES

Cregmore, Claregalway, Co. Galway
Tel: (091) 98117, Fax: (091) 98177
Contact: Pat Fahy

Creg Associates, a marketing consultancy firm, first meets with an aspiring entrepreneur for an informal confidential discussion to define the company's objectives. A proposal, outlining how these objectives could be met and how the marketing consultant could assist, is then drawn up. Proposals contain details on project targets, timing and fees.

Creg Associates provides assistance in the following areas:

* Company Development

* Marketing Policy and Planning

* National and International Market Research

* New Product Development

* New Business Acquisition

* Sourcing New Markets

* Submissions to Government Agencies

* New Product Search

* Training.

Case Study

Mullins Engineering

Mullins Engineering had been manufacturing subcontract sheet-metal customised enclosures, brackets and fittings for multinational companies for nine years. The company was founded by Joe Mullins and employed 18 people with a turnover of £0.8 million.

The owner was conscious of the company's dependence on the sub-contract sheet-metal manufacturing sector and aimed to diversify into product manufacturing. He engaged Creg Associates to help him to achieve this. More than 20 generic products and 500 relevant companies were focused on. Within a few months, when an opportunity that met all the criteria specified became available, the client company acquired a new, product-manufacturing and marketing company and integrated its production facility into the existing facility.

Mullins Engineering now manufactures and markets the product range internationally. It is one of the largest suppliers of value-added cabinets to the Irish electronics and telecommunication sectors, employing over 80 people with a turnover in excess of £14 million.

DEPARTMENT OF ENTERPRISE AND EMPLOYMENT

Kildare Street, Dublin 2
Tel: (01) 661 4444, Fax: (01) 676 2654
Davitt House, 65A Adelaide Road, Dublin 2

In January 1993, the Government established the Department of Enterprise and Employment with responsibility for all aspects of industrial policy, including planning, the development of new plans for indigenous industry, the implementation and co-ordination of new labour-market measures including training and commercial law. The restructuring brings together the former Departments of Industry and Commerce and of Labour. The intention is to create a new enterprise culture and a new climate for doing business in this country.

The objectives of the Department are:

- To promote both competitiveness in the economy and self-sustaining employment

- To monitor and improve the environment for business and to ensure that the framework of law, regulation and government policy promotes effective company performance and both public and business confidence

- To improve and upgrade the motivation, the qualifications and the flexibility of the labour force

- To ensure that markets for goods, services and labour operate in an effective way, while protecting the rights of employees and consumers

- To influence the formulation of policy in all areas which impact on enterprise and employment.

The Department has responsibility for:

- Industry, Industrial Relations and Patents

- Employment Rights and Obligations (including Occupational Safety and Health)

- Human Resources Development
- Enterprise Programmes
- Planning and Finance
- Commerce.

Enterprise Programmes Division

Small Business and Services Division
Department of Enterprise and Employment
Davitt House, Adelaide Road, Dublin 2

This division has responsibility to establish, fund and evaluate appropriate agency mechanisms and programmes that encourage the creation of self-sustaining employment.

It establishes appropriate county-level structures which will operate in liaison with relevant regional and national authorities and foster a spirit of enterprise at local level. The aim is, in its contribution to the competitiveness of the Irish economy, to oversee the development, funding and implementation of innovation, science and technology policy.

The main programmes division includes:

- Industrial Development Legislation, Liaison with Industrial Development Agencies (Forbairt/SFADCO)
- Revised Agency Structures, County Enterprise Boards
- National Standards and Quality — policy and administration
- National and International Programmes in Science and Technology.

The following are some of the relevant areas dealt with by the Department of Enterprise and Employment. (For a more detailed listing, contact the Department, see its Mission Statement, or see the Annual Report of the Department.)

- Agency Structures (Forfás, Forbairt, and IDA Ireland)
- Business Taxation Issues
- Competitiveness/Employment Protection Unit
- County Enterprise Boards
- EU Enterprise Policy

- EU Tariff Suspension Scheme (chemicals/pharmaceuticals and electronics)

- FÁS Policies

- ICC Currency Exchange Risk Scheme — this is overseen by the Department

- IDA Budget and Programmes

- IDA International Services Programme

- Industrial Relations

- Industry R&D Grants/EU Framework Programmes

- Intellectual Property (Patents, Trade Marks and Copyright)

- Occupational Safety and Health

- Sectoral Development

- SFADCO Budget and Programmes

- Standards — EU Directives

- Structural Funds — Industry and Human Resources.

Task Force on Small Business

The employment potential of small business is now recognised. Since the 1980s small business has been a net creator of jobs while large business has been a net shedder of jobs. This has been a worldwide trend and while Ireland has kept pace with developed countries such as Germany in the number of start-up companies, we have fallen behind in the number of companies that develop to become fast-growth companies. Furthermore, the interests and concerns of small business and services were not getting the attention they deserved and there was no Government Department with overall responsibility for the promotion and development of smell business and services.

In recognition of this, the Government established two Task Forces to review both the state of small business and the potential of services. The reports, published at the end of 1993 and in early 1994, contain over 200 separate recommendations for changes in Government policies (40 of which have been fully or partially implemented). The reports found, firstly, that increasingly when Irish people find jobs, it is in the small business sector, and, secondly, that the key problem facing small business in Ireland is addressing the high rate of business failure here. The changes proposed range from taxation issues to the removal of administrative burdens and the general improvement of incentives which will lead to an increase in the creation of jobs in the small business and services sectors.

The Small Business and Services Division was established in the Department of Enterprise and Employment in June 1994 to act as a single policy focus. While the immediate agenda has been set by the Task Force Reports, the mission and objectives of the Division are to improve the operating environment for small businesses and services firms by:

- Reducing the above-average level of business failure

- Increasing the ratio of fast-growth businesses

- Putting small business and services to the fore in public policy-making.

The Task Force Recommendations are addressed not only at Government but also at financial institutions among others. A dialogue has already been established with the main banks. Since publication of the Task Force Reports there has been a noticeable improvement in the range and quality of facilities available to small business. All financial institutions are anxious to participate in, and to contribute to, tripartite schemes with the State, EU and financial institutions participating.

Mr Richard Bruton TD, Minister for Enterprise and Employment, is anxious to respond appropriately to the issue of late payment. This matter is currently being examined with a view to bringing forward workable legislation in the current year, which will improve the business environment for small business.

Competitiveness and Employment Protection Unit (CEPU)

Competitiveness and Employment Protection Unit (CEPU)
Frederick Building, South Frederick Street, Dublin 2
Tel: (01) 676 1570, Fax: (01) 679 5710
Contact: Tom Sheehan/Arthur McAlinden/Noel Monaghan

The Competitiveness and Employment Protection Unit (CEPU) was established in August 1993 to co-ordinate and oversee the provision of assistance to firms in difficulty. Firms that contact the Unit are given the full support and advice available under the whole range of state programmes for industry and business. However, the Unit is not a means of providing subsidies.

SEE ALSO: AREA PARTNERSHIP COMPANIES
BUSINESS EXPANSION SCHEME
COUNTY ENTERPRISE BOARDS
FÁS, THE TRAINING AND EMPLOYMENT
    AUTHORITY
FORBAIRT
REGISTRY OF BUSINESS NAMES
REVENUE COMMISSIONERS
SHANNON DEVELOPMENT

DESIGN DESK

4 Lower Mount Street, Dublin 2
Tel: (01) 676 5518, Fax: (01) 661 9879
Contact: Ed Parkinson

Design Desk is a design and marketing consultancy. It deals in the areas of design, packaging, promotions, brochures and advertising. Design Desk discusses with clients what their product should achieve, what the content will be, how it should be presented and the overall image it should portray.

A few rough sketches displaying a number of options are shown to the client to establish the precise direction of the project. Subject to approval of the sketches, a full-size rough is produced to show how the real item will look. This is followed by artwork, photography, illustrations, colour proofs or whatever is necessary for the production of the item, which Design Desk will manage for its clients.

The time taken for completion of any project can vary from a few hours for a press ad, to several weeks for a range of packaging or a large brochure. Before commencing a project Design Desk will submit a quotation showing a breakdown of the costs involved.

Case Study

Design Desk was approached by two business people who wanted to set up a business selling Irish products into America.

After a number of discussions on the direction that the marketing the company should take, it was decided to place an ad in a New-York-based weekly paper to gauge the likely response to the new service.

The logo was first priority. After submitting a number of options and discussing the merits and faults of each, a logo was developed which incorporated elements from the first options submitted. When the logo was approved a complete range of stationery was produced.

Design Desk then designed and produced the ad which was sent to the paper. The initial response was encouraging with a reasonable number of orders coming in. A freephone number was then added to the ad, which increased the number of orders received.

When it was established that there was a good response to the service, a brochure was designed showing the range of products available. It was designed using two colours in an A3 size (300 x 420 mm, 12" x 16.5" approx.) which helped keep production costs in line at the early stages of the company's development. The brochure incorporated a response-paid order form which aided quick response from customers. The brochure was mailed to all respondents to the ads and used extensively in the marketing campaign. When it became clear that there was a sound base for the new venture and sufficient funds built up, a full-colour brochure was produced.

This was possible because there was a solid marketing plan in place. As part of the plan, the selling prices included the costs of marketing the service, producing the brochures, ads, freephone costs, etc.

As the relationship grew, Design Desk was able to offer a number of suggestions which helped the client in the marketing and development of their business. Design Desk enjoys helping clients to achieve success — after all, success breeds success.

DUBLIN CITY ENTERPRISE BOARD

Liffey House, 24–28 Tara Street, Dublin 2
Tel: (01) 677 3066, Fax: (01) 677 0497
Contact: Tom Gibney/Vanessa Carey

In September 1993, the Government announced details of the 35 County Enterprise Boards to be established throughout the country, covering County and Urban Local Authority Areas. Dublin City Enterprise Board is one such board, comprising a chairperson and 13 members. It reflects a balance of interests, embracing elected representatives of the City Council, representatives from the main public-sector agencies, business, trade union and community interests. The board members have been appointed to serve for a three-year term.

Grant-aid is available to assist in the establishment of small-scale economic projects, with the primary aim of facilitating the creation of sustainable jobs and the development of economic infrastructure at local level. The approach taken by Dublin City Enterprise Board to achieve this aim follows the initiatives outlined under the County Enterprise Boards (see p. 69).

Grant levels, grant payments and assistance criteria are the same for each of the 35 Enterprise Boards. Hence, grants will support:

- Individual, group or community projects providing products or services that have the capacity to achieve commercial viability

- The preparation of feasibility studies and business plans aimed at assessing the viability of projects.

Promoters of projects wishing to be considered for assistance should contact the relevant Enterprise Officer who will advise as to whether the project is suitable in the first instance for consideration by the Evaluation Committee of the Enterprise Board. (Application forms are available from Tom Gibney at the address above.)

Project promoters should be able to demonstrate that their project is in the commercial sphere, is capable of attaining economic viability without ongoing support and, in particular, demonstrates:

- That there is a market for the proposed product or service

- That adequate overall finance will be available to fund the project
- That they possess the management and technical capacity to implement the proposed project.

In addition, promoters must comply with existing policies on tax clearance, the certification of subcontractors and related matters. Normally applicants submit a comprehensive business plan in support of their application for assistance.

SEE ALSO: COUNTY ENTERPRISE BOARDS
LOUTH COUNTY ENTERPRISE FUND
MONAGHAN COUNTY ENTERPRISE FUND
TIPPERARY SOUTH RIDING COUNTY
ENTERPRISE BOARD
WATERFORD CITY ENTERPRISE BOARD

Dublin Institute of Technology

Kevin Street, Dublin 8
Tel/Fax: (01) 475 6650
Contact: Dr Peter Kavanagh

Bolton Street, Dublin 1,
Tel: (01) 402 3616, Fax: (01) 872 7879
Contact: Dr Pat McCormack

The Dublin Institute of Technology comprises:

- Bolton Street College

- Kevin Street College

- The College of Marketing and Design, Mountjoy Square

- The College of Commerce, Rathmines

- The College of Catering, Cathal Brugha Street

- The College of Music.

The individual colleges should be contacted for further information on the courses available.

The Dublin Institute of Technology established the Bolton Trust, which in turn runs the Powerhouse as a resource for entrepreneurs. Companies that rent space at the Powerhouse can draw on the skills of the Institute's 400 lecturers.

Dublin Institute of Technology at Kevin Street

Kevin Street College provides services in research and development, consultancy and design, and can assist in obtaining funding for projects nationally and from the EU. The technological areas covered are:

- Chemical and Food Processing

- Electrical, Electronic and Software Engineering

- Biotechnology.

The Institute also provides training courses for industrial clients. These courses include:

- Safety Management
- Environmental Management
- Industrial Control Systems
- QA Management.

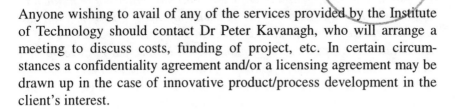

Anyone wishing to avail of any of the services provided by the Institute of Technology should contact Dr Peter Kavanagh, who will arrange a meeting to discuss costs, funding of project, etc. In certain circumstances a confidentiality agreement and/or a licensing agreement may be drawn up in the case of innovative product/process development in the client's interest.

Case Study

Recently, the Institute of Technology was approached by Turmec Engineering — an Irish marine engineering company employing approximately 60 people — to assist in the development and design of a process to help to reduce pollution related to fish processing. A project team was formed and funding was obtained through the Forbairt (formerly Eolas) Applied Research Programme. Funding on an extension of the process, with collaboration by transnational partners, is currently being sought from the EU through the LIFE programme. A prototype has been completed and a series of plant trials will be undertaken.

Dublin Institute of Technology at Bolton Street

The college at Bolton Street aims to promote and facilitate co-operation between the Institute and Industry and Commerce in Ireland. This co-operation can take a number of forms:

- Collaborative R&TD, supported under national and/or EU programmes
- Short training programmes for personnel in industry and commerce
- Consultancy projects
- Exchange of personnel including higher education/industry staff exchanges, and student and graduate placement.

These four activities can be pursued within each of the wide range of technological and business-expertise areas in which the College at Bolton Street specialises, and which fall generally within the Construction, Engineering, Transport and Printing Industries.

Case Study

Fountain and Landscapes Ltd.

A small indigenous company with international clients, Fountain and Landscapes Ltd. was involved in the design of theme parks, specialising in water features. The company approached the DIT Bolton Street with a conceptual design of a fountain clock which it intended to develop and market. Assistance was required in the mechanical design of the operating mechanism for such a fountain, and the College at Bolton Street was able to collaborate in this with Fountain and Landscapes. The fountain clock is now in production and an example is on display at the National Garden Exhibition, Kilquade, Co. Wicklow. Fountain and Landscapes has also exhibited fountain clocks at the Chelsea and Hampton Court Flower Show and has secured sales as far away as Singapore and California, as well as in Ireland and the UK.

SEE ALSO: FOOD PRODUCT DEVELOPMENT CENTRE
                 POWERHOUSE

DUNDALK EMPLOYMENT PARTNERSHIP

Carlton House, Dublin Street, Dundalk, Co. Louth
Tel: (042) 30288, Fax: (042) 30552
Contact: John Butler

Dundalk Employment Partnership was set up in 1991 by the local community to help long-term unemployed people to get back into the workforce or set up their own business, by giving them the skills and training necessary to do so. Dundalk is one of the 12 pilot areas selected for the area-based response to long-term unemployment, outlined in the Programme for Economic and Social Progress (PESP).

The Dundalk Employment Partnership has a Business Development Officer who will provide business advice and support to individuals, co-operatives and community groups, so that they can develop their projects. The assistance is given on the development of a business plan and on completion of submissions for various sources of finance.

Advice and a small amount of funding are available from the Partnership for long-term unemployed entrepreneurs who take the initiative to develop new product ideas and liaise with various organisations who can offer the relevant expertise in the development of the product.

The Partnership will consider taking an equity stake on providing loans. However, it will act as lender of last resort only if a company fails to get finance from other sources. Priority in all cases is given to long-term unemployed entrepreneurs.

The Area Enterprise Allowance Scheme means that long-term unemployed people who live in Dundalk (or any of the 12 designated PESP areas) and wish to start their own business will be entitled to keep their social welfare payments and any secondary benefits for the first 12 months subject to their business proposal being approved. They will also be entitled to retain part of their Social Welfare benefits in the second and third year of business.

The services of the business development officer are available free of charge to people within the Dundalk Urban area or to entrepreneurs proposing to employ people from the area.

In 1993, the Partnership published a grant and loan guide called *Funding for Your Organisation* which retailed at £9.25. A new and up-to-date edition will be published in 1995.

Case Study

Small Steps, Paula Gribben, Dundalk

Small Steps is an early-development clinic for children under five years of age who have learning disabilities. The clinic takes place in the child's home and the service covers the Dundalk, Drogheda, and the mid-Louth region.

Paula Gribben, the owner of the business, was formerly long-term unemployed. She approached the Dundalk Employment Partnership with her business proposal. Assistance in putting together a business plan for the idea was provided by the business development officer. The marketing manager also provided assistance.

The Partnership approved the application and Paula therefore retains all her Social Welfare benefits for the first year and part of these benefits for the second and third years. The Partnership gave Small Steps a loan of £1,000 to support the venture. Paula also availed of a Taxation Advice Seminar and a short "Start Your Own Business" evening course in conjunction with FÁS and the Dundalk Partnership. In addition, a free book-keeping service was provided by the Partnership.

Paula's plans for the future include establishing a toddler and a pre-school group. To achieve this, Small Steps will require premises and equipment, and will have to employ one other professional RNMH and two care staff.

SEE ALSO: AREA PARTNERSHIP COMPANIES
             BALLYMUN PARTNERSHIP
             THE ENTERPRISE TRUST
             FÁS, THE TRAINING AND EMPLOYMENT
                  AUTHORITY
             FINGLAS BUSINESS INITIATIVE
             GET TALLAGHT WORKING CO-OPERATIVE
                  SOCIETY LTD.
             MEITHEAL MHAIGH EO
             PLATO

EAMON DUNDON & ASSOCIATES

Argus House, Greenmount Office Park
Harold's Cross Bridge, Dublin 6W
Tel: (01) 453 2550, Fax: (01) 453 2554

Consultancy Services offered for small business include:

- Feasibility Studies
- Business Planning and Strategy
- Market Planning
- New-Product Searching
- Computer Selection
- Software Applications
- Pricing options
- ISO 9000: Training and Implementation
- Techniques of Total Quality
- World Class Manufacturing.

ENTERPRISE LINK

Wilton Park House
Wilton Place, Dublin 2
Tel (01) 660 2244, Fax: (01) 668 6813
Contact: Jane Touhey/Janet Swinburne

- Enterprise Link is single contact for all sources of support to start-up and small business in Ireland.

- It is an initiative of the Department of Enterprise and Employment, operated by Forbairt information staff

- The 1850 phone number ensures that a call can be made from any-where in the country for 11.5p.

Services include:

- Referrals to state agencies and private sources of enterprise support throughout the country using a specially designed database of support organisations

- A computerised logging system to ensure that records exist for each call so that follow-up is possible

- Factsheets on topics of interest to new businesses — available on a variety of issues from patents to business plans.

THE ENTERPRISE TRUST

1 Fitzwilliam Place, Dublin 2
Tel: (01) 661 9800, Fax: (01) 661 9255
Contact: Philip Mullally

The Enterprise Trust was established by the employer bodies — IBEC, ICOS and CIF — to co-ordinate employer input in support of the overall strategy for local economic and social development.

Role

To encourage and facilitate employer involvement in local enterprise strategies and initiatives and to translate commitment into practical action and financial support.

Aim

The focus of local enterprise strategies is on innovation and the aim is to generate opportunities leading to more viable business, and to ensure that unemployed people benefit from these opportunities.

Operation

Encouraging resources and providing advice at local level. Tax benefits apply to employers who contribute to local enterprise initiatives through the Enterprise Trust.

Results

- A local Innovation Fund, formed to prime innovative actions
- Integrated plans for enterprise and environmental development
- Sectoral development strategies
- Strategies to support new enterprises
- Strategies to grow selected SMEs (Plato — see separate entry)
- Strategies to form clusters and foster co-operation between SMEs.

SEE ALSO: AREA PARTNERSHIP COMPANIES
BALLYMUN PARTNERSHIP
DUNDALK EMPLOYMENT PARTNERSHIP
FÁS, THE TRAINING AND EMPLOYMENT
    AUTHORITY
FINGLAS BUSINESS INITIATIVE
GET TALLAGHT WORKING CO-OPERATIVE
    SOCIETY LTD.
MEITHEAL MHAIGH EO
PLATO

ENVISION MARKETING CONSULTANTS

Cathedral Buildings, Lower Abbeygate Street, Galway
Tel: (091) 68185, Fax: (091) 68510
Contact: Paul Ryan

Envision Marketing Consultants provide marketing services to companies ranging from multinationals to small indigenous businesses. Having worked with clients under programmes operated by boards including the former IDA, Bord Fáilte and FÁS, Envision's consultants have experience in meeting the requirements of entrepreneurs/owners of small businesses.

Envision can be of particular help to small businesses/entrepreneurs when problems arise such as a decline in turnover, superior performance of competitors, or when customers' complaints appear to be increasing.

Case Study

Frank Forde developed a household-safety product which he believed had considerable market potential. He approached Envision in order to obtain advice on how to realise the product's potential.

As a first step, Envision, in conjunction with Frank Forde, agreed a detailed feasibility-study work-plan (including costings and timings). The proposal for the study was submitted to Forbairt in order to seek a subsidy, which was subsequently granted.

The objectives of the feasibility study were:

- *To solicit the overall reaction to the product of security experts, distributors and potential customers*

- *To estimate the size of the market for the product (in order to guide sales forecasts and establish capital, production and cash-flow requirements)*

- *To investigate and identify international opportunities for the product through international agency and licensing agreements*

- *To develop a marketing strategy which would:*

    1) *Profile the target markets*

2) *Determine the optimum approach to packaging, promoting, pricing and distribution, based on market research findings.*

The feasibility study produced positive results and Envision continues to work closely with Frank, again based on an agreed brief. Envision is currently involved in assisting him in setting up his business and is guiding the launch of the product.

To date, Envision has:

- *Developed a business plan for use by Frank to negotiate with potential investors (i.e. banks and state agencies)*

- *Recruited personnel for the new business*

- *Identified an appropriate computer system and trained personnel to use it*

- *Developed and organised a range of necessary business information systems (e.g. telemarketing, customer database, installer agreements and installation procedures)*

- *Negotiated insurance premia reductions from insurance companies in respect of the product.*

Envision provided in excess of one consulting day per week to Frank Forde during the course of the feasibility study which was conducted over a six-month period. The current assignment is also based over a six-month period, though Envision's input is considerably reduced.

EOLAS, THE IRISH SCIENCE AND TECHNOLOGY AGENCY

Glasnevin, Dublin 9
Tel: (01) 837 0101, Fax: (01) 837 9620

EOLAS, the Irish Science and Technology Agency, was the state agency responsible for the development, application and promotion of science and technology. Forbairt has now taken over the responsibilities of EOLAS. The address remains the same.

SEE ALSO: FORBAIRT

ERNST & YOUNG

Ernst & Young Building, Harcourt Centre
Harcourt Street, Dublin 2
Tel: (01) 475 0555, Fax: (01) 475 0599
Contact: Entrepreneurial Services Department
Eamonn Doherty, Peter Mullock, Brian Redmond, Joe Devine

Ernst & Young provides a full range of support to entrepreneurial companies from concept to maturity. The firm assists in the preparation of business plans and financial projections. It also advises on sources of finance (including introductions to and liaison with banks and state agencies) and on partnerships and strategic alliances.

Extensive advice is given on corporate structure, staff recruitment and training, remuneration and incentive schemes. The financial services provided include accounts preparation and tax planning. Ernst & Young also assists with the establishment of costing, accounting and quality-management systems and controls. Continual assistance is given with expansion planning, including the raising of working and long-term capital.

EUROPEAN COMMISSION

Jean Monnet Centre, 39 Molesworth Street, Dublin 2
Tel: (01) 671 2244, Fax: (01) 671 2657
Contact: Tim Kelly

The information service has a comprehensive range of EU publications including a complete set of the *Official Journal of the EU* (formerly EC) covering current legislation and new proposals. The public has access to a well-stocked reference library. Audiovisual material on the EU is available on loan. To supplement the information service of the office, the Commission has established a number of European Documentation Centres in Irish universities (Dublin, Maynooth, Cork, Galway and Limerick).

The European Centre for Information and Promotion of Rural Development provides an information service on agriculture and rural development issues. The Centre is located in the Economics Department of University College, Galway (contact Mary Owens, tel: (091) 24411).

The European Commission in Brussels can, on its own initiative, use part of the Structural Funds budget to carry out measures of significant interest to the community.

Some of the programmes of interest to smaller companies include:

INTERREG II

INTERREG is a community initiative through which help is given to small and medium-sized enterprises (SMEs) and co-operatives, in particular via technology transfer and marketing support services. What distinguishes the range of measures that may be supported under INTERREG is the contribution they make to establishing lasting co-operative frameworks for action in areas where efforts were previously fragmented by the existence of a national border.

Local authorities implement many of the programmes — for example, the Department of Finance, Seán O'Sullivan/Richard McElligott (see pp. 106–9). The areas eligible for assistance under INTERREG are the whole of Northern Ireland (apart from the city of Belfast) and Counties Cavan, Donegal, Leitrim, Louth, Monaghan and Sligo in the Republic of Ireland. In addition, the South East region of

Ireland can co-operate with Dyfedd and Gwynedd in Wales. Application forms for the INTERREG Programme under any of the five initiatives — tourism, agriculture, fisheries and forestry, human resources, environmental protection and regional development have the following requirements:

- Project details — including intended geographical location

- Present provision in the area of the service/activity being proposed

- Forecast usage/demand

- How the project meets the objectives of the INTERREG programme

- Main beneficiaries and their location

- Whether the activity is a joint North/South project or a stand-alone application

- Identity of the lead partners in the project

- Estimated number of jobs created

- How the project makes use of the region's natural resources

- Whether the project has been published in an official EU journal

- Publicity arrangements.

Contact points for each of the main groups are:

Tourism

Northern Ireland:

Department of Economic Development
Tourism Branch, Netherleigh House
Massey Avenue, Belfast
Tel: (08) (01232) 763 244
Contact: Mr T. Hunter/Mrs L. Bell

Republic of Ireland:

Bord Fáilte, The Irish Tourist Board
Baggot Street Bridge, Dublin 2
Tel: (01) 676 5871
Contact: Jim McGuigan

Department of Tourism and Trade
Kildare Street, Dublin 2
Tel: (01) 661 4444
Contact: Paul Appleby

Agriculture/Fisheries/Forestry

Northern Ireland:

Department of Agriculture
Co-ordination Division, Dundonald House
Upper Newtownards Road, Belfast
Tel: (08) (01232) 650 111, ext. 569
Contact: Ms J. McLernon

Republic of Ireland:

Department of Agriculture and Food
Agriculture House, Kildare Street, Dublin 2
Tel: (01) 678 9011
Contact: Paul O'Keeffe, Seán Ó Broin

Fisheries Measure
Finance Co-ordination Unit
Department of the Marine, Leeson Lane, Dublin 2
Tel: (01) 678 5444
Contact: Declan Doyle

Forestry Measure, Forest Service
Department of Energy, Leeson Lane, Dublin 2
Tel:(01) 676 3636
Contact: Séamus Ryan

Human Resource Development

Northern Ireland:

Department of Education
Rathgael House, Balloo Road
Bangor, Co. Down
Tel: (08) (0247) 270 077
Contact: Ms J. Ingram

Training and Employment Agency
Clarendon House, Belfast
Tel: (08) (01232) 244 300
Contact: M. Pinkerton

Republic of Ireland:
ESF Section
Department of Enterprise and Employment
Adelaide Road, Dublin 2
Tel: (01) 661 4444
Contact: Pat Hayden, Joe McDermott

Environmental Protection

Northern Ireland:
Department of the Environment
Progressive House, Belfast
Tel: (08) (01232) 328 161
Contact: Mr I.N.L. Jones

Department of the Environment
Calvert House, Belfast
Tel: (08) (01232) 230 560
Contact: Dr G. Alexander

Republic of Ireland:
Department of the Environment
O'Connell Bridge House, Dublin 2
Tel: (01) 679 3377
Contact: John Harte

Regional Development

Northern Ireland:
Department of Finance and Personnel, EU Branch
Parliament Buildings, Stormont, Belfast
Tel: (08) (01232) 763210, ext. 2112
Contact: Mrs C. Blakley/Mrs C. Cavanagh

Republic of Ireland:

(for road projects only)
Department of the Environment
O'Connell Bridge House, Dublin 2
Tel: (01) 679 3377
Contact: Phil Hopkins

(all other projects)
EU (Structural Funds) Section
Department of Finance
Upper Merrion Street, Dublin 2
Tel: (01) 676 7571, ext. 2439
Contact: Seán O'Sullivan, Richard McElligott

Also:

EU Branch INTERREG
Department of Finance and Personnel
Parliament Buildings, Stormont
Belfast BT4 3SW

EU Structural Funds Unit
Department of Finance
Upper Merrion Street, Dublin 2

EUROFORM

This programme encourages investment in training and employment creation. The initiative is designed to reinforce other related community programmes which deal with training and job opportunities generated by technological change, namely LEONARDO, LEDA and ERGO.

TELEMATIC SYSTEMS OF GENERAL INTEREST

Promotes advanced communication within SMEs and helps them to create or develop such services themselves.

STRIDE

Helps to develop links between research centres and industry.

RETEX

Aims to accelerate the diversification of economic activities in areas heavily dependent on the textile and clothing sector and to encourage the adjustment of commercially viable businesses in all industrial sectors. The co-financed measures include improving access to venture capital and loans.

Other EU grants and loan schemes of interest include:

Business Development

- CDI — promotes long-term contractual arrangements between SMEs and African, Caribbean and Pacific (ACP) firms

- Eurotech Capital — aims to assist SMEs in meeting the financial needs of transitional advanced technology

- USLI — provides the financial support to improve and upgrade existing large-scale installations.

Cinema and Television

- MEDIA 92 — aims to assist audiovisual pilot projects in distribution, production, training and finance

- EDFO — films produced in EU and distributed in three or more EU countries may qualify for a loan

- BABEL — funds 50 per cent of the cost of dubbing and subtitling of approximately 12 films per year.

Energy

- NON NUCLEAR ENERGY — focuses on models for energy and environment: for example, fossil fuels. Various energy programmes are envisaged for the period, 1994–98, but details have yet to be finalised.

Food Technologies

- FLAIR — aims to contribute to the improvement of food safety and quality for the consumer, and to the strengthening of food science and technology

- Finance

- European Investment Bank (EIB) — provides long-term loans for capital investment projects: for example, industry, energy, infrastructure, tourism and services related to the production sector.

Marine

- FISHERIES — aims to develop fishery management, fishing methods, aquaculture and upgrading of fishery products.

A further grant of interest to small businesses concerns Local Enterprise Initiatives. This scheme aims to help entrepreneurial women to set up co-operatives or other employment creation initiatives. It runs until 1995 and grants of £1,100 per full-time job created are available. At least two jobs must be created to avail of this scheme and no more than five will be grant-aided. Men may be employed by the business, but the decision-making process must be undertaken by women. (For further information, contact Patricia Brand, LEI, Brand & Associates, 1 Westland Square, Dublin 2, Tel: (01) 677 9199.)

EC Grants Guide (published by KPMG Stokes Kennedy Crowley and the Small Firms Association, price: £15) gives more information on all of the European programmes listed.

Chartered accountants Arthur Andersen have also produced a booklet, *A Business Guide to Funds,* which includes information on EU grants.

The Small Firms Association has published:

- *A Comprehensive Guide to Government and EC Support Programmes*

- *Budget Lines of Use to Small and Medium-sized Industries.*

Structural Funds

Funds may be available under the EU Structural Funds (comprising the European Regional Development Fund, the European Social Fund, and the European Agriculture Guarantee and Guidance Fund). (For further information, apply to the EU Commission at the above address.)

Note

The EU's definition of small and medium-sized enterprises (SMEs) quoted in the *EC Grants Guide*: a small or medium-sized enterprise is defined as an independent business (fewer than 25 per cent of its shares can be held by one or more large companies), which has no more than

250 employees, and either turnover less than ECU 20 million (IR£14.9 million) or total assets net of depreciation less than ECU 10 million (IR£7.4 million).

SEE ALSO: BORD FÁILTE
                AN BORD TRÁCHTÁLA
                EUROPEAN INFORMATION CENTRE
                LEADER PROGRAMME
                SHANNON DEVELOPMENT
                STRATEGIC PROGRAMME FOR INNOVATION
                        AND TECHNOLOGY TRANSFER
                        (SPRINT)
                WOMEN'S LOCAL EMPLOYMENT INITIATIVES
                        (LEI)

EUROPEAN INFORMATION CENTRES

For relevant address, see below

There are six European Information Centres, based in Dublin, Limerick, Sligo, Waterford, Cork and Galway. EICs were established in co-operation with existing organisations that already advised firms. Each EIC has a staff specially trained to access and provide information to small and medium-sized firms on all aspects of EU affairs likely to interest local business. There is no formal link between EICs and BICs but the organisations do refer clients to each other (BICs provide help specifically to business start-ups).

The Centres provide information on:

- European Union legislation

- EU programmes and policies

- Copies of EU tenders

- Public procurement

- Finding a partner for a European venture

- Locating overseas subcontractors

- Assistance with export procedures and customs formalities

- Labelling requirements

- Opportunities in European research and development programmes

- Locating contacts in the European Commission.

ADDRESSES

EIC
Eastern Region
An Bord Tráchtála, Merrion Hall
Sandymount, Dublin 4
Tel: (01) 269 5 011, Fax: (01) 269 5820

Mid-Western Region
Shannon Development
The Granary, Michael Street, Limerick
Tel: (061) 410 777, Fax: (061) 361 903

North-Western Region
Sligo Chamber of Commerce
Harbour Office, Custom House Quay, Sligo
Tel: (071) 61274, Fax: (071) 60912

South-Eastern Region
Waterford Chamber of Commerce
An Bord Tráchtála Office
Western Industrial Estate, Cork Road, Waterford
Tel: (051) 72639, Fax: (051) 79220

South-Western Region
Cork Chamber of Commerce
An Bord Tráchtála
68–69 South Mall, Cork
Tel: (021) 509 044, Fax: (021) 271 347
Contact: Tara Dennehy

Western Region
Galway Chamber of Commerce and Industry
Hardiman House, 5 Eyre Square, Galway
Tel: (091) 62624, Fax: (091) 61963

SEE ALSO: AN BORD TRÁCHTÁLA

EUROTECH CAPITAL

European Commission, DG XVIII/A4
Wagner Building, Rue Alcide de Gasperi
L-2920 Luxembourg
Tel: (00) (352) 43 01 36 246, Fax: (00) (352) 43 63 22
Contact: Joel Berger, Giorgio Chiarion Casoni

The Financing of Transnational High-Technology Projects

- A minimum of 20 per cent of the investment capacity of the members of the network is reserved for European small and medium-sized enterprises (SMEs), which undertake transnational high-technology projects (THTPs).

- At present, the Network has an overall investment capacity of ECU 200 million for companies developing THTPs.

- Companies announce their projects to the Eurotech Capital Network through a free entry form.

- Projects introduced by SMEs developing THTPs and seeking finance include information on their management team, their product and their financial situation.

- On receiving a suitable project, an investor establishes direct contact with the project's promoter.

Priority is given to small and medium-sized enterprises seeking start-up or development finance and to public or private sector organisations seeking venture capital to form spin-off companies. In order to be eligible, a company should:

- Have fewer than 500 employees

- Be involved in high technology

- Be transnational (i.e. there should be exchange of knowledge between that company and partners in at least two member states)

- Be based in a member country of the EU.

The sort of information the investors require includes:

- Type of finance sought

- Company and contact details

- Business description

- Product description

- Marketing objectives

- Financial overview

- Management details.

Types of Finance Available

Seed Finance

Finance provided to companies to aid in the research and development of a concept before a business has reached the start-up stage.

Start-up Finance

Finance provided to companies to develop and market a new product.

Early-Stage Finance

Finance provided to companies that have completed the product-development stage and require further funds to initiate commercial manufacturing and sales.

Expansion Finance

Finance provided for the growth and expansion of a company that has begun to generate a profit. Capital may be used in this situation to finance increased production capacity, market or product development and/or to provide additional working capital.

How to Apply

To apply for venture capital through Eurotech Capital, a company should submit a development proposal on a standard Eurotech Capital proposal form, which can be obtained by sending contact details to the above address. If a member of the Eurotech Capital Network (an investor) is interested, a company will be approached directly to provide full information. Private discussions will commence thereafter.

The Eurotech Capital Network: 13 Financial Institutions

Finanziaria Italiana di Partecipazione Spa (FIP)/Italy
Società Finanziaria di Partecipazione Spa (SOFIPA)/Italy
Innolion/France
Instituto Nacional de Industria (INI)/Spain
Sofinnova S.A./France
Euroventures Benelux Team N.V./Belgium/The Netherlands
Gilde Investment Funds/The Netherlands
Eurosud Capital/France/Italy
Techno Venture Management (TVM)/Germany
Biotechnology Investments Limited (BIL)/United Kingdom
Danish Development Finance Corporation (DDFC)/Denmark
Alta Berkeley Associates/United Kingdom
Finovelec/France

FARRELL GRANT SPARKS

Chartered Accountants
Molyneux House, Bride Street, Dublin 8
Tel: (01) 475 8137, Fax: (01) 475 2044
Contact: Tim Fenn/Jerry Lambe

This firm of chartered accountants has a Small Business Unit to assist small business clients in maintaining efficient and up-to-date financial records, thereby ensuring timely access to accounting management and other information. Tax planners advise start-up businesses on the most tax-efficient structuring of a company's finances and ensure that entrepreneurs are registered for VAT, PAYE, PRSI, etc. Throughout the year clients are advised on tax deadlines and the payment of taxes.

The Corporate Finance Division in Farrell Grant Sparks advises the promoters of a business in devising strategic development plans. It monitors the implementation of these plans on an ongoing basis to ensure continued positive development and growth.

Through contacts with the providers of capital, assistance in raising finance is provided to meet each company's requirements. The firm's experience in negotiating terms with financial institutions is of particular value to entrepreneurs.

Farrell Grant Sparks also provides company secretarial services to handle the registration of companies, the preparation and filing of annual returns and accounts in the Companies Office, and the preparation of minutes to statutory directors' and annual general meetings.

To avail of these services an individual can call the firm directly and set up a meeting with the relevant personnel.

Case Studies

Softworks Computing Ltd.

The Smurfit Job Creation and Enterprise Fund has invested £150,000 in Softworks Computing Ltd. following negotiations between the Fund Managers and Farrell Grant Sparks, advisors to Softworks.

Softworks was established in 1990 to exploit a market niche for user-friendly software to monitor attendance, absence and overtime. Its product, Clockwise, was launched in 1992 and has already been successful for many prestigious customers, including Smithwicks Brewery, Premier Periclase (CRH) and the Educational Building Society.

Following the initial development of the product, Softworks required investment to fund the sales and marketing drive which would fuel the company's growth. Farrell Grant Sparks and Softworks compiled an investment proposal and identified suitable sources of funds and potential investors. The investment of £150,000 by the Smurfit Fund, in return for 30 per cent of Softworks' shares, is the result of this work.

Byrark Fabrications Ltd.

The promoters of this venture were referred to Farrell Grant Sparks with an idea for a new business that would manufacture security products. A business plan was drawn up to raise finance through both leasing and commercial banks. Farrell Grant Sparks assisted the promoters in forming a company and proceeded to register the new business for VAT and PAYE. In late August 1991, Byrark commenced trading from the former IDA (now Forbairt) Enterprise Centre in Tallaght. The company specialises in the manufacture of a number of different security products and has been successful both in exporting and in replacing imported products previously manufactured outside the state.

Byrark succeeded in increasing its workforce to 10 in its first 15 months of trading. Farrell Grant Sparks is in contact with the company on an ongoing basis to assist in meetings and negotiations with banks, the Revenue and Forbairt.

FÁS, THE TRAINING AND EMPLOYMENT AUTHORITY

(For a detailed listing of local FÁS offices,
see pp. 128–35)

FÁS, the Training and Employment Authority assists:

- Individuals starting up a business

- Newly established companies

- Small firms

- Expanding companies, particularly small and medium-sized enterprises.

Assistance is provided through a package of services including:

- Employment and Recruitment Services

- Training Programmes

- Advisory Services to Business

- Support for Co-operative and Community-based Enterprises.

Recruitment Services

FÁS offers a comprehensive recruitment service to employers at its Employment Services Offices nationwide (see list at end of chapter). From its extensive jobseeker database, FÁS can match vacancies with suitable candidates. A shortlist of applicants can be compiled and referred to the employer. Screening and interview facilities are also available on request. Job vacancies are advertised throughout the FÁS network of offices and on RTE Aertel (teletext) service.

Employers who have difficulty recruiting from the Irish labour market (for example, for vacancies with specific technical sills, overseas experience or language requirements) can use the FÁS European Employment Service (EURES). The EURES network of European advisers and computer database can match job requirements with potential applicants throughout the European Union.

For further information, contact any FÁS Employment Services Office (see list at end of chapter).

Training Programmes

Starting a New Business

For individuals thinking of setting up a business, FÁS runs a Business Appraisal Training Programme. This 10-week course is available to unemployed people on a full-time basis, and a training allowance is paid to participants by FÁS. It is also available to others as an evening course, on a fee-paying basis.

The course aims to develop and evaluate business ideas and to assess the strengths and weaknesses of participants in setting up and running a business. The course covers marketing, finance, sales, book-keeping, taxation, banking, computers, business plan, and enterprise-skills development.

Following the Business Appraisal Training Programme, participants have access to further support services including technical training, enterprise workshops, resource materials and ongoing business advice.

For further information, contact any FÁS Employment Services Office or FÁS Training Centre.

New Companies

Through the Services to Business Division, FÁS helps new companies to develop human-resource policies and training programmes. The Services to Business Division also assists by arranging for the provision of training directly, where appropriate.

FÁS Advisors initially meet with company representatives to discuss:

- The human resource plan for the venture

- Available levels of skills

- The skill levels required

- Training grants available

- Areas where FÁS can assist directly in providing training.

A detailed training plan is drawn up and the appropriate level of grant-aid is recommended to IDA Ireland or Forbairt, as appropriate. FÁS also assists with its implementation. For further information, contact Regional FÁS Office (Services to Business Division). (See list at end of chapter.)

Small Firms

The number of small firms throughout Ireland is growing, and helping small firms to set-up, survive and develop is a FÁS priority. Services include:

- Advice and assistance provided by Regional Advisors

- Special Management Development Programme for small businesses run in association with Forbairt. This modular programme, which identifies barriers to development and provides a basis for secure and profitable growth, is tailored to the needs of individual companies and is provided in-house on a one-to-one basis with the owner/ manager

- Training Support Scheme, which is a grant scheme biased towards small firms particularly owner/manager development (see below)

- A wide range of evening courses specifically aimed at small firms, available through FÁS Training Centres.

Established Business

FÁS offers a range of services and training programmes to established businesses, including assistance to companies in:

- Identifying and implementing training needs

- Training existing employees

- Training potential employees within the workplace

- Training apprentices.

Training Support Scheme

The Training Support Scheme aims to assist small and medium-sized enterprises (up to 500 employees) to improve their competitiveness in the national and international marketplace. It is aimed at improving the skills of existing employees at all levels from operative to management.

This scheme is open to firms engaged in manufacturing industry, internationally-traded services, physical distribution, wholesale, retail and motor. Non-manufacturing construction firms that trade internationally are eligible. Evidence must be available that the training need has been clearly identified and that this need is linked to a business plan or strategy, using a Business Development Training Plan framework.

Grants are approved, subject to availability of funds, for the development of personnel at all levels and all occupations in the following key priority areas:

- Strategic Planning

- Management

- Information Systems

- Technology

- Marketing/Languages

- Productivity

- Quality/Service

- Finance.

Grants are also available to implement training identified in the national training strategies (see below) for each business sector. Grants are normally a percentage of the training cost, with a higher percentage being paid to smaller firms.

Construction Training Incentive Scheme

The Construction Training Incentive Scheme is designed to increase and improve training within the construction sector in order to increase competitiveness, quality and productivity. It is aimed at improving the skills of existing employees at all levels from operative to management. Key training areas include:

- Management

- Quality

- Health and Safety.

Grants are a percentage of the training costs.

Levy Grant Scheme

A Levy Grant Scheme operates in the following sectors:

- Food, Drink and Tobacco

- Chemical and Allied Products

- Textiles, Clothing and Footwear.

Under the scheme for these sectors, employers with emoluments above a certain level are levied at 1 per cent of payroll costs. Using a system of self-rating of training, employers may be entitled to a Training Activity Grant equivalent to 90 per cent of levy paid.

For companies in the engineering industry that are engaged in *electronic activities*, a Levy Grant Scheme is currently in operation. A levy of 0.25 per cent of payroll costs is charged to a company with payroll over £78,000 per annum. For an employer with payroll costs below this figure, an opt-in fee of £200 is payable to allow participation in the Scheme.

The following grants are available to electronic companies that pay a levy of 0.25 per cent of payrolls costs:

- Training equipment grants — to a maximum of 75 per cent of cost or £2,500, whichever is the lesser — are available for projectors, screens, videos etc.

- Grants of up to 75 per cent of course fees — to a maximum of £4,000 in any one year for technical, administrative and supervisory training — towards the cost of approved external or in-company courses

- Grants of 50 per cent of the cost to a maximum of £2,500 per trainee for graduate and £70 per week for undergraduate training.

NOTE: these grants are subject to annual review.

Job Training Scheme

The Job Training Scheme is a quality work-based training programme provided to unemployed persons by employers, in co-operation with FÁS. It is aimed at using the training capacity and expertise within the workplace to train potential employees. The benefits for employers are a trained potential workforce and improved company performance.

The scheme provides full-time training for between 13 and 52 weeks, depending on the training required in each case. It is open to all employers with employment potential in the private sector, commercial state sector or voluntary sector, who have a capacity to provide training with certification to the required levels. Both FÁS and the employer must be satisfied that trainees can benefit from the training on offer.

Trainees receive a weekly training allowance from the employer. FÁS contribution to the allowance is 75 per cent of FÁS approved training-allowance rates.

Apprenticeship Training

The standards-based apprenticeship is based on uniform, pre-specified and industry-agreed standards, derived from analyses of current and future needs of Irish industry. It ensures the highest level of skills for individual firms and the Irish labour market generally. To help apprentices to achieve these standards, the scheme provides seven alternating phases of on-the-job and off-the-job training in conjunction with FÁS Training Centres or educational colleges.

On successful completion of the standards-based apprenticeship, apprentices will receive a National Craft Certificate, recognised both in Ireland and internationally.

The standards-based apprenticeship operates for the following trades: Carton Maker; Originator; Bookbinder; Printer; Plasterer; Vehicle Body Repairer; Aircraft Mechanic; Wood Machinist; Cabinet Maker; Brick/ Stone Layer; Sheet Metal Worker; Painter/Decorator; Agricultural Mechanic; Refrigeration Craftsperson; Construction Plant Fitter; Metal Fabricator; Heavy Vehicle Mechanic; Toolmaker; Plumber; Motor Mechanic; Fitter; Carpenter/Joiner.

A range of support services is provided by FÁS including:

- Apprentice Training Packs for both employer and apprentice

- Training and development for in-company apprentice supervisors and assessors

- On-the-job monitoring, which includes advice and assistance to employers on all aspects of apprenticeship

- Training Allowance paid by FÁS for apprentices attending off-the-job phases in the following sectors: Construction; Motor; Printing and Paper; Engineering (excluding Electronics). This allowance is paid from an Apprenticeship Fund established as a result of Apprenticeship Levy contributions from these sectors of industry.

- To promote the entry of women and to encourage an increase in the recruitment of women into the designated apprenticeships, FÁS offers a bursary to employers. The bursary applies only to sectors contributing to the Apprenticeship Levy.

Advisory Service for Businesses

FÁS provides companies with specialist advice and assistance in training and development matters. The basis for this service is understanding that the success of businesses depends mainly on the knowledge and skills of those who manage and work in them; and that the knowledge and skills of the people of all levels in business can be improved through development and training.

FÁS Service to Business advisers throughout the county have extensive experience in business, combining an understanding of the business environment with an in-depth knowledge of human resource development. Particular emphasis is placed on improving the capability of Irish businesses, especially small to medium-sized firms, to compete successfully in the Single European Market and the wider international environment.

National Training Strategies

At national level, FÁS formulates national training strategies, with the assistance of advisory sectoral committees for Engineering; Construction; Food, Drink and Tobacco; Chemicals and Allied Products; Textiles, Clothing and Footwear; Printing and Paper; and Services. To give additional focus to small firms, a special training advisory committee has been established to respond to and assist small firms with their growth and development.

A key objective for FÁS is the production of human resource intelligence for the various business sectors. Studies are commissioned in the industrial and commercial sectors. Steering groups to oversee these studies are established from the relevant Industrial Training Committees and outside agencies. Action plans to implement the findings and recommendations are developed and are given priority in delivery of FÁS services to business. Copies of studies may be purchased from FÁS Services to Business Division, 27–33 Upper Baggot Street, Dublin 4.

Support for Co-operatives and Community-based Enterprises

Community Enterprise Programme

The FÁS Community Enterprise Programme offers community groups and co-operative groups a comprehensive package of advice and finance to help them to become involved in enterprise and the creation of economically viable jobs. It helps community groups to identify and develop business ideas and to progress these ideas to commercial reality, by providing training, advice and financial assistance.

Types of Community Enterprises

- A community-owned company

- A community-run co-operative

- A workers' co-operative

- A community-run business advice and support centre.

Help and Support

A package of training and advisory supports plus financial assistance is available including:

- Training to meet the needs of individual groups at different stages of development e.g. idea generation, business start-up and management

- Advice and signposting of sources of information

- Feasibility-study grants

- Enterprise Worker grants

- Management grants.

How to Apply

FÁS will consider projects from any community group that feels it has the energy, commitment and dedication to turn an idea into a viable business and provide jobs for people within the community.

Projects are assessed on the basis of:

- Commercial viability of the business idea

- Job-creation potential

- Background of the sponsoring group

- The condition that no displacement of other businesses will occur as a result of the business proposal.

For further information and assistance on progressing a community-based business idea, contact Regional FÁS Office (External Training Division).

For details of FÁS assistance to Workers' Co-operatives, see section on FÁS Co-operative Development Unit.

FÁS EMPLOYMENT SERVICES AND REGIONAL OFFICES:

FÁS Employment Services Office (Arklow)
Government Buildings, Castlepark
Arklow, Co. Wicklow
Tel: (0402) 39509, Fax: (0402) 39413

FÁS Employment Services Office (Athlone)
Town House Centre, St Mary's Square
Athlone, Co. Westmeath
Tel: (0902) 75288, Fax: (0902) 75291

FÁS Employment Services Office (Ballina)
Riverside, Church Road, Ballina, Co. Mayo
Tel: (096) 21921/21211, Fax: (096) 70608

FÁS Employment Services Office (Ballybofey)
Main Street, Ballybofey, Co. Donegal
Tel: (074) 31233, Fax: (074) 31446

FÁS Employment Services Office (Ballyfermot)
Ballyfermot Hill, Ballyfermot, Dublin 10
Tel: (01) 626 6211, Fax: (01) 626 4135

FÁS Employment Services Office (Bantry)
Warner Centre, Barrack Street
Bantry, Co. Cork
Tel: (027) 50464, Fax: (027) 50203

FÁS Employment Services Office (Blanchardstown)
The Brace Centre, Main Street
Blanchardstown, Dublin 15
Tel: (01) 820 1011, Fax: (01) 821 1635

FÁS Employment Services Office (Bray)
Royal House, Main Street, Bray, Co. Wicklow
Tel: (01) 286 7912, Fax: (01) 286 4170

FÁS Employment Services Office (Carlow)
Kennedy Street, Carlow
Tel: (0503) 42605, Fax: (0503) 41759

FÁS Employment Services Office (Carrick-on-Shannon)
Government Buildings, Shannon Lodge
Carrick-on-Shannon, Co. Leitrim
Tel: (078) 20503, Fax: (078) 20505

FÁS Employment Services Office (Castlebar)
Units 7 & 8, Humbert Mall
Castlebar, Co. Mayo
Tel: (094) 22011, Fax: (094) 22832

FÁS Employment Services Office (Cavan)
Magnet House, Farnham Street, Cavan
Tel: (049) 31767/32532, Fax: (049) 32527

FÁS Employment Services Office (Clondalkin)
Westward House, Main Street
Clondalkin, Dublin 22
Tel: (01) 459 1766, Fax: (01) 457 2878

FÁS Employment Services Office (Clonmel)
6 Mary Street, Clonmel, Co. Tipperary
Tel: (052) 24422, Fax: (052) 24565

FÁS Employment Services Office (Coolock)
Unit 1A, Northside Shopping Centre
Coolock, Dublin 17
Tel: (01) 847 5911, Fax: (01) 847 5770

FÁS Employment Services Office (Cork)
Government Buildings
Sullivan's Quay, Cork
Tel: (021) 544 377, Fax: (021) 968 389

FÁS Employment Services Office (Drogheda)
14 North Quay, Drogheda, Co. Louth
Tel: (041) 37646, Fax: (041) 38120

FÁS Employment Services Office (Dublin)
D'Olier House, D'Olier Street, Dublin 2
Tel: (01) 671 1544, Fax: (01) 679 8240

FÁS Employment Services Office (Dublin)
27–33 Upper Baggot Street, Dublin 4
Tel: (01) 668 5777, Fax: (01) 660 9259

FÁS Employment Services Office (Dundalk)
78–79 Park Street, Dundalk, Co. Louth
Tel: (042) 32311, Fax: (042) 36311

FÁS Employment Services Office (Dún Laoghaire)
18/21 Cumberland Street
Dún Laoghaire, Co. Dublin
Tel: (01) 280 8488, Fax: (01) 280 8476

FÁS Employment Services Office (Ennis)
42 Parnell Street, Ennis, Co. Clare
Tel: (065) 29213, Fax: (065) 28502

FÁS Employment Services Office (Finglas)
Unit 14c, Finglas Shopping Centre, Finglas, Dublin 11
Tel: (01) 834 6222, Fax: (01) 834 6386

* FÁS Employment Services Office (Galway)
Island House, Cathedral Square, Galway
Tel: (091) 67165, Fax: (091) 62718

FÁS Employment Services Office (Kilkenny)
Irishtown, Kilkenny
Tel: (056) 65514, Fax: (056) 64451

FÁS Employment Services Office (Killarney)
Unit 1, Kenmare Place, Killarney, Co. Kerry
Tel: (064) 32466, Fax: (064) 32759

FÁS Employment Services Office (Letterkenny)
Ramelton Road, Ballyraine Industrial Estate,
Letterkenny, Co. Donegal
Tel: (074) 22200, Fax: (074) 24840

FÁS Employment Services Office (Limerick)
18 Davis Street, Limerick
Tel: (061) 228 333, Fax: (061) 412 326

FÁS Employment Services Office (Longford)
7 Market Square, Longford
Tel: (043) 46820/46821, Fax: (043) 45702

FÁS Employment Services Office (Mallow)
25 O'Brien Street, Mallow, Co. Cork
Tel: (022) 21900, Fax: (022) 22582

FÁS Employment Services Office (Monaghan)
16 Church Square, Monaghan
Tel: (047) 81511, Fax: (047) 83441

FÁS Employment Services Office (Mullingar)
Church Avenue, Mullingar, Co. Westmeath
Tel: (044) 48805, Fax: (044) 43978

FÁS Employment Services Office (Navan)
Tara Mall, Trimgate Street, Navan, Co. Meath
Tel: (046) 23630/23925, Fax: (046) 21903

FÁS Employment Services Office (Nenagh)
Connolly Street, Nenagh, Co. Tipperary
Tel: (067) 31879, Fax: (067) 31167

FÁS Employment Services Office (Newbridge)
6 George's Street, Newbridge, Co. Kildare
Tel: (045) 31372/31090, Fax: (045) 34446

FÁS Employment Services Office (Newcastlewest)
Government Buildings
Gortboy, Newcastlewest, Co. Limerick
Tel: (069) 62411, Fax: (069) 61561

FÁS Employment Services Office (Portlaoise)
4 Meehan House, James Fintan Lalor Ave
Portlaoise, Co. Laois
Tel: (0502) 21462, Fax: (0502) 20945

FÁS Employment Services Office (Roscommon)
Castle Street, Roscommon
Tel: (0903) 26802, Fax: (0903) 25399

FÁS Employment Services Office (Shannon)
Industrial Estate, Shannon, Co. Clare
Tel: (061) 471133, Fax: (061) 472613

FÁS Employment Services Office (Sligo)
Government Buildings, Cranmore, Sligo
Tel: (071) 43390, Fax: (071) 44120

FÁS Employment Services Office (Swords)
34 Main Street, Swords, Co. Dublin
Tel: (01) 840 5252, Fax: (01) 840 3751

FÁS Employment Services Office (Tallaght)
Westpark, Old Bawn Road
Tallaght, Dublin 24
Tel: (01) 452 5111, Fax: (01) 452 5591

FÁS Employment Services Office (Thurles)
Government Buildings, Stradavoher,
Thurles, Co. Tipperary
Tel: (0504) 22188, Fax: (0504) 23574

FÁS Employment Services Office (Tralee)
17 Lower Castle Street, Tralee, Co. Kerry
Tel: (066) 22155, Fax: (066) 22954

FÁS Employment Services Office (Tralee)
Industrial Estate, Monavalley, Tralee, Co. Kerry
Tel: (066) 22155, Fax: (066) 23065

FÁS Employment Services Office (Tuam)
High Street, Tuam, Co. Galway
Tel: (093) 28066, Fax: (093) 28068

FÁS Employment Services Office (Tullamore)
Church Street, Tullamore, Co. Offaly
Tel: (0506) 51176/21921, Fax: (0506) 21964

FÁS Employment Services Office (Waterford)
28 Patrick Street, Waterford
Tel: (051) 72961, Fax: (051) 70896

FÁS Employment Services Office (Wexford)
Henrietta Street, Wexford
Tel: (053) 23126/23936, Fax: (053) 23177

FÁS TRAINING CENTRES

(* Regional Offices)

* FÁS Training Centre (Athlone)
Garrycastle, Athlone, Co. Westmeath
Tel: (0902) 75128/74481, Fax: (0902) 74795

* FÁS Training Centre (Baldoyle)
Baldoyle Industrial Estate, Baldoyle, Dublin 13
Tel: (01) 839 1144, Fax: (01) 839 1362

FÁS Training Centre (Ballina)
Riverside, Church Road, Ballina, Co. Mayo
Tel: (096) 21921, (096) 70608

* FÁS Training Centre (Ballyfermot)
Ballyfermot Hill, Ballyfermot, Dublin 10
Tel: (01) 626 6211, Fax: 626 4135

FÁS Training Centre (Cabra)
Bannow Road, Cabra, Dublin 7
Tel: (01) 838 0122, Fax: (01) 838 8788

* FÁS Training Centre (Cork)
Rossa Avenue, Bishopstown, Cork
Tel: (021) 544377, Fax: (021) 544291

FÁS Training Centre (Dublin)
57–60 Jervis Street, Dublin 1
Tel: (01) 872 6877, Fax: (01) 872 6182

* FÁS Training Centre (Dundalk)
Industrial Estate, Coes Road, Dundalk, Co. Louth
Tel: (042) 32311, Fax: (042) 32117

FÁS Training Centre (Finglas)
Poppintree Industrial Estate
Jamestown Road
Finglas, Dublin 11
Tel: (01) 834 8311, Fax: 834 6336

FÁS Training Centre (Galway)
Industrial Estate, Mervue, Galway
Tel: (091) 751260, Fax: (091) 753590

FÁS Training Centre (Leitir Cheanainn)
Gaoth Dobhair, Na Doire Beaga
Leitir Cheanainn, Co. Dhún na nGall
Tel: (075) 31211, Fax: (075) 31114

FÁS Training Centre (Letterkenny)
Ballyraine Industrial Estate
Ramelton Road, Letterkenny, Co. Donegal
Tel: (074) 22200, Fax: (074) 24840

* FÁS Training Centre (Loughlinstown)
Wyattville Road
Loughlinstown, Co. Dublin
Tel: (01) 282 1811, Fax: (01) 282 1168

* FÁS Training Centre (Raheen)
Industrial Estate
Raheen, Co. Limerick
Tel: (061) 228333, Fax: (061) 228820

FÁS Training Centre (Shannon)
Industrial Estate
Shannon, Co. Clare
Tel: (061) 471133, Fax: (061) 472613

* FÁS Training Centre (Sligo)
Ballytivnan, Sligo
Tel: (071) 61121, Fax: (071) 69506

FÁS Training Centre (Tallaght)
Cookstown Industrial Estate
Belgard Road, Tallaght, Dublin 24
Tel: (01) 4516411, Fax: (01) 4516021

FÁS Training Centre (Tralee)
Industrial Estate, Monavalley
Tralee, Co. Kerry
Tel: (066) 26444, Fax: (066) 23065

* FÁS Training Centre (Waterford)
IDA Industrial Estate, Cork Road, Waterford
Tel: (051) 72961/2/3/4/5, Fax: (051) 70896

FÁS Training Centre (Wexford)
Whitemills Industrial Estate, Wexford
Tel: (053) 43602, Fax: (053) 41718

SEE ALSO: FÁS CO-OPERATIVE DEVELOPMENT UNIT

FÁS CO-OPERATIVE DEVELOPMENT UNIT

27–33 Upper Baggot Street, Dublin 4
Tel: (01) 668 5777, Fax: (01) 668 2691

The primary objective of the Co-operative Development Unit, located at FÁS, is the creation in Ireland of a strong commercially viable worker co-operative sector. The CDU staff provide training, business/co-operative advice, promotion and financial assistance. This initiative works through a process of project/sector identification, market evaluation, business planning and training, with the aim of establishing worker co-operatives with a high chance of success.

The CDU is a member of CECOP, the European Federation of Worker Co-operatives, which gives access to, and influences, the latest developments in the European co-operative sector.

A Development Officer is assigned by the Unit to each group. This officer carries out an assessment of the proposed goods or services of the group to show if the plan is viable, and if so, where the market is. The development officer then advises the group in preparing a business plan which should outline:

• The capacity of the group to manage the project and to produce the goods or supply the services

• The commercial viability of the proposed business

• The financial package required to support the start-up and ongoing requirements of the business.

After start-up, the CDU will help on a practical level with training in business and co-operative skills, and with ongoing business advice and monitoring.

The Unit has extensive experience in employee buyouts/company conversion. It can give specialist advice on:

• How to set up a buyout team

• Carrying out an initial feasibility study on a proposed buyout

• Designing a democratic structure to benefit the whole workforce.

- Designing the new company's legal structure to ensure worker control

- Sources of finance, including grants

- Developing a business plan for the new company

- The role of trade unionists in the new company

- Negotiating with the existing owners in a buyout situation.

The CDU can provide financial assistance at all stages of co-operative development, from business planning and research to expansion of trading operations.

CDU Worker Co-operative Grant Package

The grant package invests start-up financial support in emerging worker co-operatives and provides development grants for existing worker co-operatives. For the purpose of grant approval, a worker co-operative is considered to be a "legally incorporated body which stipulates in its Rules or Memo and Articles, clauses which substantially reflect the co-operative principles as determined by the International Co-operative Alliance (ICA) and in which the Board of Management/Board of Directors are or are controlled by the Worker Members/Shareholders". Applications for grant support should be in the form of a business plan.

Grants available include:

- Feasibility-Study Grant Support up to £5,000

- Start-up Grants — Co-operative Management Grant:

    1) Towards the employment cost of a full-time manager. (Employment costs = Gross wage + Employers' PRSI). Grants can cover up to 70 per cent of the cost of employing a manager (up to £18,750). This grant may alternatively be used towards the costs of identified management skills, e.g. finance, marketing, sales.

    2) In exceptional cases, the Management Grant can be renewed in the second and third years, though this is done on a reducing scale. Total finance available for Management Grants over the first three years cannot exceed £36,000.

    3) The resources needed for co-operative development, such as the acquisition of new capital equipment, legal costs, trade

fairs, promotional materials up to a maximum of £3,000 per project or 50 per cent of actual costs, whichever is the lesser (exclusive of VAT).

- Wage subsidies — 60 per cent of employment costs of the employees of the co-operative to a maximum grant of £100 per week per member. This grant applies for one year and is not renewable.

- Training Grants — up to 75 per cent of the cost of direct training fees where such training is an integral part of the business plan

- Development Grants are available to worker co-operatives which have successfully traded for at least one year independent of grant-aid from the CDU:

    1) Feasibility-Study Grant to determine the commercial viability of planned expansion project

    2) Wage subsidies may also be available for additional recruitment at the expansion stage.

CDU Worker Co-operative Revolving Loan Fund

The Worker Co-operative Revolving Loan Fund was established by the Co-operative Development Council and the Enterprise Trust. The loan fund is administered through the Tallaght Trust Fund. The maximum loan available from the Fund to an individual worker co-operative is £50,000 and should not exceed 50 per cent of the total required. It should also be of a capital nature. The minimum loan available is £1,000. An annual loan arrangement fee is applied to all loans. This fee is set at 5 per cent and reviewed at agreed times.

FÁS also provides an application form for grant-aid from the Worker Co-operative Fund, which is managed by the Irish League of Credit Unions. It is for persons who are members of a credit union and also bona fide members of a registered worker co-operative. A maximum grant of £750 per eligible member of a credit union may be available under the Fund, with a maximum grant of £3,000 in any one year to a particular worker co-operative. Further grants may be available after one year's trading. However, a decision to approve a grant is totally at the discretion of the League Board whose decision will be final. Applicants should include the following with their application form:

- Copy certificate of registration of the co-operative

- Copy of the rules of the co-operative

- Copy of the latest audited accounts of the co-operative

- Copy of any feasibility study.

Applications should be addressed to:

General Secretary, Irish League of Credit Unions
Castleside Drive, Rathfarnham, Dublin 14
Tel: (01) 490 8911 (Contact: Grace Perrott)

The CDU publishes a *Worker Co-operative Trade Newsletter* and an *Annual Trade Directory* which are available on request.

Case Studies

Recoverable Resources

Recoverable Resources, set up in Dublin in 1989, now employs seven people in the marketing, recovery and export sale of used beverage cans to the can manufacturers of Europe. The co-operative covers the greater Dublin area where the volume of used drinks cans ensures the commercial viability of the project. Recoverable Resources accounted for 293 tonnes recovered in 1991.

Tullamore Meats

Tullamore Meats, a phoenix co-operative, grew out of the ashes of the Midland Butter and Bacon Company. The latter company closed its doors in 1989, making the entire workforce redundant. Nine of the former workers decided that there was still a market for the high quality sausages and puddings produced by their former employer. With their own redundancy money, contributions from the community, and assistance from FÁS and the IDA, they formed Tullamore Meats and commenced production in 1990. Today the co-operative has established a firm foot-hold for its products in the Midlands region.

CDU REGIONAL CO-ORDINATORS

Dublin North
FÁS Training Centre
Industrial Estate, Baldoyle, Dublin 13
Tel: (01) 839 1144, Fax: (01) 839 1362
Contact: Mr Pat Fitzsimons

Dublin South
FÁS Training Centre
Wyattville Road, Loughlinstown, Co. Dublin
Tel: (01) 282 1811, Fax: (01) 282 1168
Contact: Mr Ron O'Connor

Dublin West
FÁS Training Centre
Ballyfermot Hill, Dublin 10
Tel: (01) 626 6211, Fax: (01) 626 4135
Contact: Mr Jim Casey

South-East
FÁS Employment Service Office
Irishtown, Kilkenny
Tel: (056) 65514, Fax: (056) 64451
Contact: Mr Finbarr O'Neill

South-West
FÁS Training Centre
Rossa Avenue, Bishopstown, Cork
Tel: (021) 544 377, Fax: (021) 544 291
Contact: Mr Jim St Leger

Mid-West
FÁS Training Centre
Industrial Estate, Raheen, Limerick
Tel: (061) 228 333, Fax: (061) 301 992
Contact: Mr Michael Collins

Midlands

FÁS Training Centre
Garrycastle, Athlone, Co. Westmeath
Tel: (0902) 75128, Fax: (0902) 74795
Contact: Mr Danny Weston

West

FÁS Training Centre
Industrial Estate, Mervue, Galway
Tel: (091) 751 260, Fax: (091) 753 590
Contact: Mr Padraic Lydon

North-West

FÁS Training Centre
Ballytivnan, Sligo
Tel: (071) 61121, Fax: (071) 69506
Contact: Mr Peter Dunne

North-East

FÁS Employment Service Office
14 North Quay, Drogheda, Co. Louth
Tel: (041) 37646, Fax: (041) 38120
Contact: Mr Oliver Flood

SEE ALSO: CENTRE FOR CO-OPERATIVE STUDIES
IRISH LEAGUE OF CREDIT UNIONS
REGISTRAR OF FRIENDLY SOCIETIES

FINGLAS BUSINESS INITIATIVE
(A DIVISION OF THE FINGLAS PARTNERSHIP)

Rosehill House, Finglas Road, Dublin 11
Tel: (01) 836 1666 Fax: (01) 864 0211
Contact: David Orford

One of the 12 PESP initiatives, the Finglas Business Initiative has a number of programmes to offer to small businesses and entrepreneurs.

Mentor Programme

The Finglas Business Initiative has over 100 retired business people on a mentor panel where they act as mentors to existing and start-up businesses. Mentors are available to advise businesses on a regular basis.

Support for Start-up Businesses

Business Information Service

Advice is available on all aspects of business start-up:

- Sources of finance and grants

- Assistance with projections and business plans

- Assessment of business ideas.

Loan Finance

- Assistance with loan applications.

- Special low-interest loans available in certain circumstances.

Book-keeping Service

The services of a qualified book-keeper to set up a company's accounts system. Up to 30 hours of assistance at no cost.

Special Payments Scheme

For people living in the Finglas area who have been more than 12 months on the Live Register, there is a special Area Allowance Payments Scheme, under which someone becoming self-employed can retain full Social Welfare and secondary benefits for 12 months.

Seminars

Seminars will be run on a regular basis for the owners of new businesses. Topics will cover finance, books and records, taxation, sales and marketing, staff, and legislation for employees.

To qualify for these programmes, the following conditions must be met:

- The applicant must be establishing a business in Finglas (the promoter may live outside the area).

- The proposed business must not be in direct competition with an already established business in the area.

- The business idea must be considered viable.

Support for Established Businesses in Finglas

Confidential Report Service

If a company needs to expand or diversify but is not sure in which direction to proceed, or if a company is experiencing trading difficulties, professional advice is available from the Finglas Business Initiative.

For businesses approved under this scheme, the Finglas Business Initiative will provide a consultant to prepare a detailed report on the business and make appropriate recommendations. The Finglas Business Initiative will also provide advice on how to implement the recommendations made in the report.

Skills Development Training

For employers in the Finglas area whose staff need further training, the Finglas Business Initiative can provide:

- Grants towards the cost of approved courses

- Advice and information on training courses

- Where appropriate, temporary staff to relieve staff on courses.

Business Seminars

The Finglas Business Initiative, in conjunction with the Finglas Chamber of Commerce, will run on a regular basis seminars of relevance to local businesses. Anyone with a particular topic they would like to see covered can contact the Finglas Business Initiative at the above address.

Business Data Base

The Finglas Business Initiative maintains a comprehensive data base on businesses in the Finglas area, and it can help anyone requiring information on a company in that area.

Case Study

Specified Moulds Limited.

When Finglas-man Pat Todd learned that the company he worked for had gone into liquidation, it could have meant the dole queue. Pat however, decided that he was going to take his future in his own hands. He arranged to meet David Orford of the Finglas Business Initiative, and explained that he planned to make an offer to the liquidator of the company, for the equipment. David explained that the first thing Pat would need was a business plan. He introduced him to the Dublin Business Innovation Centre, which agreed to assist Pat jointly with the Finglas Business Initiative. A business plan was produced, Pat was advised on how to negotiate with the company liquidator, and the landlord of the company's premises was approached with a view to taking over the lease on the premises.

Within three months Pat had formed his own company, Specified Moulds Ltd. The new company purchased all the production equipment from the old company and a factory premises was secured Pat was finally in business running his own company.

A year later, Pat Todd is looking to the future with confidence and is talking to the Finglas Business Initiative about his plans for expansion. He is currently producing moulds for some of the top companies in Ireland, and over the next year he hopes to secure orders that are currently being sent abroad. He hopes that this will entail increasing his highly-skilled staff from two to four.

SEE ALSO: AREA PARTNERSHIP COMPANIES
              BALLYMUN PARTNERSHIP
              DUNDALK EMPLOYMENT PARTNERSHIP
              THE ENTERPRISE TRUST
              FÁS, THE TRAINING AND EMPLOYMENT
                  AUTHORITY
              GET TALLAGHT WORKING CO-OPERATIVE
                  SOCIETY LTD.
              MEITHEAL MHAIGH EO
              PLATO

FIONTAR

Dublin City University, Dublin 9
Tel: (01) 704 5614, Fax: (01) 704 5690
Contact: Professor Finbarr Bradley, Ms Nicola Nic Pháidín

Dublin City University has developed an innovative degree programme, the B.Sc. in Airgeadas, Ríomhaireacht agus Fiontraíocht (Finance, Computing and Enterprise). This degree presents students with qualifications in areas of computing, finance and enterprise development, along with fluency in French, German or Spanish. What is exceptional about the degree programme, however, is that it is conducted entirely through Irish. The purpose of running an Irish enterprise degree programme is to strengthen and assert the link between Irish speakers and an Irish enterprise culture. This degree is designed both for those seeking professional employment and for those intending to set up their own companies.

Fiontar, which administers the degree, is a special centre established at DCU, whose research and teaching agenda focuses on a range of cross-disciplinary areas conducted in Irish.

The degree is of four years duration, and in the latter part of their fourth year, students will be involved in the development and design of a technical product or service, and the simulated or actual start-up of an enterprise.

Eighteen students began the course in 1994. Many came from Irish-medium schools but, interestingly, a number received their secondary education at English-medium schools.

Entry Requirements

Applicants should note that there are several special entry requirements for admission to this degree course. (Full details from above address.)

FIRST STEP

Jefferson House, Eglinton Road
Donnybrook, Dublin 4
Tel: (01) 260 0988, Fax: (01) 260 0989
Contact: Patrick Kearney

First Step was set up in 1990 by Mrs Norma Smurfit, who brought together prominent members of the Irish business community to harness the goodwill of the private sector. First Step works through existing community enterprise groups, and in parallel with state support agencies, without any committees or bureaucratic structures. If a project has the potential to create more jobs in disadvantaged areas, and an examination of it reveals no basic flaw, the entrepreneur may subsequently be given financial and/or practical assistance.

Seed funding for projects or people with no security can be provided by First Step. It may fund projects up to a maximum of 50 per cent of the start-up costs. However, evidence of matching funds may be required. Grants can be made available towards prototype development or feasibility studies. First Step also has a panel of successful business people prepared to give some free time to a young enterprise in the critical start-up years.

Personal and credit references as indicated to each project promoter by the assessment officer concerned will be required. A business plan/ feasibility plan can be included with applications, stating the total cost of the project, and enclosing the CVs of the management team.

When First Step approves a loan for a project the following conditions apply:

- The loan is interest-free, with conditions of repayment as set out in the letter of approval.

- The Directors have the right to insist on guarantor(s) for any loan.

- A moratorium of no more than three months is allowed on loan repayments.

- First Step has the right to appoint a mentor of its choice to any project. Project applicants are deemed by virtue of their application for funds to have agreed to co-operate fully with any mentor appointed.

- The Directors reserve the right to apply such other conditions as they may deem appropriate to any loan that may be advanced.

- All approved projects, by virtue of their application, permit First Step to use their project for publicity and fund-raising activities.

- In the case of any breach of the listed conditions, First Step has the right to insist on immediate payment of any loans and, if necessary, to call in any guarantee.

- In the event of default on any repayment, First Step will recall the entire loan and call in all guarantees.

Project funding for First Step comes entirely from the private sector, both at home and abroad, with the exception of the EU-funded project (Horizon) in Dublin's inner city. First Step uses this fund to trigger other available resources, whether from the state or the European Commission. All funds given for projects go entirely to those projects, without any deduction for administration.

First Step is designed to support projects where the promoters come from socioeconomic disadvantaged backgrounds. Project promoters must demonstrate that they have been unsuccessful in raising the necessary finance from commercial sources. First Step is not an alternative to commercial bank finance, but rather a lender of last resort.

Excluded Enterprises

In addition to the general criteria above, there are certain areas of activity which First Step does not support. The following are not currently eligible:

- Projects which, in the opinion of the Board, could raise their own finance through other sources

- Courier projects within the Dublin area

- Taxi and hackney projects

- Publishing projects

- Worker co-ops

- Feasibility/training study funding

- Financial guarantees to third parties.

The Directors reserve the right to amend the above list at any time.

First Step/Bank of Ireland Scheme

An extra dimension was added to First Step's lending capacity in October 1994 when Bank of Ireland agreed to match approved First Step projects with interest-free loans up to a total of £1 million over a four-year period. Effectively, this means that First Step can now approve individual projects up to a total of £25,000 on the basis that 50 per cent of the funding is provided by Bank of Ireland.

In addition to financial assistance, Bank of Ireland has also made available specialist personnel as well as a bank of experienced business mentors to assist with new First Step projects. (Contact: Colm O'Doherty, Tel: (01) 260 0988.)

First Step Back to Work Fund

This new £500,000 pilot scheme has been launched by First Step and the Department of Social Welfare. The scheme will provide small-scale seed capital for the long-term unemployed who have a business idea.

SEE ALSO: BANK OF IRELAND ENTERPRISE SUPPORT
UNIT

FOOD PRODUCT DEVELOPMENT CENTRE

Dublin School of Catering,
Cathal Brugha Street, Dublin 1
Tel: (01) 874 6058, Fax: (01) 874 8572
Contact: Carmel Murphy

A Food Product Development Centre has been established at the Dublin Institute of Technology, Cathal Brugha Street, to develop innovative food concepts. The Centre has access to over 200 DIT staff comprising food technologists, professional chefs and marketing personnel.

Project ideas in consumer value-added foods are researched and developed in the following sectors: fruit and vegetable, fish, dairy, meat, poultry, convenience, snack and speciality foods. Research is carried out on the product, the production system, packaging, marketing and economics. Technical assistance is provided through the range of food science and technology facilities which exist throughout the Dublin Institute of Technology. Design and photographic services are available in marketing new food concepts.

The Centre's services include:

- Sensory assessment (consumer and specialist panels)

- Ingredient sources and testing

- Shelf-life studies

- Market research

- Packaging, labelling and concept-testing

- Advice on recipe development and design and marketing of new food products

- Quality audits for catering industry.

SEE ALSO: DUBLIN INSTITUTE OF TECHNOLOGY

FORBAIRT

Wilton Park House, Wilton Place, Dublin 2
Tel: (01) 660 2244, Fax: (01) 660 5019

Glasnevin, Dublin 9
Tel: (01) 837 0101, Fax: (01) 837 9620

Organisational restructuring has taken place among the state industrial development agencies. This restructuring became effective from 1 January, 1994. The new state body, Forbairt, took over from the Industrial Development Authority (IDA) and EOLAS. Hence:

- *Forfás* is responsible for overall industrial policy co-ordination and for increasing the level of linkages between indigenous and foreign-owned firms. To achieve this, Forfás will co-ordinate the work of the different agencies (Chief Executive: John Travers).

- *Forbairt* (includes the former Eolas) is responsible for assisting indigenous Irish industry — small businesses and entrepreneurs included (Chief Executive: Dan Flinter).

- *IDA Ireland* is responsible for investing overseas investment into Ireland (Chief Executive: Kieran McGowan).

Forbairt is a state-owned and funded body to facilitate the development of Irish business and to provide a range of science and technology services and programmes for enterprise in Ireland. Industrial development and technology services to Irish industry are provided by Forbairt, which is an amalgamation of the Irish industry function of the former IDA, and EOLAS. Forbairt can only assist projects in manufacturing or internationally traded services. Projects are assessed individually on their merits but must be commercially viable and show a clear market opportunity. Projects which may infringe directly on existing Irish manufacturers or which operate in a sector where there is already over-capacity will not be assisted by Forbairt.

To help new and existing small business, Forbairt provides a variety of assistance designed to meet each company's individual needs. In addition to financial assistance, this can include advice on developing business ideas, developing management capability, establishing business contacts, etc. The aim of Forbairt is to help companies to build the management and capability to set up and develop significant businesses.

Assistance is available under a number of programmes.

Feasibility-Study Grant Programme

This programme provides advice and financial assistance towards examining the feasibility of a business idea.

Small Business Programme

This provides financial assistance for manufacturing projects creating permanent jobs, which clearly demonstrate market opportunities, are based on import substitution, and which are not infringing directly on existing domestic manufacturers or operating in a sector where there is already over-capacity. This assistance can be either employment or capital grants, depending on the size and needs of the project.

Manufacturing companies include those which make products:

- For export
- Which will be sold in sectors of the Irish market subject to international competition (import substitution)
- Of an advanced technological nature for sale to internationally trading or skilled sub-supply firms.

Mentor Programme

Under this programme, experienced business executives are matched as mentors with small companies to advise on every aspect of starting and developing a business, and at no cost to the company.

Management Development Programme

This is designed to help strengthen the internal management of a company by providing advice and assistance with installing management systems, business planning, strategic planning, and recruiting specialist business skills.

The Enterprise Development Programme

This is a special programme of assistance to attract senior managers to set up management potential projects.

International Services Irish Programme

This provides a special package of incentives and support facilities for companies involved in a range of internationally traded services.

Research and Development Programme

Under this programme also, companies can obtain assistance towards the cost of acquiring new technology and developing new products and processes.

In considering grant applications, Forbairt will look at:

• The need for financial assistance

• The commercial viability of the project

• The economic benefits which the project would generate in Ireland

• The resources (management, finance, raw materials, etc.) available to promote the project.

These factors will decide the amount and make-up of grant-aid. In addition to cash grants, Forbairt may also provide advice and access to its international network of business contacts.

Enterprise Preparation Programme

Forbairt offers an Enterprise Preparation Programme, aimed at managers leaving senior positions within industry to set up on their own. In Dublin, Forbairt runs this programme in conjunction with the Irish Management Institute, and in Galway, with the Western Management Centre. (For further details of this programme, local Forbairt offices should be contacted — see addresses below.)

Feasibility-Study Grants

Researching an idea before starting a business can be expensive, not least because during this time an entrepreneur may not be earning anything. Someone trying to get a manufacturing business off the ground may be eligible to apply for a feasibility-study grant.

Under the Feasibility-Study Grant Programme advice and financial assistance is available towards examining the feasibility of a business idea. Funding is available for market research, preparation of costings and financial projections, assessment of manufacturing processes, plant, equipment, etc., and sourcing raw materials. The feasibility study may also include negotiations with potential joint venture partners and negotiation of manufacturing licences. Grants are available up to a level of 50 per cent of the agreed cost of the research stage — up to a maximum of £15,000 per study — and is handled by Forbairt.

Criteria for Getting a Grant

An applicant must:

- Be an individual, community group or company

- Be investigating a new manufacturing product or process

- Apply before beginning the study

- Carry out most of the work in the Republic of Ireland

- Not repeat work that has previously produced negative results (whether carried out by the applicant or someone else)

- Not seek aid from any other state body for the expenditure which will be incurred in this project.

Feasibility-study grants are also available for international services projects. If a study is in an area already known to have over-capacity, it is unlikely to receive a grant.

Eligible studies include:

- Market research

- Preparation of costings and financial projections

- Assessment of manufacturing processes

- Assessment of suitable plant, equipment, etc.

- Sourcing of raw materials

- Negotiation with potential joint-venture partners

- Negotiation of manufacturing licences.

To apply for a feasibility-study grant, it is necessary to submit an application to Forbairt (or any regional Forbairt office — see addresses below). An Bord Tráchtála (ABT) becomes involved subsequently if there is an overseas marketing element, to offer guidance on the design and implementation of a market research exercise, and to offer the use of its library.

The application process involves providing much of the information that would be included in a business plan, as well as a separate explanation of the work involved in the feasibility study and the costs involved. The application includes a summary of anticipated expenditure broken down between general research and export market research.

The feasibility grant will agree costs under a number of headings — for example, travel, market research or prototyping. A promoter who spends more than anticipated will not get grant-aid on the excess. Therefore, in making an application, it is essential that:

- Estimates are accurate

- Each item of expenditure is justified

- Some margin is included, in case estimates are cut back in arriving at the amount to be grant-aided — though it is not advisable to be too greedy and run the risk of losing out on the grant altogether.

The format suggested for an application is:

- Information on promoter:
    — Promoter's name
    — Address
    — Present position
    — Qualifications
    — Work history
    — Background
    — Business objectives (if existing company).

- Details of project to be examined:
    — Products
    — Customer/Markets
    — If exports are proposed, are they necessary for profitability initially?
    — Competitors
    — Relevance of product to company's existing business (where relevant)
    — Estimated size of investment (including working capital)
    — Promoter's capital availability
    — Estimated employment
    — The critical issues for the project (for example, technical development and performance; obtaining planning per-mission; finding equity partners).

- Present status of project, including work carried out to date

- For each separate stage of the study, details of:
  — Work to be done.
  — By whom/time involved/cost and details of travel and other special expenditures.

- Where consultants will be involved, the name of the consultant (a few quotations should be obtained), the exact work to be undertaken, standard costs per week and number of weeks, and any special expenses agreed

- For prototype expenditure, the number of units proposed, the material and labour cost per unit and a justification of the number of units

- Details of any export market research to be carried out.

The grant is considered under two headings — Home Market Research and Export Market Research. When setting out the order in which the study will be undertaken, it is important to label these two stages carefully (if they both apply), with sub-stages within these stages clearly indicated. Application for assistance must be made prior to the commencement of the study. The majority of the work must be carried out within the state.

If an application is accepted (this can take up to two months during which time the study may not proceed), a letter of offer will be sent. This should be read carefully. Applicants should query any parts of it that they do not understand. It will be against this document, not the original application, that expenditure will be checked before any grants are paid out. It is important to be sure what the terms of the grant-aid are and to keep to them. Applicants should also be sure to sign and return the letter of offer within the time period indicated — otherwise the grant-aid may lapse.

Then — and only then — can work on the study begin. It must not be started before grant approval is obtained.

When the study is completed, a report and a note of costs, including receipts, must be submitted. If the grant is for more than £2,500, an auditor's certificate of expenditure must also be submitted when making a claim.

To enable an auditor to complete such a certificate, it will be necessary to keep a careful record of expenditure and all receipts. Before the money is issued, the validity of expenditure will be checked against the completion of the various stages indicated in the application.

In some instances, part of the grant (usually less than half) will be paid before the study is fully complete, if an interim report is submitted with supporting claims documentation.

The feasibility-study grant is an important tool in developing a business. For those eligible, it is definitely worth applying for a grant, since it spreads some of the costs of the research stage. In addition, it will be possible to avoid making some of the basic mistakes, by drawing on Forbairt's expertise in dealing with many other companies.

Small Business Programme

The Small Business Programme evolved as a result of provisions in the Underdeveloped Areas Act, 1952, and the Industrial Grants Act, 1959, and the establishment of designated areas which were perceived as being particularly in need of grant assistance. In April 1967, a special Small Business Division was established in IDA (now Forbairt) to implement a Department of Industry and Commerce (now Department of Enterprise and Employment) pilot scheme to assist small manufacturing firms. Over the next decade, the scheme spread to become nationwide in its application and covered all product areas except beef, dairy and related products.

The programme is administered through eight regional Forbairt offices, each of which has a Small Business team. Regional Small Industry Boards, within each office, can make decisions on projects in their regions involving grants of up to £300,000 in designated areas and £225,000 in non-designated areas.

To ensure that regional decisions do not distort the national policy, and that Forbairt grant-assistance policy keeps pace with national developments, a central unit in Dublin, the Small Business Division Central Policy Unit, monitors all projects.

The Small Business Programme comprises four arms:

- Start-ups (mainly manufacturing)

- Irish international traded services

- Enterprise Development Programme

- Development of existing companies.

The manufacturing start-up and Irish internationally traded services programmes are the most likely to be of interest to start-up companies. The Enterprise Development Programme operates by attempting to attract senior managers from existing jobs to join with a group of others to form a high-potential Irish company.

The Small Business Information Centre is a source of advice for people who want to start their own manufacturing business. Each Forbairt office has a Small Business Information Centre. Entrepreneurs who wish to discuss their planned business venture must fill out a questionnaire, to which Forbairt specialists will respond. A public phone information line is provided to help with queries on the questionnaire.

Other Forbairt programmes exist, but may be of limited interest to start-ups. These programmes include:

- *Capability Building Programme*, where a company identified as having a high growth potential is singled out for input of additional time and expertise from Forbairt staff, who will help it to deal with any barriers to growth.

- *National Linkage Programme*, aimed at components suppliers or potential components suppliers to foreign manufacturers. The objective is to increase the quality of firms so that more will act as suppliers, thereby increasing the Irish-made component of products manufactured by foreign companies in Ireland. The programme also aims to build formal links between Irish suppliers and larger, often multinational, purchasers.

- *Graduate Placement Schemes*, covering three schemes managed by the Irish Goods Council, Forbairt and FÁS to place new graduates with companies where both graduate and company may benefit. The schemes fund half of a graduate's salary for a 12-month period.

Assistance Given

The assistance given by Forbairt includes:

- Employment grants — up to a maximum of £4,000 per person for start-up companies employing up to 15 people

- Capital grants — for machinery and buildings

- Leasing grants — for machinery

- Interest subsidy grants — to reduce the interest on loans raised to finance the business

- Loan guarantees — to cover loans raised to finance asset investment or working capital.

Other forms of assistance include:

- Feasibility-study grants — to individual and existing firms to research new project ideas and to undertake market research to validate
the potential of the proposal before making a commitment in fixed
asset investments (see above)

- Product and process development grants — grants of up to 50 per
cent of the cost of developing or improving a product and process,
subject to a maximum of £250,000 per project and paid on the basis
of audited and inspected expenditure (This point is expanded under
Product Development Licensing.)

- Training grants — administered in conjunction with FÁS, with grants
of up to 50 per cent of the cost of training additional staff for expansion projects involving significant technological change

- Management development grants — FÁS and Forbairt have joined to
develop and fund management training programmes that aim to train
managers of small companies to install management information systems and business and strategic planning systems. Forbairt generally
pays 90 per cent of costs. The chances of obtaining such a grant are
good, as Forbairt regards such training as strengthening a company.
The four key business areas that the programme can address are:
records and management systems, business planning, strategic planning and strengthening the management team.

Increasingly, and particularly where it is making a major commitment to
a company's development, Forbairt looks for a stake in the business.
This stake is usually in the range of 5–15 per cent. The idea is that
Forbairt investments in successful businesses should not be a one-way
traffic but should, in time, provide funds, through ongoing dividend payments and/or sale of the shares, which can be used to fund development
in other businesses.

Product Development Licensing

One way to overcome the costs involved in researching and developing
new products and processes is to negotiate a licensing agreement with
another company that already has the required technology. Agreements
such as these can help Irish companies to gain entry to achieve significant growth in export markets. Forbairt can provide financial assistance
towards acquiring this new technology.

- Application for assistance must be made prior to the commencement of the project.

- The project must involve a reasonable degree of innovation relative to the company's existing level of technology.

- The project must have a reasonable prospect of commercial success.

- The product/process must be produced or applied within the state.

- The parties to the licence agreement must be independent entities.

It is necessary to include the following with an application:

- A brief history of the company — making reference to the licensor and the performance of the new product in its home market

- Product development strategy — company's objectives for the next 2–5 years

- Description of the proposed product or process

- Commercial viability — the existing market capability, the target market, market share and turnover projections for the new product should be outlined

- Technical viability — the key points in the licence agreement: patent/ copyright protection, familiarisation/training period, technical assistance and termination clauses should be outlined. What is the overall investment required to commercialise the new product or process (i.e. the investment in the licence, R&D, fixed assets, working capital and training)?

Other organisations with relevant expertise include Teagasc, An Bord Tráchtála (ABT) and the Higher Education Institutions. The grant assistance available includes:

- Licensor charges — patent rights, technical assistance, prototype components and licence options in the form of downpayments, royalties, etc.

- Licensee costs — wages and salaries, travel and subsistence

- Consultancy fees — specialist advice on technology, patents and copyright.

International Services Irish

Forbairt provides a special package of incentives and support facilities for companies involved in internationally traded services.

The main areas of business to which this grants package relates are: software development, technical and consulting services, media recording services, publishing houses, international and financial services, commercial laboratories, administrative HQs, healthcare services and research and development services. These companies must have the ability to compete successfully in the export market.

In making an application, a promoter should submit:

- A short history of the company

- Details of services to be provided by the new operation

- Details of the markets and market share for the company's services

- Details of market research undertaken

- Details of strategy to achieve market entry and development

- Information on the location of the project

- Assessment of accommodation required

- Details of equipment needed and estimated cost

- Employment projections

- Details of management/technical control of the company

- Details of finance required and cash-flow projections for three years.

The successful applicant may qualify for the following:

- A feasibility grant of up to 50 per cent of the cost of researching and assessing the viability of project

- Employment grants payable for full-time jobs created. An agreed amount will be paid per job in two instalments — 50 per cent on certification that the job exists and 50 per cent one year later

- Research and development grants of up to 50 per cent of the cost of an approved development project

- Tax write-off for investments up to £25,000 for qualifying individuals under the Business Expansion Scheme

- Maximum 10 per cent tax if the company is engaged in computer services

- Business parks if the company is in the service industry.

As with the other Forbairt programmes, capital grants, training grants, rent-subsidy grants, management development grants, advisory mentor/ patron programmes and advice and consultancy for projects are available. Forbairt also seeks some repayment of full grant packages. In companies with significant development potential, Forbairt may take an equity stake in return for the grant package.

Research and Development Grants

IDA Ireland and Forbairt jointly administer the Research and Development Grants package. Commercial, strategic and technical aspects are appraised.

Commercial Background and Strategy

The following information must be supplied by a promoter seeking assistance:

- Name and address, title of the project, brief history and objectives of the company in relation to turnover, profit, markets, growth rate and product areas to be developed. The proposed strategy initiatives to achieve these objectives should also be included.

- In describing the products and processes used, the manpower and financial resources that will be allocated to product development over the next 2–3 years must be defined. If the product involves a process development, what are the expected unit- and total-cost savings? What is the anticipated contribution to turnover/profit that will derive from the new or improved product?

- In stating its principal markets, the company's marketing capability in terms of products, markets served, distribution system and market share should be outlined. It should be stated who the company's main competitors are and what their size is. The company's marketing plan for the new product should also be described and it should be indicated whether the target market is growing or declining.

- The competitive advantage of the new product should be outlined, along with any evidence that there is a demand for the product, who the intended customers are and who conducted the market research. Forbairt will need to know if the promoter has ever undertaken any previous product development or technology acquisition, and if so what the commercial outcome was.

Product or Process to be Developed

- Again, the promoter needs to describe the proposed product or process but here must define the technical objectives such as performance specifications or unit costs. Details should also be given of any preliminary technical feasibility or research studies completed on the project to date.

- Where appropriate, any alternative development options available should be described and it should be explained how a choice was made and how this choice compares with that of the main competitors.

- The steps that have been taken to secure the company's position in regard to patents, licences, registered designs or copyright should be detailed.

- Details should be given of the project plan indicating associated costs and whether these are the company's own staff costs or those of subcontractors or consultants. The plan should be summarised in diagrammatic form such as a bar chart. The CVs of key project team members, or relevant information regarding their technical backgrounds, should be provided.

  Note: Eligible costs include wages/salaries, overheads, travel and subsistence, materials, technical consulting fees, purchase/rent of facilities and or equipment.

- Details should be given of any management control reports, proposed review points, or prototypes which will be available for inspection in the course of or on completion of the project.

  Note: Support can be provided for the employment of Product Development Managers to help the planning and implementation process.

- A summary of overall project costs should be provided under the relevant eligible expenditure headings as given.

As with all other state grants, expenditure incurred by a company before making its application cannot be supported, and the majority of work must be carried out within the state. Projects must also represent a reasonable degree of innovation relative to the company's existing level of technology and they must have a reasonable prospect of commercial success. All applications should be sent to the local Forbairt Small Business Manager.

Technology Transfer

By twinning each regional Forbairt office with an overseas IDA Ireland office, Forbairt can help companies to find partners for joint ventures, licensing agreements and technology transfers. Under this scheme, grants of up to 50 per cent are available for technology acquisition.

Small Factory Workspace

For some businesses, getting the right workspace cheaply can be a major step in the right direction. Forbairt provides this kind of assistance. Most are single units of up to 1,000 square metres, or special incubator units for start-up projects. Incubator units are usually flexible in size, and offer secretarial and other back-up services on the same site.

Forbairt has a number of workspace units that may be available from time to time. The contact point for people who want to rent these units is the local Forbairt regional office. Assisted workspaces include:

- Forbairt Enterprise Centre, Pearse Street, Dublin 2 — a refurbished mill and specially constructed units, totalling 20,000 square metres. The size of units varies

- Forbairt Enterprise Centre, North Mall, Cork — similar to Pearse Street, Dublin, though smaller in scale

- Forbairt, Whitestown Business Centre, Tallaght, Dublin 24

- Forbairt Enterprise Centre, East Wall Road, Dublin 3

- Forbairt Enterprise Centre, Gardiner Street, Dublin 1

- Forbairt Enterprise Centre, The Liberties, Dublin 8

- Waterford Food Centre — specially for small food projects, the Centre has 100,000 square feet of space and is located on the Waterford Industrial Estate. It provides central office, technical and hygiene services to projects based there.

Each Forbairt office has a Small Business Information Centre. Entrepreneurs who wish to discuss their planned business venture must fill out a questionnaire, to which Forbairt specialists will respond. A public phone information line is provided to help with queries on the questionnaire.

Technology Services to Industry

Forbairt stimulates the Irish economy through programmes of investment in science and technology, carried out in industry, third-level colleges and in other specialised research centres. In addition, it provides a
range of technical and consultancy services to Irish industry. These,
combined with the investment programmes, are aimed at raising the
level of technological competence and competitiveness in Irish industry.
EOLAS, the Irish Science and Technology Agency, was the state agency
responsible for the development, application and promotion of science
and technology. However, EOLAS has now become part of Forbairt.

Forbairt operates a number of programmes of particular relevance to
new and existing small firms, including the National Technology Audit
Programme

National Standards Authority of Ireland (NSAI)

The National Standards Authority of Ireland is a division of Forfás and,
in consultation with industry sectors, it develops and publishes standards
to meet increasingly stringent market requirements for quality, design,
personnel and safety of products.

National Technology Audit Programme

The National Technology Audit Programme is designed to assist companies in assessing the current status of their technology and in identifying how it can be improved to reduce costs and increase competitiveness.

The average cost of a technology audit is £4,000. The audit is grant-
aided by Forbairt, through the Department of Enterprise and Employment, reducing the net cost to a small company to approximately £1,000.
Small and medium indigenous companies with a definite product range
are eligible.

Technology Management Programme

The Technology Management Programme offers grant assistance to
companies wishing to employ an experienced technical person. A salary
supplement over three years is available (50 per cent of salary up to
£10,000 in Year 1, £5,000 in Year 2 and £2,500 in Year 3), plus an
additional £5,000 for technical consultancy.

Tech Start Programme

The Tech Start Programme offers grant assistance to companies that take on a technically qualified graduate to carry out an agreed work pro-gramme. A salary support of £5,000 for a degree holder (£4,500 for a diploma holder) is paid for one year, plus an additional £2,000 for external consultancy. Small Irish-owned companies with little or no technical capability, but with potential to develop, are eligible.

Forbairt Scheme for Assistance with Inventions

Forbairt can offer to fund a patent programme for an invention, covering 100 per cent of the patent costs, subject to agreement with the inventor on a division of royalties resulting from the sales of the patented product or process. Where a patent programme is being funded, Forbairt will normally also assist with legal fees associated with drawing up licensing agreements. Inventions developed by industry, private individuals, government-sponsored research, universities or colleges are eligible.

Forbairt has a network of eight regional offices nationwide — in Dublin, Cork, Waterford, Athlone, Limerick, Sligo, Dundalk and Galway — serving Irish-based industry and acting as a gateway to a wide range of technical support, information and development services in Ireland and overseas.

Published by Forbairt, *Technology Ireland* includes a selective diary, listing the important science and technology shows, seminars, exhibi-tions and events in Ireland and abroad. There is also a useful listing of technology transfer opportunities in Europe.

There are Forbairt offices in Athlone, Cork, Dundalk, Galway, Limerick, Sligo and Waterford, as well as in Dublin.

OTHER ADDRESSES

Forbairt Enterprise Centre
Gloucester Place, Gardiner Street, Dublin 1
Forbairt Enterprise Centre
Pearse Street, Dublin 2
Tel: (01) 677 5655, Fax: (01) 677 5487

Forbairt Enterprise Centre
East Wall Road, Dublin 3
Tel: (01) 855 2333

Forbairt Enterprise Centre
Main Road, Tallaght, Dublin 24
Tel: (01) 451 6962

Forbairt Enterprise Centre
North Mall, Cork
Tel: (021) 397 711, Fax: (021) 395 393

Forbairt Regional Office — County Kerry
57 High Street, Killarney, Co. Kerry
Tel: (064) 34133, Fax: (064) 34135

Forbairt Regional Office — Donegal region
Portland House, Port Road
Letterkenny, Co. Donegal
Tel: (074) 21155, Fax: (074) 21424

Forbairt Regional Office — Dublin region/East region
Wilton Park House, Wilton Place, Dublin 2
Tel: (01) 660 2244, Fax: (01) 660 5095

Forbairt Regional Office — Midlands region
Auburn, Dublin Road, Athlone, Co. Westmeath
Tel: (0902) 72695, Fax: (0902) 74516

Forbairt Regional Office —— North West region
Finisklin Industrial Estate, Sligo
Tel: (071) 61311, Fax: (071) 61896

Forbairt Regional Office — North East region
Finnabair Industrial Estate, Dundalk, Co. Louth
Tel: (042) 31261/39031, Fax: (042) 39034

Forbairt Regional Office — South West region
Industry House, Rossa Avenue
Bishopstown, Co. Cork
Tel: (021) 343555, Fax: (021) 343444

Forbairt Regional Office —— South East region
Forbairt Industrial Estate, Cork Road, Waterford
Tel: (051) 72911, Fax: (051) 72719

Forbairt Regional Office — West region
Forbairt Industrial Estate, Mervue, Galway
Tel: (091) 751 111, Fax: (091) 751 515

SEE ALSO: BORD FÁILTE
AN BORD TRÁCHTÁLA
DEPARTMENT OF ENTERPRISE AND
    EMPLOYMENT
ENTERPRISE LINK
FÁS, THE TRAINING AND EMPLOYMENT
    AUTHORITY
IRISH MANAGEMENT INSTITUTE
SHANNON DEVELOPMENT
ÚDARÁS NA GAELTACHTA

FRIEL STAFFORD

Chartered Accountants
13 Fitzwilliam Square, Dublin 2
Tel: (01) 661 4066, Fax: (01) 661 4145
Contact: James Stafford

Friel Stafford is a firm of Chartered Accountants specialising in Corporate Recovery and Business Planning for start-ups. One of the firm's niches is advising prospective purchasers on how to negotiate the purchase of a business from receivers/liquidators or shareholders. The firm's specialisations have enabled it to develop a close working relationship with banks and grant-giving organisations.

The firm believes in giving pragmatic advice to its clients and is not afraid to advise a client that a particular business plan may not be successful.

Services offered to the potential entrepreneur include:

- Formulation of a business plan

- Assistance with market research

- Development of a marketing strategy

- Introduction to possible equity investors

- Finance/grant applications

- Company formations

- PAYE/VAT registration.

Friel Stafford does not charge for an initial consultation.

GERMAN-IRISH CHAMBER OF INDUSTRY AND COMMERCE

46 Fitzwilliam Square, Dublin 2
Tel: (01) 676 2934, Fax: (01) 676 2595
Contact: Cariona Neary

The German-Irish Chamber of Industry and Commerce is a contact point for Irish companies that wish to establish business links in Germany. The Chamber provides information and consultancy on marketing and legal issues relating to transnational business. The full-time staff of nine people includes marketing experts as well as both a German and an Irish lawyer.

German Firms Seeking Irish Representatives

As a recognised consultancy for German firms, the Chamber receives a constant flow of enquiries from German companies seeking Irish partners. Through these enquiries the Chamber is able to offer a wide range of products and services from Germany to Irish distributors and agents, many of whom are small and medium-sized companies.

Irish Firms Entering the German Market

The Chamber can provide background information on major markets in Germany. There is also a comprehensive range of specialist databases and directories providing addresses of manufacturers, associations and distributors available. The Chamber can provide listings or set up initial contacts with German companies on behalf of Irish firms. It works with a whole range of Irish companies, including firms from the clothing, food and construction sectors, and assists companies with the strategic problems of finding an agent and setting up a business.

The specialist services of the Chamber include representation at the Cologne and Düsseldorf Trade Fairs. The Chamber is the official information centre for the Dual System Germany — which administers the licence to carry the "Green Dot" recycling symbol used on sales packaging in Germany. Companies with products destined for the German retail market can receive assistance from the Chamber in applying for the licence to print the Green Dot on their packaging.

Services to Firms Already Established in Germany

The Chamber can also provide many services to Irish companies that already have an involvement in the German market, including a VAT refund service, debt collection service and advice on the regulatory systems existing in various sectors.

Legal Services

Through its Legal Department and in-house lawyer the Chamber can provide expertise in a wide range of areas of both Irish and German law. These include advice on/negotiation of agency and distribution agreements and/or related contracts such as joint ventures/franchises, and also advice on all aspects of German/Irish commercial law relevant to Irish companies doing business with Germany.

How to Avail of the Chamber Services

Companies must have worked out a strategy for the German market before contacting the Chamber. An initial meeting will then be arranged to discuss how the German-Irish Chamber can help them. A quotation for the charges will follow.

Membership of the Chamber

While it is not necessary to be a member of the Chamber to avail of its services, members are entitled to avail of the German-Irish Chamber services at reduced rates.

GET TALLAGHT WORKING CO-OPERATIVE SOCIETY LTD.

Enterprise Centre, Main Road, Tallaght, Dublin 24
Tel: (01) 459 9159, Fax: (01) 452 6708
Contact: Michael Johnson, Chief Executive

Get Tallaght Working (GTW) is a community-based co-operative established in 1984 with the specific purpose of implementing action to alleviate the unemployment problem in Tallaght. It actively supports the development of enterprise, self-employment and co-operative development as real long-term answers to the economic and social problems of Tallaght.

The Tallaght Partnership contracts GTW to provide enterprise-support services on its behalf. The Partnership has also developed a project known as PLATO Tallaght (see separate listing) which works with existing small and medium-sized businesses in Tallaght.

The core purpose of GTW is to provide practical assistance to individuals/groups to enable them to establish and maintain commercially viable enterprises. GTW currently employs five people full-time.

Advice and Information

Individuals or groups with a business idea receive advice and support from GTW in preparing a business plan and developing their project to start-up stage. GTW also provides information on training, grants, loans, finance, marketing, business contacts and related matters.

Workspace

Since 1988, with support from the former IDA (now Forbairt), GTW has operated incubator workspace units within the former IDA (now Forbairt) Enterprise Centre at Main Road, Tallaght. These premises are provided at a competitive cost to new and emerging businesses, at a location where direct help can be provided by GTW.

Finance

GTW assists people in obtaining grants and seed capital from various sources, and can process applications to the Tallaght Trust Fund which provides low-interest loans on a revolving basis to unemployed people with a viable business idea.

Business Advisory Panel

GTW operates a Business Advisory Panel, which provides technical assistance to emerging businesses in Tallaght. The panel comprises local volunteer business executives who work jointly and on a one-to-one basis to help solve specific problems in new or existing small businesses.

Lobbying Activities

Various policy proposals on the development of Tallaght have been presented by GTW, including the need for a Development Team for the area, local government reform and the potential of the Tallaght Regional Technical College. It continues to monitor economic and social conditions in Tallaght and contributes to debate at local and national level on these and related issues.

Enterprise Development Programme — NEST

Over a two-year period, selected individuals (with priority given to the long-term unemployed) with a business idea, but without business or related experience, are given intensive support to research and develop their idea and to start up in business. Training inputs, close monitoring, weekly group meetings and one-to-one support are all included, with the aim of minimising the failure rate.

Business Development Service

This service helps existing small businesses to grow and expand and can involve assistance with such things as marketing, planning, finance, and product development. Help is also provided to companies that are experiencing difficulty, to enable them to continue operating.

In addition to the services outlined above, GTW has added three new programmes:

- NEST (New Enterprise Support Thrust) Programme: this is a pilot initiative developed by GTW and funded by the Enterprise Trust and the Tallaght Partnership, designed exclusively for the long-term unemployed, to enable them to set up their own business, through personal development and developing business skills, and by building self-confidence. Current training and development programmes for the long-term unemployed are designed to help people to re-enter the job market as employees. NEST offers the entrepreneurial option — based on the premise that entrepreneurs are not only born but, given the right environment and support, can also be made.

- Marketing Development Programme: this assists start-ups and existing small businesses in conducting effective market research and preparing and implementing marketing plans.

- External Trade Programme: this assists small and medium-sized companies in Tallaght in opening new markets in Northern Ireland and Great Britain.

Individuals can contact GTW directly to arrange for an initial consultation. There are no preconditions.

During 1994, GTW assisted 381 individuals with advice and information. This resulted in the establishment of 126 new businesses creating 140 new jobs. Many of these were small companies — in many cases one-person operations. Of these new businesses, 32 per cent were in the service/distribution category, 16 per cent were in the transport sector, and 15 per cent were in manufacturing. The remainder were spread over construction, printing/publishing, catering/food and retailing.

Eight out of 10 project promoters were men and the predominant age group for both men and women was 25–50. Over two-thirds of the project promoters were long-term unemployed.

Case Studies

Rosey Lee Products

Michael Martin had been unemployed for over two years. He developed an idea for recycling tea bags into high quality garden compost. Get Tallaght Working helped him to develop a business plan, obtain finance and make a grant submission to the former IDA, now Forbairt. His business is now established as Rosey Lee Products and employs five people with immediate plans to employ three more.

Tracers

Tracers was started five years ago by the brother and sister team of Kieran Phelan and Esther Dempsey. It was formed initially to provide a computer maintenance service, but Kieran and Esther soon realised that

*the marketing of video games would provide greater business oppor-
tunities.*

*They first occupied a small unit in the IDA Enterprise Centre, with
the help of the Get Tallaght Working Group who provided them with an
Incubator licence. The business took off and Tracers soon moved to a
larger unit with their occupancy moving from 230 square feet to 600
square feet. They also took on two extra staff, with Kieran concentrating on sales and marketing whilst Ester specialised in administration and purchasing. Once again, Tracers outgrew its workspace and
Get Tallaght Working allocated it a 1,000-square-foot ground-floor
unit, which Tracers fitted out with a purpose-built office suite storage
and display area. Last year they took on a marketing assistant with the
help of the Leader Programme. They also became a client of PLATO —
a Belgian business development initiative brought to Ireland by the
Tallaght Partnership. Recently, Esther became a trustee of the Tallaght
Trust Fund, which was set up to provide seed capital for fledgling
enterprises in the Tallaght area.*

SEE ALSO: AREA PARTNERSHIP COMPANIES
                 BALLYMUN PARTNERSHIP
                 DUNDALK EMPLOYMENT PARTNERSHIP
                 THE ENTERPRISE TRUST
                 FÁS, THE TRAINING AND EMPLOYMENT
                      AUTHORITY
                 FINGLAS BUSINESS INITIATIVE
                 MEITHEAL MHAIGH EO
                 PLATO

GREENFIELD CO-ORDINATORS LTD.

Enterprise House
Aiden Street, Kiltimagh, Co. Mayo
Tel: (094) 81040, Fax: (094) 81708
Contact: Mary Keane/Catherine O'Boyle

Business Background

Greenfield Co-ordinators Ltd. is a business and training consultation service established in 1991. As a result of changing market forces there is a growing demand for advice and direction regarding enterprise start-up and business restructuring. The business was initiated under the umbrella of IRD Kiltimagh Ltd., Co. Mayo, a community-based company with the objective of stimulating economic development.

The association of the team members with successful community development projects and the achievements of IRD Kiltimagh Ltd. brought a new demand from community leaders and organisations seeking to prepare planning documentation for their communities. As a result, Greenfield Co-ordinators Ltd. became involved in community facilitation and training, and the preparation of integrated community (economic and social) development plans.

In more recent times, the company team has broadened its market base and now offers its services throughout Ireland.

Greenfield Co-ordinators is a FÁS-approved training organisation, and participates in the FÁS mentoring programme. Greenfield Co-ordinators has undertaken work on behalf of Forbairt, Údarás na Gaeltachta, Ireland West Tourism, the Leader Programme, and County Enterprise Boards.

Mission Statement

Greenfield Co-ordinators Ltd. is a consultation service which advises and helps existing and potential entrepreneurs and community activists to develop their ideas into viable and successful business and community ventures.

Community Development Plans and Training Programmes
Successful clients include:

- Arrow Community Development Ltd., Sligo

- Killeshandra Community Council Ltd., Killeshandra, Co. Cavan

- Aislann Chill Chartha Teo, Co. Donegal

- Dunkellin Country Ltd., New Inn, Co. Galway — Community Structures Co-ordination.

- Bohola Co. Mayo — Community Resource and Needs Survey.

Community Projects — Feasibility Studies
Successful clients include:

- The Market House Centre, Carrick-on-Shannon, Co. Leitrim

- The Allihies Wilderness Sanctuary, Allihies Co. Cork

- The Bohola Primary Processing Project, Bohola, Co. Mayo

- The Farm Fresh Food Processing Project, IRD Kiltimagh Ltd., Co. Mayo.

Tourism Enterprises — Business/Marketing Plans and Feasibility Studies
Successful clients include:

- UISCE ($10°$ West) Outdoor Activities Centre, Belmullet, Co. Mayo

- Barleyhill Equestrian Centre, Bohola, Co. Mayo

- Cill Aodáin Hotel, Kiltimagh, Co. Mayo

- Cloonnacauneen Castle, Galway

- The Abbey Hotel, Roscommon

- Naturally West Holidays Ltd. (Holiday Marketing Company) Kiltimagh, Co. Mayo

- Knock International Airport, Co. Mayo

- Tourism Marketing Programmes, France/UK/Ireland.

Service Options

Greenfield Co-ordinators Ltd. offers the following service elements:

- Business and Marketing Consultation
- Business and Marketing Training Programmes
- Business Plans
- Feasibility Studies
- Marketing Plans
- Market and Marketing Research
- Preparation and Production of Reports
- Completion of Grant Applications (County Enterprise Board, LEADER Programme; ERDF; FEOGA; ADM; other European incentives)
- Community-Development Training
- Community Resources and Needs Audits
- Community Development Studies
- Community Economic and Development Plans.

GUARANTEED IRISH LTD.

1 Fitzwilliam Place, Dublin 2
Tel: (01) 661 2607, Fax: (01) 661 2633
Contact: John McCarthy

The concept of Guaranteed Irish was initially introduced for the manu-facturing sector, to provide an effective means for the consumer to identify Irish-made products.

The familiar logo of the "G" with the "I" appears on thousands of products from hundreds of manufacturers.

In 1993, Supporting Guaranteed Irish was introduced to accommo-date the many companies and organisations in the service sector wishing to be identified with the aims and objectives of Guaranteed Irish Ltd.

Research carried out during 1993 showed that 30 per cent of all adults stated that they were "a lot more likely" to buy a brand that they were considering buying if it had the Guaranteed Irish symbol (findings: AGB Adelaide). The findings show the Guaranteed Irish symbol to be an effective marketing tool.

Criteria

To apply for the guaranteed Irish mark, application should be made to the organisation at the above address. Details on the product or service will be requested, and an inspection will follow. Inspection covers:

- Process/service

- Finished product

- Commitment to after-sales service

- Other relevant details.

Companies or products applying for the mark must manufacture their product or provide their service in this country.

An annual subscription is payable to Guaranteed Irish Ltd., and this is based on the number of people employed. The annual subscription can be as little as £60 for very small companies.

Case Study

Beeline Healthcare Ltd.

Beeline Healthcare Ltd. is the manufacturer of vitamin supplements and winner of the 1993 "Up and Running" business competition featured on RTE. The company attributes its success in Irish market share of health products to the Guaranteed Irish mark. Beeline is based in Clondalkin, Co. Dublin, and supplies the leading multiple groups, independent stores, healthfood shops and pharmacies. Beeline was awarded the Guaranteed Irish mark in 1988 and it is marked effectively on its range of products.

GUINNESS WORKERS EMPLOYMENT FUND LTD.

St James's Gate, Dublin 8
Tel: (01) 453 6700,
Contact: Honorary Secretary (Mornings)

The Guinness Workers Employment Fund Ltd. has been in existence since 1958. To date, it has lent more than £860,000 and helped in the creation of 350 jobs. Guinness workers and pensioners make a voluntary subscription of 20p a week, which is then used to provide small businesses with financial assistance.

Most of the businesses assisted are in the manufacturing and crafts sectors and are ideally producing a new product or are a direct Irish import substitution. The average financial assistance amounts to a term loan of £5,000 with interest being charged at the time of writing at 9 per cent: normally interest rates are below those charged by the commercial banks.

The preconditions are listed as:

- Good Entrepreneur

- Good Idea

- Good Plan

- Inability to obtain capital through normal channels of finance.

Entrepreneurs must submit applications on the Fund's official application form, which calls for financial information on the planned business and other information normally included in a business plan.

HACKETT & ASSOCIATES

Victoria Road, Greystones, Co. Wicklow
Tel: (01) 287 4938, Fax: (01) 287 7555
Contact: Joseph Hackett

Evaluating a Product

Anyone considering investing in the manufacture or distribution of a new product needs to know — *Will enough people buy it?* Hackett & Associates can prepare an unbiased report based on verifiable facts and figures to assist in making a decision.

Hackett & Associates start by preparing a first Product Screening Report that concentrates on technological feasibility and market compatibility. They then establish the existing market size and trends, assess the competition's strengths and weaknesses, technological developments and possible constraints. From this information, they compute the market share that is available to an entrepreneur and predict the time scale required to reach a break-even sales figure.

When Hackett & Associates are satisfied that a market could be created for a product, they ask: *Why will people buy it?* The company has developed a model programme to give entrepreneurs an in-depth analysis of the comparative merits or demerits of a product. This generates cogent reasons for predicting success or failure in the market place.

The *product viability* is then examined. Does it have *differentiation* to establish its reason for being? Does it have *relevance* to the personal needs of enough people? Can it establish *esteem*, a measure of regard from customers? Can it win *brand structure* by gaining *familiarity*? These are attributes of strong and enduring products that deliver the vital element, *customer satisfaction*.

Hackett & Associates consider the possibility of *market failure* and alert entrepreneurs to avoidable pit falls. Extensive research shows that principal reasons for product failure are:

- Lack of advertising support (3 per cent)
- Lack of trade acceptance (15 per cent)
- Perceived as poor value (15 per cent)
- Faulty product or packing (67 per cent).

The completed analysis will be a valuable report on the market viability if the product.

Evaluating a Product for a Buyer

Hackett & Associates also provide a service to buyers, whereby they assess the competence of suppliers to provide *customer satisfaction*. The trade status and durability of suppliers, their reliability and service-performance capabilities are compared with those of other suppliers and, where applicable, the product manufacturer.

Hospital Product and Service Evaluation Brief

Hackett & Associates assess the competence of suppliers to provide satisfactory equipment or services.

HAYDEN BROWN

Chartered Accountants
Grafton Buildings, 34 Grafton Street, Dublin 2
Tel: (01) 677 1951, Fax: (01) 677 1308
Contact: Stephen Brown

Hayden Brown is a firm of chartered accountants whose main clients are small to medium-sized, family-run businesses. The firm is currently involved in a new initiative aimed at helping businesses at planning and early-trading stages. By providing the entrepreneur with advice and information, Hayden Brown will help a new company through the difficult stages of setting up in business.

The services offered to the potential entrepreneur include:

- Formulation of a Business Plan

- Cash-Flow Projections

- Finance/Grant Applications

- Company Formation

- PAYE/VAT Registration

- Personal and Corporate Tax Planning.

An initial consultation with Hayden Brown is free of charge.

HOOD ASSOCIATES

Merrion Place, Dublin 2
Tel: 676 2248, Fax: (01) 676 2249
Contact: Oliver Hood

Hood Associates was established in 1984. The company provides innovative support to Irish industry in product development and has a reputation for expertise in plastics technology, manufacturing processes, ergonomics, mechanical and detail design and styling. With a leading-edge 3-dimensional engineering solid- and surface-modelling CAD system, the clients of Hood Associates have access to the very latest technology. The company has extensive experience across a broad range of industry sectors (more information or a brochure can be obtained on request). Hood Associates clients, (some of whom have gone on to receive the European Community Design Prize, and awards in the IDA Wang Competition and RTE's "Up and Running", among others). Hood Associates' work is to ISO 9000.

Case Study

Itec Security

In 1985 Itec Security, now part of Aritech, came to Hood Associates with a security vibration sensor which was in need of rationalisation. As Itec did not want to be involved in the launching of a new product on the market, the external appearance was left virtually unchanged and the designers from Hood Associates concentrated on the internal workings of the sensor. The new sensor gave improved performance and was very much easier to install. In addition, a revolutionary new anti-tamper device was invented which has since become an industry standard. The resulting "Universal Sensor" became Itec's bestselling product, and is still on the market today.

ICC BANK

72–74 Harcourt Street, Dublin 2
Tel: (01) 475 5700, Fax: (01) 671 7797

ICC Bank is a state-owned specialist business bank. It provides a wide range of financial services to businesses, in particular to small and medium-sized enterprises.

The main service provided by ICC Bank is loan finance to business. Facilities include short, long and medium-term loans, fixed and variable. ICC Bank loans tend towards short-term finance, though its long-term loans continue to offer a longer repayment period than the commercial banks. ICC Bank also offers international trade and foreign exchange services, as well as a complete treasury service, including a comprehensive deposit-taking system. It also has a specialist savings and investment subsidiary for customers — ICC Investment Bank. Subsidiary companies of ICC Bank provide corporate finance, venture capital and BES investment opportunities.

In assessing a formal request for facilities for small established businesses ICC requires a sound business plan, two years' audited accounts, projections and a marketing plan. The ability, experience and quality of the promoter are also important factors. For start-up situations ICC requires a business plan with realistic projections for the business in the future.

OTHER ADDRESSES

ICC Bank
ICC House, 46 Grand Parade, Cork
Tel: (021) 277 666, Fax: (021) 270 267

ICC Bank
Unit 113, Eyre Square Centre
Eyre Square, Galway
Tel: (091) 66445, Fax: (091) 66811

ICC Bank
ICC House, Charlotte Quay, Limerick
Tel: (061) 317 577, Fax: (061) 311 462

ICC Bank
86 The Quay, Waterford
Tel: (051) 57331, Fax: (051) 57336

IDEAS FORUM

[BUSINESS RESEARCH AND TRAINING SERVICES]

Hogan House
15/16 Hogan Place, Dublin 2
Tel: (01) 661 3022, Fax: (01) 661 3130
Contact: Mary Egan, Jim Campbell, Mike Fitzgerald

Ideas Forum offers a unique business research and training service, which has been designed to help companies of all sizes — from start-up to major corporations — to develop their own ideas. Ideas Forum can also provide organisations with ideas or opportunities for development.

The service is unique in that it offers more than 20 years' experience of business research, in all main industry sectors, both in Ireland and overseas, and acts as the Irish research service for one of the main international business information services. Ideas Forum has particular skills in conducting industry/business, rather than consumer research projects, and another unique feature of the service is that the founder of the business is the only published author on the subject in Ireland.

While Ideas Forum services organisations of all sizes, as a small operation itself, it has a special interest in helping smaller or start-up businesses. The staff appreciate that the cost of research may intimidate smaller operators, but, with their knowledge of sources and research skills, they can customise research to suit clients' budgets and needs.

Ideas Forum is currently in the process of developing a database of business development ideas/opportunities for use by clients.

Examples of services available include:

- Industry surveys
- Identification of opportunities for markets, products and technologies
- Finding licence/joint-venture partners
- Telephone and personal research
- Customer audits
- Searches of official documentation (e.g. Land Registry, Registry of Deeds, planning applications, Company Registry, EU, etc.)

Initial consultation is free of charge.

INDUSTRIAL DEVELOPMENT AUTHORITY (IDA)

Wilton Park House, Wilton Place, Dublin 2
Tel: (01) 668 6633, Fax: (01) 660 5107

The work of the IDA in relation to Irish-owned companies is now performed by Forbairt.

IDA Ireland is responsible for attracting overseas investment into Ireland.

SEE ALSO:　　　FORBAIRT

INDUSTRIAL LIAISON CO-ORDINATION GROUP

c/o Waterford RTC
Cork Road, Waterford
Tel: (051) 75934, (051) 78292
Contact: Dr Erik Lunde

The Industrial Liaison Co-ordination Group offers the small business owner and the entrepreneur access to:

- Support in the design and/or technology of product/process/service development

- Specialised advice and training.

The service has access to an array of facilities and equipment in higher-education colleges, as well as support funding from the relevant state agencies, such as Forbairt and FÁS. The networking of the colleges around the country gives the small business owner or entrepreneur access to amenities available at all the colleges in the network.

There are currently over 250 industrial projects active within the colleges. All receive financial support through the Applied Research Programme set up by Forbairt.

To avail of any of the services offered by the Group, individuals should contact the college, by phone or fax at the above numbers. Follow-up contact usually takes the form of a discussion about the proposed collaboration.

If support funding is sought by an individual or group, application forms must be completed. For certain types of grant, a cash contribution from the company is required. In the case of a direct consultancy, the company pays the college an agreed fee.

SEE ALSO: DUBLIN INSTITUTE OF TECHNOLOGY

THE INNOVATION CENTRE

National Technological Park
Limerick
Tel: (061) 338 177, Fax: (061) 338 065

The Innovation Centre was established in 1980 by Shannon Development, in partnership with the University of Limerick. It provides a wide range of supports directed towards the formation and development of new, technology-based, export-orientated, indigenous, growth companies. The Innovation Centre is a member the European Business and Innovation Centres Network (EBN).

Facilities for would-be entrepreneurs include:

- Project development assistance — a team of experienced executives based in the Centre assists and advises on all aspects of business creation and venture start-up.

- Training in entrepreneurship:

  — *Entrepreneurs' Programme* — a comprehensive training-based programme, comprising six months' part-time training and consultancy, directed towards the formation of venture teams by the Programme's participants, for the purpose of the development and launch of new high-technology, export-orientated, and indigenous businesses.

  — *New Venture Briefings for Entrepreneurs* — a series of short briefing sessions covering a wide range of key topics to appeal to those interested in developing new or expanding existing firms with growth potential. Topics for the briefing sessions include:

    - Developing a saleable, technology-based product

    - The venture-team approach to business success

    - Licensing, technology transfer and intellectual property

    - Focus on international service businesses, etc.

  — *START Programme* — a short evening programme, run by Shannon Development throughout the Shannon region, to introduce people to the essential elements for successful, new business formation and development. Topics covered include:

- Sourcing business ideas
- Business planning
- Project development
- State supports available to new businesses.

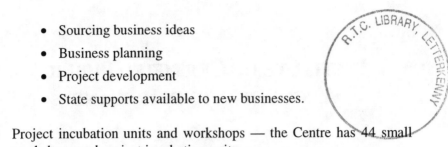

- Project incubation units and workshops — the Centre has 44 small workshops and project incubation units.

- Training, conference and meeting room facilities, including catering.

- Secretarial services — word processing, fax, receptionist and photo-copying.

- Project-development assistance on-site.

SEE ALSO: SHANNON DEVELOPMENT
WOMEN'S BUSINESS DEVELOPMENT CENTRE

INSTITUTE OF CERTIFIED PUBLIC ACCOUNTANTS IN IRELAND

9 Ely Place, Dublin 2
Tel: (01) 676 7353, Fax: (01) 661 2367
Contact: Denis Hevey

The CPA Institute is a body of accountants and auditors, recognised in Ireland by the Companies Act, 1990, and also throughout the European Union because of its inclusion in the EC Directive on the Mutual Recognition of Professional Qualifications.

Institute members provide accountancy services in all business sectors including small business. Services to entrepreneurs include:

- Feasibility studies

- Business plans

- Funding applications

- Auditing

- Taxation

- Financial advice.

In addition, the Institute will make representations on behalf of entrepreneurs to government and other regulatory bodies when matters of concern arise.

INSTITUTE OF CHARTERED ACCOUNTANTS IN IRELAND

87–89 Pembroke Road, Ballsbridge, Dublin 4
Tel: (01) 668 0400, Fax: (01) 668 0842
Contact: Eugene McMahon

11 Donegall Square South, Belfast BT1 5JE
Tel: (08) (01232) 221 600, Fax: (08) (01232) 230 071

The members of the Institute of Chartered Accountants in Ireland provide advice and assistance to individuals who are either thinking of starting a business, or are already established and developing. The Institute is the largest professional accountancy body in Ireland and members are required to report annually on the steps they have taken to keep their knowledge up-to-date with new technical developments affecting professional practice. Members provide advice in the following areas:

- Starting a business

- Running a business

- Accounting systems

- Secretarial and book-keeping services

- Auditing

- Taxation

- Government grant applications

- Bank submissions — profit and cash-flow projections

- Personal financial planning

- Farm financing and accounting

- Farm taxation.

INTEGRATED RESOURCES DEVELOPMENT DUHALLOW

James O'Keeffe Institute
Newmarket, Co. Cork
Tel: (029) 60633, Fax: (029) 60633
Contact: Maura Walsh, Manager

IRD Duhallow was set up by the people of Duhallow as a rural development company in 1989. IRD Duhallow strives for social, economic and environmental sustainability and growth in Duhallow, by capitalising on resources, strengthening culture, fostering pride and a sense of identity, strengthening the capacities of communities and groups and meeting the challenges of change. The single greatest achievement of IRD Duhallow through the LEADER Programme has been its success in firmly embedding in the minds of local communities the concept of self-help and bottom-up development.

In 1991, IRD Duhallow was selected to participate in the EU LEADER Pilot Programme. Duhallow's LEADER grant allocation was £1.29 million and this has yielded a total investment of £4 million in the region, with 68 community and private projects benefiting from this fund.

IRD Duhallow secured the EU EUROFORM Programme in 1993. The EUROFORM Operational Programme is a community initiative involving transnational projects seeking to develop new skills, new qualifications and new employment opportunities.

IRD Duhallow has applied for LEADER II and awaits confirmation of approval. Under the measures laid down by the EU Commission for LEADER II, IRD Duhallow will enact the following measures.

Measure A: Acquisition of Skill

- Establishing a team of animators

- Programme development

- Dissemination of information

- Social research.

Measure B1: Technical Support for Rural Development

- Administration and running of the group

- Support feasibility studies

- Initiation and co-ordination of projects

- Provision of technical support for sub-committees.

Measure B2: Vocational Training and Recruitment Assistance

- Community development training

- Training for SMEs

- Training for tourism

- Identification and development of new skills

- Food business development training

- Employment grants and training

- Focus on rural women and families.

Measure B3: Rural Tourism

- Marketing

- Culture and heritage

- Eco-tourism

- Amenities and attractions

- Angling

- Activity holidays

- Increase in accommodation base.

Measure B4: Small Firms, Crafts Enterprises and Local Services

- Aid to new business development, diversification and expansion

- SME networks and local innovation

- Access to technology

- Business support mechanisms

- Increased quality standards

- Marketing

- Revolving loan fund.

Measure B5: Exploitation and Marketing of Local Agricultural Forestry and Fishery Products

- Encouragement of value-added products

- Farm business appraisal scheme

- Increase in quota levels — viability

- Supplementary/alternative enterprises

- Support for new processes

- Slaughter and process facilities

- New technology.

Measure B6: Preservation and Improvement of the Environment and Living Conditions

- Village and town enhancement

- Alternative energies

- Cultural and social development

- Development of derelict buildings/sites

- Social action programmes

- Recycling and environmental preservation

- Rural resettlement.

Measure C: Transnational Partnerships

- Identification of suitable partners

- Research and development of initiatives

- Project management development programme

- Exchange of expertise and experience

- Participation in transnational seminars

- Joint marketing initiatives.

Case Study

Duhallow Food Training Centre

The Food Training Centre which opened in Boherbue in October 1994 is, as the name implies, a facility catering for the training needs of those planning a future in the Food Industry. A Food Hygiene Course, leading to City and Guilds/FÁS certification, was conducted in 1993/1994. On 31 March 1995, in Newmarket, the nine successful participants were presented with their certificates by Ivan Yates, TD, Minister for Agriculture.

The building was renovated with the assistance of EU LEADER funds. This involved upgrading the building to food-grade standard and subdividing it into four Food Incubator Units. All of the units are currently occupied and there are applications to take up units when they become vacant.

Greenacres Foods, owned by Ms Rita Ahern, occupies two units and employs five people. Because of expansion of her business, Ms Ahern plans to move to a larger premises before the end of the year. Her venture has been particularly successful, as has Ms Ahern on a personal basis, having in March 1995 received the Irish Permanent Young Business Woman of the Year Award.

The Irish Venison Co-op uses one unit for development of new pâté and salami product

A local "home baker" has taken the fourth unit and is operating a very successful business with good demand for her excellent quality produce.

The initial period of operation of the Food Centre has been very successful, and plans are well-advanced to initiate training programmes for young entrepreneurs in the food industry, in conjunction with the National Food Biotechnology Centre and the Department of Food Science and Technology at UCC. Work is also ongoing with Teagasc, Moorepark, on the development of a dairy-based product to be marketed in the near future.

The Food Training Centre employs a full-time manager, Mr Dan Murphy (Tel: (029) 76375), who, as well as overseeing the commercial and training aspects of the Centre, offers advice on a consultancy basis to a number of Food Enterprises in the region.

INTERNATIONAL FUND FOR IRELAND

PO Box 2000, Belfast, BT4 3SA
Tel: (08) (01232) 768 832, Fax: (08) (01232) 763 313

PO Box 2000, Dublin 2
Tel: (01) 878 0655, Fax: (01) 871 2116

The International Fund for Ireland was established in December 1986, following the signing by the British and Irish Governments of the Anglo-Irish Agreement. The contributors to the Fund are the USA, Canada, New Zealand, Australia and the European Union. The six counties in which the Fund operates are Cavan, Donegal, Leitrim, Louth, Monaghan and Sligo. The objectives of the Fund are to promote economic and social advance and to encourage contact, dialogue and reconciliation between Nationalists and Unionists throughout Ireland.

The International Fund for Ireland runs seven programmes.

Disadvantaged Areas Initiative

- The Community Regeneration and Improvement Special Programme (CRISP) operates in towns and villages of Northern Ireland with a population of up to 10,000 in areas of particular disadvantage.

- The Community Economic Regeneration Scheme (CERS) assists community groups in Northern Ireland with proven ability to generate economic growth and job creation, by providing premises in disadvantaged areas for economic/commercial purposes, including retail and other services.

- The Border Towns and Villages Scheme involves a variety of Fund programmes for the community-led economic and physical regeneration of border towns and villages in the Republic.

Business Enterprise

- Workspace accommodation is provided for small businesses at various enterprise centres.

- The Revolving Business Development Fund is a support scheme for local business development organisations. It administers revolving funds, providing loans for small businesses.

- Local Business Development Teams is a scheme to support the appointment of business development officers by local enterprise-development organisations.

- Community Business is a scheme to support the development of community business in disadvantaged areas.

- Various marketing initiatives are funded in Northern Ireland and in the Republic to stimulate investment and open up new market opportunities. Cross-border projects include:

  — All-Ireland Trade Show in Washington DC and in Russia — to promote all Ireland products.

  — Food Enterprise & Export Development (FEED) Belfast/Dublin — focuses on the development of new products and export markets.

  — Joint IDB/ITB Subcontract Exhibition Belfast/Dublin — organisation of four subcontract exhibitions to help in promoting cross-border trade.

  — Televised quality promotion, Upper Galwally, Belfast — all-Ireland competition promoting enterprise awareness and total quality management in business.

  — Joint IDB/ITB trade promotion in Boston to strengthen trade between Ireland and the US.

  — ACUMEN Cross-Border Development Programme to increase cross-border trade.

Tourism

- Hotel and Guesthouse Improvement Scheme — assistance is given to lower-grade hotels and guesthouses in the border counties of the Republic to improve accommodation and facilities.

- Hotel Improvement Scheme — assistance for improvements to one- and two-star hotels (opened prior to 1986) in Northern Ireland.

- Licensed Guest Inns — assistance for public houses and restaurants that have an established catering trade and whose owners want to develop visitors' facilities, such as bedrooms, etc.

- Community-Sponsored Amenities Development Scheme — development and restoration of various centres.

- Young Entrepreneurs Scheme — assistance is given to encourage young entrepreneurs to develop tourism-based businesses.

- Joint Marketing — for Northern Ireland and the Republic in Europe, North America, Britain and Australia/New Zealand.

Urban Development

A programme to stimulate viable economic activity in the commercial centres of towns and villages in the North and in the six southern border counties, by bringing vacant and derelict buildings and sites back into productive use. Top priority is given to projects located in the most disadvantaged towns, especially in CRISP-designated towns.

Rural Development

An initiative to support community-driven economic development in disadvantaged rural areas in Northern Ireland and the border counties of the Republic.

Science and Technology

The Programme supports the development of industry–university links and cross-border collaboration in research and development and infrastructural projects, in order that the research capability of Irish universities can be harnessed to the development of commercially exploitable technologies.

Wider Horizons

- Young Workers'/Young People's Projects, which include work-experience opportunities in Canada, France, Denmark, Germany, Ireland, the Netherlands and the USA.

- Managers'/Entrepreneurs' Programme, which includes partnership arrangements and work-experience programmes in the USA, and in England, Scotland, Denmark, Germany, the Netherlands, France and other parts of Europe.

The Fund is also involved with flagship projects, two of which have now been completed — Navan Fort and the Erne/Shannon Waterway. It also operates a Community Relations Programme, designed to provide practical support for initiatives and projects that will improve relationships between the communities in the North and between North and South. It has two investment companies, which provide seed capital on normal commercial criteria, both to existing enterprises and start-up projects. These companies, trading under the names Enterprise Equity (NI) Ltd. and Enterprise Equity (Irl) Ltd., are based in Belfast and Dundalk respectively. They were set up to stimulate business development in Northern Ireland and the border counties of Cavan, Donegal, Leitrim, Louth, Monaghan and Sligo in the Republic.

The Fund's Business Enterprise Programme is managed by the Department of Foreign Affairs in the Republic and the Department of Economic Development in Northern Ireland. Only border counties in the Republic are eligible for assistance from the Fund.

One of the main components of the Programme continues to be the assistance provided to local community enterprise groups towards the provision of workspace accommodation and the establishment of business-loan funds to assist the establishment and growth of small businesses. The International Fund for Ireland has assisted a total of 43 enterprise agencies in Northern Ireland and has established four new enterprise centres in the Republic. (For a more detailed listing of the various enterprise centres and schemes available, contact either of the addresses above.)

SEE ALSO: LOUTH COUNTY ENTERPRISE FUND
MONAGHAN COUNTY ENTERPRISE FUND

IRISH BUSINESS AND EMPLOYERS' CONFEDERATION

Confederation House, 84/86 Lower Baggot Street, Dublin 2
Tel: (01) 6601011 , Fax: (01) 6601717

The Irish Business and Employers' Confederation (IBEC) represents and provides economic, commercial, employee relations and social affairs services to some 4,000 companies and organisations from all sectors of economic and commercial activity. IBEC works to shape policies and influence decision-making in a way that develops and protects members' interests and contributes to the development and maintenance of an economy that promotes enterprise and productive employment.

European Orientation Programme

The European Orientation Programme aims to encourage Irish exporting companies to improve their marketing/production/intelligence skills. It sponsors graduates on a training programme, comprising three months' in-company, three months' language training in an EU country, and six months in a commercial environment similar to that of the sponsoring company, also in an EU country.

A grant of 50 per cent of the Programme costs is available from Forbairt/An Bord Tráchtála for sponsoring companies. Successful candidates receive a bursary of £8,000 to cover travel, lodgings, etc. Irish manufacturing and internationally-traded service companies are eligible. Other companies may participate, but have to pay the full amount of £9,000 (which includes a programme management fee).

SEE ALSO: AN BORD TRÁCHTÁLA
              FORBAIRT

IRISH CRAFT AND GIFT EXHIBITORS

Temple Hall, Blackrock, Co. Dublin
Tel: (01) 283 1021, Fax: (01) 288 9483
Contact: Ron Finlay Mulligan/Ida Kiernan

Irish Craft and Gift Exhibitors provides Irish manufacturers with an opportunity to participate in inexpensive hotel shows in the USA. The group consists of 20–25 companies, which have been exhibiting together for 19 years. The exhibitors invite a mailing list of approximately 400 US shops/buyers to view and place orders at hotel shows.

The work of the exhibitors' group involves regular communication with An Bord Tráchtála. Applications are welcome from established and reliable manufacturers who can deliver when stated. Within a small group, product duplication may have to be taken into account. There are no special forms to complete — the initial application is in writing and a discussion is then arranged.

A list of past exhibitors is available from the above address.

SEE ALSO: AN BORD TRÁCHTÁLA

IRISH LEAGUE OF CREDIT UNIONS

Castleside Drive, Rathfarnham, Dublin 14
Tel: (01) 490 8911, Fax: (01) 490 8915
Contact: Grace Perrott

The Irish League of Credit Unions (ILCU) has a worker co-operative fund through which it can grant-aid credit union members who are members of such co-ops. A maximum grant of £750 per eligible member of a credit union may be available under the Fund, with a maximum grant of £3,000 in any one year to a particular worker co-operative. Further grants may be available after one year's trading. It has also provided sponsorship, along with FÁS and the Northern Ireland Co-operative Development Agency, for the Worker Co-operative Enterprise awards.

There is a strong belief in credit unions that providing support for employment initiatives at the local level is an important role for them to play in community development. By joining a credit union, members will:

- Be encouraged to save on a regular basis, thereby building up a fund of money for their own benefit and that of other members

- Have access to a source of credit at a reasonable rate of interest

- Own and control their own credit union, and therefore gain greater control over their personal finances.

Entrepreneurs or owners of small businesses will be treated in the same manner as individual members of a credit union. Policies regarding loans for business purposes may vary from union to union. Loans are generally provided for provident and productive purposes, and interest is charged at not more than 1 per cent per month on the reducing balance (12.68 per cent APR). Eligibility for loans will be judged on ability to repay and on the member's savings and repayment record.

To become a member of a credit union, it is necessary to be over 16 years of age, and to be within the common bond (that is, that members of a credit union have something "in common" with other union members), usually living in the same area, or working for the same employer within the same industry sector. On approval for membership of a credit union, an application form must be completed, a small entrance fee paid (usually £1 or less) and a share purchased (£1 generally). There are currently 526 local credit unions, which are affiliated to the League in the 32 counties.

Case Study

Smarett Limited

Smarett Limited, trading as North West Busways, is a 100-per-cent-owned worker co-operative providing bus services in the north-western part of Donegal. The company was formed by four bus drivers made redundant in March 1992. The drivers each invested £4,000 to help establish the business.

The company currently operates three buses, providing a scheduled passenger service from Inishowen to Letterkenny, with plans to introduce new routes to Derry. The co-operative's buses are also available for chartered hire. The company operates a passenger service, licensed by the Department of Transport. It plans to expand the routes to improve its service of the transport needs of residents and visitors in the Donegal/Derry region.

Smarett Limited was a joint winner of the 1992 New Worker Co-operative of the Year award, run by the FÁS Co-operative Development Unit with the support of the ILCU, which helped the company to acquire a vehicle for use on the new cross-border service.

SEE ALSO: REGISTRAR OF FRIENDLY SOCIETIES

IRISH MANAGEMENT INSTITUTE

Sandyford Road, Dublin 16
Tel: (01) 295 6911, Fax: (01) 295 5147

The aim of the Irish Management Institute (IMI) is to provide members with training programmes to suit the needs of their companies. The following are details of some of the programmes available for the small business owner.

Business Development Programme for Small Businesses

This Development Programme is for owner/managers of small manufacturing or certain service companies with a strong commitment to expanding their business. It is sponsored by a number of companies and development agencies, and is now being run under licence from the IMI in eight European countries.

The objective of the Programme is to increase participants' ability to develop their business by focusing on the practical challenges and opportunities that they face.

The Programme includes:

- How participants can make a realistic assessment both of themselves and their companies

- How to identify practical and profitable ways to expand a business

- How to find new customers and new markets, and develop new products

- How to draw up comprehensive development plans for a business in the areas of finance, production, personnel and marketing

- How to improve efficiency.

The Business Development Programme consists of a monthly two-day residential workshop, with a one-day follow-up visit each month to participants' companies. A survey is made before the Programme begins, to ensure that the content is tailored to the needs of participants, and regular progress reviews ensure that it is relevant and practical.

The number of participants on the Programme is limited to 18, and these are carefully selected, based on their commitment to, and the potential of, their businesses. Care is taken to ensure that while there are common interests among participants, none are in direct competition.

Marketing Plan for Small Businesses

This course is designed for executives in small businesses who are responsible for developing a marketing plan.

The objective is to create a more effective marketing plan by integrating all the market-related activities that take place. The course covers the fundamental elements of marketing and explains:

- How to develop a successful marketing strategy
- How to define the market segments
- How to use the marketing mix — product, price, promotion and distribution
- How small businesses can exploit direct marketing
- How to create a marketing plan that will deliver sales and profits objectives.

Participants will work through the steps required to develop a plan, using personal computers where necessary.

Other Programmes

Other courses available at the IMI, which are specifically designed for small businesses, include:

- Industrial Relations Negotiating Skills
- Export Development Programme.

Two recently introduced courses at the Institute are:

- Advanced Business Development Programme
- General Management Programme for Senior Managers.

In addition, Forbairt's Enterprise Development Programme, which is aimed at managers leaving senior positions within industry to set up on their own, is run in Dublin in conjunction with the Irish Management Institute. (For further details, local Forbairt offices should be contacted.)

SEE ALSO: FORBAIRT
                KPMG STOKES KENNEDY CROWLEY

IRISH PRODUCTIVITY CENTRE (IPC)

IPC House, 35–39 Shelbourne Road, Ballsbridge, Dublin 4
Tel: (01) 668 6244, Fax: (01) 668 6525
Contact: Tom McGuinness

The Irish Productivity Centre (IPC), one of Ireland's leading business consultancy agencies, helps small and medium-sized enterprises to grow from start-up to successful ventures. The IPC has a team of highly experienced advisers in marketing, production, accountancy and technology, to provide a "total care package" for clients across a broad spectrum of business sectors. The centre operates closely with all State agencies, ensuring that client companies benefit from the many support services and grants.

The IPC Council comprises representatives of the Irish Business Employers' Confederation and the Irish Congress of Trade Unions.

Services for SMEs

Having worked closely with the SME sector in Ireland for over 30 years, IPC has developed a full range of services designed to help companies not only to overcome immediate problems, but also to grow and develop into strong competitive ventures.

Initial Appraisal

This examines:

- The company's strategy and mission

- The cost base and cost drivers in the company

- The product and customer base

- Funding and financial control

- Management information.

The Solution and its Implementation

The types of activity that the IPC might undertake, with the agreement and support of the company's management and employers, would include:

- Company Assessment
- Management Organisation and Structure
- Strategic and Business Planning
- Feasibility Studies
- Grant Applications
- World Class Manufacturing and Continuous Improvement
- Product Development
- Preparation of Training Programme — external and in-house
- Information Systems and Technology
- Raising Finance
- Productivity Measurement
- Quality Systems to ISO 9000
- Market Research/Analysis/Development domestically and internationally
- Sales Management and Promotion
- Sales Analysis
- Marketing Segmentation and Planning
- Staff Recruitment.

Financial Graduate/Accountants Programme
This programme is designed and run by IPC to assist SMEs to strengthen their financial and management accounting function by employing a full-time financial graduate/accountant (FGA). Grant-aid is provided by Forbairt and Shannon Development towards the salary cost of the FGA, plus 100 per cent of the training cost to the IPC. FGAs must be registered students with a professional management accounting body and must be currently sitting, or have finished their final examinations. (For details, contact John Ryan at the above address)

International Programmes
The IPC has tendered and carried out both pilot projects and major

programmes, which have received funding from the EU, including its "Planned Growth Programme" whereby SMEs receive in-company consultancy assistance, the International Company Development Programme and the European Integrated Company Development Programme. Funding has also been received under EUROFORM — a major initiative for SMEs and the environment.

IRISH QUALITY ASSOCIATION

Merrion Hall, Strand Road, Sandymount, Dublin 4
Tel: (01) 269 5255, Fax: (01) 269 5820
Contact: Seán Conlan

The Irish Quality Association is a voluntary organisation committed to ensuring that quality is put into daily business practice. Membership of the IQA is corporate-based and includes industrial sectors, in both the manufacturing and service industries.

The IQA is well known for its improvement programmes which assess the overall adequacy of a company's quality and/or hygiene standards. In addition the IQA provides a full range of membership services designed to equip member organisations with the information necessary to sharpen their approach and streamline operations to those of the best-in-class.

Hygiene Mark

The Hygiene Mark was introduced in 1989 as an initiative to encourage businesses to pay greater attention to hygiene practices. When applying for a hygiene mark, participants are aware that no advance notice will be given of the hygiene systems audit. Hygiene Mark certification therefore assures customers that companies displaying the mark have undergone a rigorous hygiene programme.

During this hygiene test, the following areas are thoroughly assessed:

- Structural Layout

- Food Storage and Protection

- Cleaning Systems

- Insect and Pest Control

- Staff Facilities and Personal Hygiene

- Operational Hygiene

- Management of Hygiene

- General Grounds.

The "Triple Hygiene Mark"

The Triple Hygiene Mark scheme was introduced in 1991 to give recognition to firms that consistently maintained exceptionally high standards of hygiene (for three consecutive years, at least).

IQA National Hygiene Awards

These awards are presented annually to businesses in 14 different industrial categories which achieve optimum standards of hygiene. From these, one Supreme Award winner is chosen.

Quality Mark

To obtain a Quality Mark, companies must undergo stringent audits to assess the effectiveness of their quality-assurance systems. To date, 351 Irish companies are certified to the Quality Mark standard. Linked into the Quality Mark Scheme are the annual Quality Awards where the best of the Quality Mark holders are in contention for an award in their region. From these, the supreme Quality Award winner is chosen.

Education and Training

The Quality Association has developed links with third-level colleges and universities. The number of courses available in the area of quality has burgeoned in recent years, and interested students may now avail of courses for the following qualifications:

- Certificate in Elementary Quality Assurance

- Certificate in Quality Control (City and Guilds)

- Certificate in Quality Management

- Diploma in Quality Management

- Quality Assurance Degree

- Postgraduate Diploma in Quality Assurance.

In 1992, the IQA established an Education and Training Approvals Board to validate courses from educational institutions, training establishments and industry. The Association also offers, on an ongoing basis, in-house training services, and organises a number of quality-focused half-day and five-day training programmes.

IRISH SMALL AND MEDIUM ENTERPRISES ASSOCIATION (ISME)

32 Kildare Street, Dublin 2
Tel: (01) 662 2755, Fax: (01) 661 2157
Contact: Frank Mulcahy, Director

The Association's primary objective is to represent to the government, government departments, development agencies public utilities and other major influences in the business community the concerns of owner-managed businesses.

ISME intends to extend and build on its many group schemes to ensure value for money from the members' annual subscription. The group schemes in place include:

- ISME group insurance scheme — delivers savings of up to 40 per cent on annual premiums

- ISME group VHI scheme — group discount of 10 per cent on premiums

- ISME group ISO 9000 facility — cost to small firms: £3,500 less FÁS grant of 65 per cent

- ISME group ISO 9000 annual certification fee — up to 50 per cent less than National Standards Authority of Ireland (NSAI) fees

- ISME group translation service — 20 per cent less than normal commercial prices

- ISME group invoice discounting facilities — savings of up to 40 per cent are achievable; or normal discount factoring — undisclosed factoring whereby companies' debtors are managed for them in confidence; and invoice discounting

- ISME industrial relations service

- ISME credit insurance

- ISME foreign currency scheme — cutting members' costs

- ISME self-managed pension fund

- ISME group commercial mortgage facilities — savings of up to 3 per cent on the normal market costs.

- ISME group debt collection service

- ISME group leasing facilities

ISME can also reduce costs for those considering registering a patent.

Regular regional briefing sessions are organised for ISME members. In addition, ISME is offering a company "health check", whereby ISME will deploy specialists who will analyse companies' cost structures and identify where costs are out of line and where savings can be made. ISME also provides regionalised management development programmes on Solution-Based Marketing and Financial Management for SMEs.

ISME membership fees range from £200 to £400 and depend upon the number of people that a company employs. Membership is available to companies with up to 500 staff.

ISME Publications

- Quarterly Newsletters

- *Guide to Employer Obligations, Procedures & Practices*

- *EC Grants*

- *Wages & Conditions Survey*

- *Insider/Outsider*

- *How to Deal with the Revenue Commissioners*

- *Guide to Industry Support Programmes*

IRISH TRADE UNION TRUST

3rd Floor, Liberty Hall, Eden Quay, Dublin 1
Tel: (01) 878 7272, Fax: (01) 878 7128
Contact: Naomi Brennan

The Irish Trade Union Trust was set up and funded by SIPTU (Service Industry Professional Technical Union). It provides low-interest long-term loans to worker co-operatives that are SIPTU members. The loans are intended to fill the gap between initial capital investment and grant-aid. Application is made by submitting a complete business plan with financial projections.

The Trust assists in the formation of "phoenix co-operatives" and employee share-ownership plans. It provides a back-up service for groups wishing to set up co-ops — whether it be a group of unemployed people in a community who have identified a business idea that can provide employment, or a group of workers who have been made redundant and wish to take over the business from former owners. The Trust also assists local community employment initiatives and Rural Tourism Development projects.

Advice is available to worker co-operatives on the following topics:

- Legal structure — history, ethics and group dynamics

- Training, feasibility studies, business plans — guidance in compilation and assessment

- Financial costings — budgets and projections

- Introduction to state agencies

- Model Rules — assistance in drawing them up

- Registration

- Funding and other sources of help.

KPMG STOKES KENNEDY CROWLEY
BUSINESS DEVELOPMENT SERVICES

Chartered Accountants
1 Stokes Place, St Stephen's Green, Dublin 2
Tel: (01) 708 1600, Fax: (01) 708 1666
Contact: John Crawford/Terry McGowan/
Colin O'Brien/Cathy Byrne

KPMG SKC Business Development Services provides specialised business advisory services to small and medium-sized companies. These services include:

- Audit and Accountancy Services

- Company Secretarial Services

- Financial Advice

- Grant Applications

- Tax Planning and Advice

- Business Start-ups

- Operations Management — financial management, internal control re finance, debtors, production, stock control and bank position

- Training and Education — business courses on company secretarial law and other areas

- Employee Benefit — the varying mix of packages available to employees as salary, such as pensions, life insurance etc., are examined.

- Personnel Recruitment Services.

The Business Development Programme, held in the Irish Management Institute, is sponsored by KPMG SKC. This is a management course designed for Irish companies that have been successfully established for a number of years and are employing in the region of 20–25 people and have the growth potential to expand to 100 employees. Entrepreneurs in this category should contact either the IMI or KPMG SKC for further application details.

The EC Grants Guide, published by KPMG Stokes Kennedy Crowley and the Small Firms Association, gives relevant information on grants. Also published by KPMG SKC and of interest to Irish indigenous firms is *A Comprehensive Guide to Government and EC Grants*.

Case Studies

Finance

An individual with a manufacturing idea required financial planning assistance. KPMG SKC helped to develop a business plan and to obtain a Forbairt feasibility grant. It then advised on the funding options for the purchase of a factory and machinery, assisted in raising the finance with an outside equity source and helped to negotiate grants from various sources. KPMG SKC also helped to complete the necessary statutory documentation to put the funding in place.

Tax

A client had a company which was making substantial trading losses. The client was also involved with two other companies which were trading successfully. By restructuring a group of companies, the client was able to claim tax relief on the losses against the profits of the other companies.

LEADER PROGRAMME

Department of Agriculture and Food
Rural Development Division
Agriculture House, Kildare Street, Dublin 2
Tel: (01) 678 9011, Fax: (01) 661 6203
Contact: Mary Cullinan/Jo O'Donnell

LEADER is the EU initiative for rural development which enables groups in rural areas to implement their own multi-sectoral integrated business plans for the development of their areas. EU funding of £54 million is being provided for LEADER II, which will be supplemented by a significant Irish Government contribution. There will also be the possibility of further funding at the mid-term review. Investment in the following areas may be undertaken by the groups:

- Technical support to rural development including animation and group administration

- Training and recruitment assistance

- Rural tourism

- Small firms, craft enterprises and local services

- Local exploitation and marketing of agricultural, horticultural, forest and fishery products

- Preservation and improvement of the environment and living conditions.

In addition to undertaking various activities themselves, the groups may aid individuals and other groups within their operational areas who have suitable projects to offer.

For further information, contact Rural Development Division, Department of Agriculture, Food and Forestry, Agriculture House, Kildare Street, Dublin 2. Tel: (01) 607 2674.

LIFFEY TRUST

117–126 Upper Sheriff Street, Dublin 1
Tel: (01) 836 4651, Fax: (01) 836 4818
Contact: Séamus McDermott

The Liffey Trust was founded in 1984, and is a voluntary, non-political, non-profit-making organisation devoted to job creation in Ireland. It receives no state aid and relies for its funding on private companies and individuals, on raffles and functions, and on promotions of various sorts.

The Trust believes that bureaucracy hinders the setting-up and development of new enterprises, and endeavours to eliminate the obstacles that prevent would-be entrepreneurs from getting started. It has helped 120 different businesses to date and has the largest enterprise centre in Europe funded without state aid.

The Liffey Trust provides the following services to start-up businesses:

- Preparation of business plans, feasibility studies and grant applications, free of charge

- Advice on ways and means of raising finance

- Guidance on setting up accounting and control systems

- Model Rules, free of charge, for co-operatives

- Free management consultancy for the first year

- Free marketing consultancy for the first year

- Organisation of combined marketing of products

- Workspace in Dublin with free or reduced rent for new businesses while they are getting established. Food units are also provided.

- Handling of the bureaucratic procedures to help a new business:

    — To decide its legal structure

    — To become registered

    — To obtain a VAT number

— To register for PAYE and PRSI

— To obtain subcontract numbers.

- Explanations of the many different kinds of grants available.

There are no charges for the Liffey Trust consultancy services, either before or after the business is in operation. However, there is a charge for rented space — this amounts to two-thirds of commercial rates. The Trust has over 60 units, varying in size from 100 to 4,000 square feet. Many of the units are suitable for food processing.

The Trust has published a book, *Setting up a Business* (grants and everything the entrepreneur needs to know). Copies are available from the above address.

LIMERICK CHAMBER OF COMMERCE

96 O'Connell Street, Limerick
Tel: (061) 415 180, Fax: (061) 415 785
Contact: Brendan Woods

Shannon Business Centre
Shannon, Co. Clare
Tel: (061) 362 422, Fax: (061) 362 024

The Limerick Chamber of Commerce is a long-established private business organisation.

Its mission is to promote and develop a better business environment for its members within the area in which it operates. It provides an authoritative and representative voice for over 450 members in industry, trade, commerce, tourism and the professional services in Limerick and also Shannon where it established a branch office in 1989.

Limerick Chamber of Commerce is an affiliated member of the Chambers of Commerce of Ireland through which it has formal links and communications with the Irish Business Bureau and Eurochambres. It has specific business development associations established with Chambers of Commerce and Industry in Belgium, France, Germany, Greece, Italy, the UK, the USA and the Confederation of Independent States (CIS).

The Chamber's operation includes the Secretariat and Management of the Limerick Market Trustees, an extensive portfolio of open market properties including the newly restored and exciting Milk Market Project at Cornmarket Row. Through the President and Board of Directors it is represented on a wide-ranging number of local public bodies, boards, authorities and other forums through which the Chamber influences policy and decisions positively affecting the business environment and the community at large.

The Chamber provides regular opportunities for members to meet one another, which helps small business owners to make new contacts and creates a greater awareness of their companies throughout the business community.

SEE ALSO: CHAMBERS OF COMMERCE OF IRELAND

LIMERICK FOOD CENTRE

Shannon Development
Raheen, Limerick
Tel: (061) 302 035, Fax: (061) 301 172
Contact: Colman O'Driscoll

The Limerick Food Centre provides modern facilities in a pure environment for food processors, enabling them to meet exacting processing standards for the home and export markets.
The Centre offers:

- Facilities and infrastructure for food processors, including accommodation in "shell" form, which can be adapted to specific needs of individual firms, and small 300-square-foot food-processing units for the development and testing of new food products

- Food Business Incubation Centre

- Food Development Laboratory

- Food and Natural Resources Information Bank

- Fully equipped processing hall in which clients may undertake pilot batch production of their proposed products.

SEE ALSO: SHANNON DEVELOPMENT

LOUTH COUNTY ENTERPRISE FUND

Finnabair Industrial Park
Dundalk, Co. Louth
Tel/Fax: (01) 289 3052
Contact: Archie Coubrough

The Louth County Enterprise Fund was established in 1989 to administer the funds made available in Co. Louth by the International Fund for Ireland. The County Enterprise Fund offers low-interest loans to help small firms to start up or expand, as well as grants to certain community enterprises. The maximum loan available from the Fund is £15,000 which is repayable over three years, or over five years where the purchase, extension, or renovation of property is concerned.

Applications are made on the company's official form and the applicant will be required to provide a business plan. This is then circulated to the members of the Assessment Committee and considered by them. If a project appears viable, an interview will be set up with the applicant. The committee then makes its recommendation to the Board whose members decide whether or not to grant the loan.

A basic requirement for any loan offered by the Enterprise Fund is that the project be set up in Co. Louth.

SEE ALSO: INTERNATIONAL FUND FOR IRELAND
MONAGHAN COUNTY ENTERPRISE FUND

MADDEN CONSULTANTS LTD.

31 Ballytore Road, Rathfarnham, Dublin 14
Tel: (01) 490 6096, Fax: (01) 492 0368
Contact: James Madden, BE.Chem.C.Eng., MBA, MMII

Madden Consultants Ltd. is a firm of marketing consultants, strategic planners, trainers and project managers. The firm works closely with individuals and companies in researching and formulating marketing plans. The following is a list of the services provided to help organisations to realise their full potential:

Marketing Services

- Detailed Research and Competitive Analysis
- Marketing Audit
- SWOT Analysis
- Marketing Strategy Formulation and Detailed Action Programmes
- Market Research, Market Entry Plans
- Technology Transfer/Licensing.

Strategic Planning Services

- Company Audit, Environmental Analysis, Financial Modelling and Strategic Plans
- Business Planning and assistance with Grant Applications
- Feasibility Studies
- Acquisition Searches.

Training Services

- Marketing Planning, Strategic Planning and Export Planning.

Project Management Services

- Presentations to potential customers
- Assistance in selecting good distributors/agents
- Expert help from qualified staff on a contract basis.

MARKETING CENTRE FOR SMALL BUSINESS

University of Limerick
Plassey Technological Park, Castletroy, Limerick
Tel: (061) 333 644 ext. 2619/2161, Fax: (061) 330 316
Contact: Briga Hynes or Patricia Fleming

The Marketing Centre for Small Business is located at the University of Limerick. It was established in 1985 with the support of the University of Limerick, Shannon Development, FÁS, Industrial Credit Corporation and An Bord Tráchtála. The primary function of the Centre is to facilitate and assist individuals who wish to start in business, and those who are in business and wish to develop and expand further.

Over the years, the Centre has assisted a wide range of entrepreneurs in both the manufacturing and service sectors.

The varied range of services provided by the Centre includes the following:

- General consultancy and advice

- Market research and analysis

- The development of market and business plans

- Undertaking feasibility studies

- Product and pricing research

- Development of promotional strategies

- Organising workshops and seminars

- Training and Development Programmes.

The services of the Centre are specifically designed to accommodate the varying needs of the small business sector

Small Business Institute Programme.

This programme, which is promoted by the University of Limerick and Shannon Development, (the state development agency for the Shannon

Region), offers to small businesses a consultancy programme that is designed to identify and solve their business problems.

Through the Student Enterprise Centre at the University, small firms may access the resources, managerial experience and professional competences of the University and its students at an agreed nominal fee. The consultancy programme provides confidential managerial assistance to firms in manufacturing, tourism, agribusiness and the service sectors.

SEE ALSO: PLASSEY MANAGEMENT & TECHNOLOGY
                 CENTRE
                 SHANNON DEVELOPMENT

THE MARKETING INSTITUTE

South County Business Park, Leopardstown, Dublin 18
Tel: (01) 295 2355, Fax: 295 2453
Contact: Suzanne Carden

Established in 1962, the Marketing Institute is the professional representative organisation for marketing people in Ireland. It is a national organisation with seven regional councils and a national secretariat comprising a chief executive and 12 staff based in Leopardstown, Dublin. The Institute is a non-profit-making body and is also the examining body for marketing education in Ireland. Money generated is spent on developing member services and on the Institute's education programme.

The aim of the Marketing Institute is to promote the benefits of good marketing practices to the business community. By providing access to information, it also provides opportunities for individuals to improve their marketing careers. It plays a role in promoting marketing as the principal force driving any successful business, and acts as the representative body for marketing people, to provide a forum and a focus for marketing issues.

The Institute is the examining body for marketing education in Ireland. Opportunities for education are provided at every point in the marketer's career: at the initial stages, through graduation, and later through professional development in marketing.

A range of quality services for members and students, through which valuable marketing information flows, is also provided by the Institute. Services include publications and a full range of events, catering for every sector of the profession.

Membership of the Marketing Institute is available to those who meet the criteria set by the membership committee of the Institute. Associateship allows those not working directly in a marketing area, or those beginning their marketing career, to enjoy the benefits of membership.

MEITHEAL MHAIGH EO

Lower Main Street
Foxford, Co. Mayo
Tel: (094) 56745, Fax: (094) 56749
Contact: Justin Sammon, Manager

Meitheal Mhaigh Eo was established in 1991 as an Area Based Partnership Company. It is actively involved in promoting enterprise at local level, with particular emphasis on assisting the long-term unemployed to start their own business.

Area Allowance Enterprise Scheme (AAES)

This programme enables unemployed individuals with enterprise ideas to retain 100 per cent of their Unemployment Assistance and secondary benefits for the initial year in starting a business, 75 per cent in the second year and 50 per cent in the third year. Meitheal Mhaigh Eo provides technical assistance in drafting business plans and investigates sources of finance and other supports to develop business ideas. To date, over 200 new enterprises have been established, many of which have generated additional employment locally. Enterprises that have started under this scheme range from the provision of a local hackney service to designer clothing, which is being exported to Germany.

Community Employment Programme (CEP)

Meitheal Mhaigh Eo acts as sponsor for a number of FÁS Community Employment Programmes aimed at developing innovative employment and enterprise opportunities for the unemployed in the area. Projects developed to date include community arts, organic gardening and hill-walking.

Community Project Development

Meitheal Mhaigh Eo assists local community groups and individuals in developing specific business projects based on local resources. Technical assistance is provided in the form of expertise in designing action plans, and advice on project funding and other schemes available.

Information

Information is provided on the supports and services available for community groups and individuals. Meitheal Mhaigh Eo publishes a newsletter, *Community Focus*, which provides information and updates on local development, enterprise opportunities and funding sources.

SEE ALSO: AREA PARTNERSHIP COMPANIES
BALLYMUN PARTNERSHIP
DUNDALK EMPLOYMENT PARTNERSHIP
THE ENTERPRISE TRUST
FÁS, THE TRAINING AND EMPLOYMENT
AUTHORITY
FINGLAS BUSINESS INITIATIVE
GET TALLAGHT WORKING CO-OPERATIVE
SOCIETY LTD.
PLATO

MGM CONSULTANTS

2 Holmeade House, Holles Street, Dublin 2
Tel/Fax: (01) 676 7043
Contact: Declan Garvin

MGM Consultants is a management consultant firm that provides services to assist small and medium-sized Irish companies in the areas of strategic and market planning.

Strategic Plan

By examining the "fit" that exists between a company and the industry in which it competes, MGM will compile an audit of the company's resources and potential.

Market Plan

In devising a market plan for a company, MGM provides services that vary depending on the company's individual requirements. A market plan includes such aspects as market segmentation, customer service, competitor strategies, pricing, product promotion, distribution, marketing information systems, and resources.

"Hands-on" Approach

MGM believes in providing direct assistance to a client company, without disrupting existing operations within that company.

An initial consultation with MGM is free of charge and involves the preparation of a proposal, and details of cost to the company involved.

Case Study

Company A, located in the mid-west of Ireland, had been in existence for six years. The company manufactures custom products for the home market, had increased its annual turnover to £2 million, and employs 50 people full-time. The company directors were concerned about the future of the company primarily in areas of market potential, management development, and declining profitability. MGM was appointed with a brief to perform an independent audit of the company, establish the company's potential, and to identify the key issues to be resolved.

MGM Consultants analysed the company's finances, markets, operations, human resources, and the owner's objectives. The primary findings were:

- *The company's growth had been achieved mainly through word-of-mouth; the company had no marketing function or marketing plan, and senior managers were unable to estimate market size, competitor turnover, or the extent of export opportunities.*

- *Senior managers were preoccupied with the day-to-day running of the business and were unable to devote sufficient resources to strategic planning. This had resulted in the uncoordinated management decisions in terms of market targeting and investment in fixed assets, as well as a constant rejigging of company priorities and failure to follow through on management decisions. These uncertainties resulted in a decrease in profitability as turnover increased.*

Without a clear understanding of its market, the company would not be in a position to overcome its short-term vision and develop a strategic plan. With this in mind, MGM prepared an initial marketing information system. The consultants were able to demonstrate that the industry was tangible, with discrete segments having unique requirements and characteristics. These characteristics and requirements were identified for each segment and the annual purchasing volume was estimated for each segment. This segmentation was used to analyse the company's existing customer base as well as that of the company's competitors; export opportunities were also analysed for each segment.

The market information, together with the independent audit of other functional areas, provided the company with a framework for developing an overall strategic plan. This plan allowed for a focusing of effort throughout the company, and led to superior management decisions, and, ultimately, to increased profitability.

In conclusion, MGM Consultants identified Company A as similar to many small and medium-sized Irish companies. Typically, these companies will be production- — rather than market- — oriented. Turnover for such companies will have grown organically with minimal marketing resources. The companies will have reached a stage of development where senior managers are preoccupied with the resolution of short-term issues, and the longer-term development of the company is jeopardised.

MONAGHAN COUNTY ENTERPRISE FUND

Courthouse, Monaghan
Tel: (047) 82211 Fax: (047) 84786
Contact: T.A. Golden

The Monaghan County Enterprise Fund was set up with the assistance and support of the International Fund for Ireland. It is a company limited by guarantee and its board is widely representative of business, industrial, professional, farming and local community personnel. Board members act in a voluntary unpaid capacity and do not receive remuneration, dividends or fees.

The aims of the Enterprise Fund are to assist and support SMEs and to create jobs over as wide an area of Co. Monaghan as possible.

The Monaghan County Enterprise Fund administers the following schemes for the International Fund for Ireland:

Revolving Business Enterprise Fund

Under this programme loans up to £15,000 at a low rate of interest are advanced to suitable small or medium-sized projects. The International Fund has committed £370,000 to this scheme, subject to the collection of matching funds to the extent of approximately £92,000.

Workspace Scheme

This scheme assists in the provision of suitable premises for small projects. The maximum assistance in any single case is £25,000, or 50 per cent of the cost — whichever is the lesser.

Community-Based Economic Projects Scheme

The purpose of this scheme is to encourage and assist local enterprise groups in engaging in economic projects for the benefit of their communities. The maximum assistance to any single group is £20,000.

The Workspace Scheme and the Community-Based Economic Projects Scheme are totally funded by the International Fund for Ireland.

SEE ALSO: INTERNATIONAL FUND FOR IRELAND
               LOUTH COUNTY ENTERPRISE FUND

THE NATIONAL FOOD CENTRE
(A DIVISION OF TEAGASC)

Dunsinea, Castleknock, Dublin 15
Tel: (01) 838 3222, Fax: (01) 838 3684
Contact: Carmel Farrell

The National Food Centre is a division of Teagasc, the Agriculture and Food Development Authority. It provides a range of technical and marketing services to the food industry. Established in 1987, the Centre, from its facilities at Dunsinea and Raheen (Limerick), deals with all foods, with the exception of milk products. The latter are the responsibility of the National Dairy Products Centre at Moorepark, Fermoy, Co. Cork.

Research Programme

The National Food Centre maintains its own basic research programme, while at the same time supporting the private sector with contracted cost-effective applied research. Research is carried out on a confidential basis.

Consultancy and Training

Consultancy is available at all levels at the Centre, including help in market research, compiling feasibility studies and R&D grant applications. There is an extensive training programme in the areas of hygiene, quality systems and legislation. Company training courses may be delivered on site or at the Centre.

Product and Process Development

The Food Centre can assist in all aspects of product and process development from factory design and recipe formulation to full-scale factory production.

Analytical Services

The Specialist Chemical and Microbiological laboratories offer a wide range of services, including compositional analysis, sensory analysis, shelf-life testing, and complete bacteriological assessments.

The National Food Centre aims especially to assist small companies and new entrants into the food business. The Information Service is available to help with any enquiries.

SEE ALSO: TEAGASC

NATIONAL IRISH BANK LTD.

7–8 Wilton Terrace, Dublin 2
Tel: (01) 678 5066, Fax: (01) 678 5949
Contact: Brian Leydon

As part of a Small Business Loans initiative, National Irish Bank has created a Business Development Fund of IR£10 million, offering loans of between £15,000 and £175,000 to the Small Business Sector.

Features

- IR£10 million fund

- Aimed at Small Businesses with expansion or development plans

- Variable Interest Rate

- Terms available 1–7 years

- A capped interest rate, which will apply until 30 September 1996 to provide protection against the probability of a rise of interest rates above 10 per cent

- Minimum loan £10,000

- Maximum loan £175,000

- No arrangement fee to apply

- A competitive current account fee package can be negotiated.

NATIONAL MICROELECTRONICS APPLICATION CENTRE

UL Building, National Technological Park
Plassey, Limerick
Tel: (061) 334 699, Fax: (061) 330316
E-Mail: MAC@UL.IE
Contact: Dr John J. O'Flaherty

The primary activity of the National Microelectronics Application Centre (MAC) is the contract development of new and improved electronic software, telematic and information products and processes for Irish entrepreneurs and industry. If an idea falls into one of these categories, MAC can help its clients to identify, select and develop a product by:

- Discussing their market opportunity, concept, product, process or service idea with them. MAC can give a good idea of what technology is appropriate and whether it is possible at the price, size and time that the market will require. These sessions are confidential, free of charge, and without obligation.

- Doing an on-line search of world databases to identify whether a similar product exists anywhere else, to identify potential competitors, and to identify whether there are technologies that might lead to a competing product by the time they get to market with their product. This usually costs no more than a few hundred pounds.

- Conceiving, designing and building a working prototype of their product or system, as part of a feasibility study.

- Developing and building production prototypes, as part of their main developmental stage, which is usually grant-aided. This involves designing for manufacture, and sourcing appropriate state-of-the-art components to give them a competitive edge. Adhering to standards and regulations, avoiding electromagnetic interference, etc.

MAC normally works on fixed-price contracts to agreed schedules, so the entrepreneur's exposure is defined and can be budgeted exactly to the grant application. However, MAC is willing to consider any arrangement that makes commercial sense for both MAC and the entrepreneur or company.

The shareholders in MAC are Shannon Development, University of Limerick and Forfás. The company's board includes directors from the Department of Enterprise and Employment, Forbairt, Telecom Éireann and private industry

Case Studies

During the past year, MAC has worked with 300 entrepreneurs in developing their ideas for high-technology products. The following are two examples:

- *MAC persuaded a person who had been made redundant to drop his idea for a technically over-ambitious product and to concentrate instead on a much simpler but viable domestic product. He has now completed a feasibility study, and a UK company is very interested.*

- *The Centre worked with a small Northern Ireland manufacturing company looking to diversify and move into the Republic. MAC took the company through the steps of developing an electronic/ software product and worked with the company's management to develop their initial over-simple concept into a viable product proposal.*

MAC undertook a total of 65 projects and EU work in 1994. These included the development of a fault-tolerant LAN-based, stand-alone fire-damper control system, Bookcheckweighters which detect missing pages in books, a Weighfill *system used for filling babyfood containers and closed-user E-Mail/Bulletin services for specific user groups.*

In the past year MAC has also completed a feasibility study on its own Weighfill HSHA *(High Speed High Accuracy) product.*

SEE ALSO: FORBAIRT
                         SHANNON DEVELOPMENT
                         UNIVERSITY OF LIMERICK

NATIONAL MICROELECTRONICS RESEARCH CENTRE

University College, Lee Maltings
Prospect Row, Cork
Tel: (021) 904 092, Fax: (021) 270 271

The National Microelectronics Research Centre was founded in 1981 to provide support for the Irish electronics industry. The Centre is based at University College Cork and undertakes research work in electronics and related fields in conjunction with Irish and European industry, third-level institutions and research establishments.

Services available at NMRC include:

- Design — devices, processes

- Simulation — circuit, device, and process simulation

- Evaluation — failure analysis and reverse engineering

- Fabrication — discrete devices, integrated circuits etc.

- Education — industrial education seminars, diploma and part-time courses for industry

- Consultancy — product development, process development.

Those wishing to use the facilities at the Centre should contact the Commercialisation Manager there and give a brief description of the type of work they want done. In situations where the work to be done is straightforward, a quote — including work description, estimated time-scale and cost — will be provided. Where the work is more complex, a meeting between a company's staff and the Centre's technical management may be required. This meeting should determine the feasibility of the project before either the company in question or the NMRC makes any commitments.

All work carried out at the Centre will be kept strictly confidential. (For further information on facilities at the NMRC, contact the above address.)

NATIONAL REHABILITATION BOARD

24–25 Clyde Road, Dublin 4
Tel: (01) 668 4181, Fax: (01) 668 5029
Contact: Dr Arthur O'Reilly

The National Rehabilitation Board (NRB) is a government body that provides and co-ordinates services to people with disabilities. It offers a nationwide range of services to people and organisations, including employers, in areas of training and employment.

NRB offers an Employment Support Scheme, which provides financial support to employers to encourage them to employ people with disabilities whose work productivity levels are below average.

How the Employment Support Scheme (ESS) Works

- An employer offers a job to an individual with disabilities.

- The NRB measures the individual's productivity.

- The individual receives the full normal rate of pay.

- The NRB pays an ESS grant to the employer to cover the shortfall in productivity.

Who Can Apply?

A company can apply for ESS funding if:

- It hires an individual with a disability

- It hires an individual who receives either a social welfare benefit payment or the Disabled Persons Maintenance Allowance (DPMA) from the local Health Board.

Grants are also available from NRB to assist in adapting a workplace or equipment to facilitate the employment of a person with a disability.

NRB will cover the cost of a sign-language interpreter for hearing impaired persons at job interviews.

(For further information on any of the services provided by the NRB, contact your local NRB Centre or the above address.)

NEW OPPORTUNITIES FOR WOMEN (NOW)

National Co-ordination:
Department of Enterprise and Employment
Davitt House, Adelaide Road, Dublin 2
Tel: (01) 676 5861, Fax: (01) 676 9047
Contact: Freda Nolan

Support Structure:
Council for the Status of Women
32 Upper Fitzwilliam Street, Dublin 2
Tel: (01) 661 5268, Fax: (01) 676 0860
Contact: Mary Donnelly

New Opportunities for Women (NOW) is a European Union initiative that promotes equal opportunities for women in the areas of employment and vocational training. The initiative is administered by the Department of Enterprise and Employment. The existing support structure is the council for the status of women.

The operational programme under the NOW initiative agreed between the European Commission and the Department provides the framework for NOW activities in Ireland. A number of priority areas for activity have been identified including:

- Advisory and Guidance Services

- Pre-training

- New Technology

- Upgrading of Skills

- Rural Development

- Childcare

- Enterprise Creation.

Innovative pilot projects with a transnational dimension have been set up under each of the priority areas. Community groups, voluntary organisations and statutory training bodies are involved in the delivery of these projects.

Under the Enterprise Creation measure, projects that assist women in starting their own enterprises are supported. Several agencies/organisations are involved in delivering activity under this measure, including Shannon Development, Parents Alone Resource Centre, CERT, Údarás na Gaeltachta, Tallaght NOW and LEI/First Step.

NORTHERN IRELAND BUSINESS CLUB

92 Lisburn Road
Belfast BT9 6AG
Tel: (08) (01232) 683 628
Contact: Mark Crossen

The Northern Ireland Business Club was established to provide the following for small and medium-sized business owners and directors:

- Free monthly networking events

- Low-cost workshops and seminars

- Informal lunch-time meetings to discuss problems etc. with other members

- A place to voice their opinions about matters concerning them

- An opportunity to network and increase business by selling products to other members.

At club meetings, which are held once a month, members are encouraged to give fellow members a short presentation on their business and products. Active buying and selling is encouraged by the committee, and a members' stand is set up at local business exhibitions that are open to the public and non-members.

Recently the Northern Ireland Business Club launched a North/South initiative, which will give members of the Club an opportunity to increase trade links in the Republic.

SEE ALSO: CO-OPERATION NORTH

O'CONNOR, LEDDY & HOLMES

Century House, Harold's Cross Road, Dublin 6W
Tel: (01) 496 1444, Fax: 496 1637
Contact: J.D. Leddy

O'Connor, Leddy & Holmes is a firm of accountants and business consultants, which offers national and international services to Irish companies. The firm provides a range of financial and advisory services covering:

- Accountancy — all aspects

- Taxation

- Corporate Finance

- Investment Appraisal

- Reconstruction and Insolvency.

For smaller businesses, the firm can help in compiling cash-flow forecasts for banks and grant applications to government bodies.

In 1988, O'Connor, Leddy & Holmes became a member of Urbach Hacker Young International, thus providing both the firm and its potential clients with greater international resources and expertise.

An initial meeting with O'Connor, Leddy & Holmes is free of charge and is usually of one hour's duration. There are no preconditions to the setting-up of this interview.

PEMBROKE CONSULTANTS

15 Herbert Street, Dublin 2
Tel: (01) 676 3727/676 3735 Fax: (01) 676 3736
Contact: Dick Blake

Pembroke Consultants specialises in business planning and funding for start-up or expanding Irish businesses. Fees are charged on a modular basis for bringing a business concept from viability assessment through to production stage.

No charge applies to the initial meeting, which is used to gather information about the promoter and the business proposal. Based on information available, the consultant will recommend appropriate action to progress the project. Where further information is required, a structured feasibility study may need to be undertaken, covering key aspects such as product evaluation, market research, competitor analysis, technology assessment, defining management requirements and funding. Pembroke Consultants will prepare applications and provide hands-on assistance in planning and carrying out the study to best effect. A standard fee rate applies, half of which may be recouped through the approved feasibility grant.

If the proposal is viable, Pembroke Consultants will assist in the preparation of a comprehensive business plan. The consultant will make application for grants appropriate to the project and assist in the negotiation of finance from banks or equity investors.

Pembroke Consultants will assist in long-term strategic planning and help the company to build business partnerships. Professional advice on corporate tax planning and accounting is also provided by the firm.

PLASSEY MANAGEMENT & TECHNOLOGY CENTRE

National Technological Park, Plassey, Limerick
Tel: (061) 333 644 ext. 2003, Fax: (061) 330 872
Contact: Judith Conway

Plassey Management & Technology Centre is a centre for education, training and development. The Centre organises open learning courses and day and evening courses. It has a small core of professional staff who liaise with organisations to establish training and development needs. Drawing from a panel of over 300 practitioners and academics, staff at the centre will:

- Analyse training needs and develop learning objectives

- Design appropriate learning strategies and materials

- Deliver effective training and development outcomes

- Evaluate results against objectives.

The Centre's four main areas of operation are:

- Open Learning Courses — enabling participants to undertake development programmes in their own environment, with learning materials, tutorial and counselling support provided locally by the centre

- In-Company Training/Organisational Development — programmes/ strategies designed to facilitate and progress organisational training and development goals

- Public Day Courses — short courses carried out to update management and technical expertise

- Evening Programmes — part-time business and advanced technical courses offering opportunities for career development.

New Business Development Course

Plassey offers a New Business Development course, which costs £235 and lasts 10 weeks. The aim is to provide participants with an understanding of the process of starting a new business, to enable them to appreciate the opportunities, as well as the problems, faced by the owner/manager in the ongoing business. The course outline includes:

- Definition of an Entrepreneur

- Environment of Entrepreneurship

- Characteristics of the Entrepreneur

- Market Entry — alternative strategies

- Legal Forms of Ownership

- The Business Plan

- Sources of Finance

- State and Other Support Organisations

- Franchising and Direct Marketing

- Criteria for Success

- Strategic Management for the Small Firm.

Case Study

Electronic Resources

Electronic Resources was set up in the Spring of 1991 as a sales and marketing consultancy service to the Irish electronics industry. The main thrust of the business is the sale of electronic components, which has seen steady growth since commencement. The managing director of the company, Paul Stephenson, whose background is in technical sales, felt that it would be appropriate to update his skills. He therefore enrolled with Plassey Management & Technology Centre in 1989 on the Open University Professional Diploma in Management. To date, he has completed the Effective Manager, Marketing in Action and Accounting, and PC for Managers modules, and he has found these to be an invaluable help in the setting-up and in the day-to-day running of his business.

PLATO

Small Business Development Programme
Bolbrook Enterprise Centre
Avonbeg Road, Tallaght, Dublin 24
Tel: (01) 462 0317, Fax: (01) 462 1240
Contact: Máire Hunt

Plato is an international small business network whose aim is to develop the strategic management skills of small business directors. The first Plato scheme in Ireland was introduced by the Tallaght Partnership and commenced in October 1993. Currently, 80 owner/managers of small companies in the Tallaght area are taking part in the two-year programme.

One of the unique aspects of Plato is the involvement of large corporations in a Plato region. In Tallaght, 11 "parent" companies provide counselling, advice and support for small business managers.

The Plato programme includes:

- Training in all aspects of strategic and operational management

- Small business development groups

- Advice and information from management in large companies

- Networking opportunities with other small businesses in Ireland and other European countries.

The Plato programme is oriented towards companies at least three years in operation, employing 3–50 people, and which display a clear indication of growth potential. Companies can be involved in any area of business activity. Participants must be the owner-manager of their organisation.

An evaluation of companies taking part in Plato in Tallaght showed significant improvements in business performance and management skills. Companies achieved on average, an increase in turnover of 19 per cent and employment of 24 per cent. All owner-managers in Plato in

Tallaght would recommend the programme to others as highly relevant, practical and cost-effective.

A number of County Enterprise Boards are planning to offer the programme to small businesses in their region, in 1995.

SEE ALSO: AREA PARTNERSHIP COMPANIES
BALLYMUN PARTNERSHIP
DUNDALK EMPLOYMENT PARTNERSHIP
THE ENTERPRISE TRUST
FÁS, THE TRAINING AND EMPLOYMENT
    AUTHORITY
FINGLAS BUSINESS INITIATIVE
GET TALLAGHT WORKING CO-OPERATIVE
    SOCIETY LTD.
MEITHEAL MHAIGH EO

POWERHOUSE

Pigeon House Harbour, Ringsend, Dublin 4
Tel: (01) 668 7155, Fax: (01) 668 7945
Contact: Paul Douglas

The Powerhouse, which is run by the Bolton Trust, has almost 6,000 square feet of office space to let, to accommodate enterprises. The monthly rental for desk space is £43.33. Office rental rates vary with room size from £90 to £322 per month. The charge is inclusive of building services.

Powerhouse is unique among enterprise centres in that it employs a full-time Enterprise Development Manager. The manager's role is to advise and work with companies to help them succeed. In addition, the resources of the Bolton Trust — namely 400 lecturers from the Dublin Institute of Technology colleges (Bolton Street, Kevin Street, the College of Marketing and Design, the College of Commerce at Rathmines, the College of Catering at Cathal Brugha Street and the College of Music) — can be called upon to assist in a company's development.

Powerhouse also provides reception, secretarial services, telephone service, typing, desktop publishing, mailshots, photocopying, business address, security cards and electricity heating — all priced on a usage basis.

SEE ALSO: DUBLIN INSTITUTE OF TECHNOLOGY

PRICE WATERHOUSE

Chartered Accountants
Gardner House, Wilton Place, Dublin 2
Tel: (01) 660 6700, Fax: (01) 660 7638
Contact: Paul Monahan, Growing Business Group

Price Waterhouse provides a broad range of services for entrepreneurs, including:

- Audit and Accountancy Services

- Corporate Financial Advice

- Taxation Consultancy

- Customs and Trade Advice

- Management Consultancy

- Insolvency and Reconstruction Services

- Secretarial and Share Registration Services.

The specialised "Growing Business Group" provides services dedicated to developing companies, such as:

- Assistance with the preparation of business plans and financial projections

- Advice on incorporation of a company

- Advice on VAT, PAYE, PRSI and other statutory requirements

- Assistance in sourcing finance

- Assistance with grant applications

- Advice on the optimal tax structure of businesses

- Assistance with on-going business planning and financial reporting.

There is no charge for the initial consultation.
Outlining their main objective as being to identify and build on

opportunities to develop their clients' prosperity, Price Waterhouse reprinted in 1993 *Doing Business in the Republic of Ireland,* and has example business plan and planning checklist documents available, free of charge.

OTHER ADDRESSES

Price Waterhouse
Gardner House, 1 South Mall, Cork
Tel: (021) 276 631, Fax: (021) 276 630

Price Waterhouse
Gardner House, Bank Place, Limerick
Tel: (061) 416 644, Fax: (061) 416 331

PROJECT DEVELOPMENT CENTRE

17 Herbert Street, Dublin 2
Tel: (01) 661 1910, Fax: (01) 661 1973
Contact: Margaret Whelan or Jo Ann Campbell

An initiative of the Dublin Institute of Technology, the Centre has been in operation since 1983. Its rationale is the fostering of entrepreneurial flair among Irish graduates.

The Enterprise Development Programme (EDP) is a practical support run by the Project Development Centre for graduates who wish to start their own businesses. The Programme is open to graduates of any discipline who have a business plan based on innovative ideas or new technology.

Two Enterprise Development Programmes are run each year, starting in January and July. Formal modules and training workshops take on average two or three days per month, allowing ample time for the actual development of the enterprise. The Programme is funded under the European Social Fund. Each participant is eligible for a weekly grant allowance, while the Centre provides the requisite desk space, phone, fax and computer facilities.

Training takes the form of hands-on experience in carrying out the product development, the marketing and financial studies of the project, and in the development of the business to a commercial stage. Each participant carries out work on their own individual innovative business. The Programme also benefits from a highly integrated mentor system, with weekly meetings designed to help the participants to avoid problems and clear any difficulties.

Participants are based in the Project Development Centre or at their own offices.

Applications for the Programme are invited in both May and November and should take the form of a two to three-page business proposal and a CV. Applicants must go through a rigorous selection programme and must show a commitment to the enterprise.

Since 1991, the Centre has been responsible for the launching of up to 90 innovative businesses and over 300 jobs, with increasing potential through further growth and spin-offs.

Case Study

Bia Nua Ltd.

Brian Murphy is the classic case of someone having a good business idea, a great deal of commitment and virtually nothing else when he first applied for the Enterprise Development Programme. A trained food technologist, Brian had worked within the baking sector in the UK for a number of years before returning to Ireland in 1992. He had successfully identified in the Irish market a niche for gluten-free products. He started the Enterprise Development Programme in January 1993 and was chosen as one of the four finalists for the Centre's fifth enterprise award competition.

During the Programme, he successfully set up and launched the Bia Nua company, and now has a range of products available on the market. The EDP Programme facilitated the establishment of this small, but expanding, business and provided the promoter with the necessary support and counselling to persevere with his idea.

SEE ALSO: DUBLIN INSTITUTE OF TECHNOLOGY

QUALITY ASSURANCE RESEARCH UNIT

University College, Galway
Tel: (091) 24411 Ext. 2222, Fax: (091) 29413/25700
Contact: Annette Dolan

The placement programme at UCG for Diploma in Quality Assurance participants involves the placement of trainee professionals in industry and services through the Quality Improvement Scheme. This placement scheme is a two-way learning process, involving the improvement of quality systems within the participating company and the development of the trainee quality professionals. Diploma participants attend lectures each Monday and work in a participating company for the remainder of the working week.

Diploma participants are graduates in science and engineering. The programme emphasises the practical aspects of Quality Assurance and Total Quality Management, covering the technological and managerial aspects of quality, by means of formal lectures and tutorial sessions. All participants of the course are required to undertake a quality-related project. (Further information relating to this course can be obtained from the above address.)

REGIONAL TECHNICAL COLLEGE, GALWAY

Dublin Road, Galway,
Tel: (091) 753 161, Fax: (091) 751107
Contact: Andrew D'Arcy

Regional Technical College, Galway established a Research and Consultancy Unit in 1984 to encourage the development and growth of existing businesses and to support initiatives in enterprise projects in the region. This Unit currently provides assistance to initiatives in the following five areas:

- Engineering

- Science

- Hotel and Catering

- Business Studies

- Art and Design.

A number of assignments carried out by the Unit have been in the area of enterprise development, including courses under the EUROFORM and NOW programmes to help individuals and groups to establish themselves.

The College has a large professional staff and the Research and Consultancy Unit has access to college facilities for industrial and business applications. The Unit provides services for the "start-up" phase and for the ongoing development of business.

For the entrepreneur just starting up in business, the Unit offers:

- Enterprise Development Courses

- Feasibility Studies

- Market Research

- Prototype Samples Development

- Draughting for Patenting

- Draughting for Production

- Product Design

- Computer Software Development.

For established business, in addition to the above list, the Unit can help with:

- Quality Control

- Production Planning

- Training, etc.

RTC Galway runs a range of courses, which are open to the public and which are relevant for business and industry.

REGISTRAR OF FRIENDLY SOCIETIES

Ship Street Gate, Dublin Castle, Dublin 2
Tel: (01) 661 4333, Fax: (01) 679 5226
Contact: Pat Corcoran

A co-operative society can be formed by any group of seven or more people over the age of 18, and can be registered with the Registrar of Friendly Societies. The advantage of registration is limited liability. Moreover, state grant applications and banks often require a co-operative to register. If a co-operative applies for registration through one of the organisations listed below, and avails of its model rules, the fee will be approximately £240–£500. However, if a co-operative wishes to submit its own rules, then the Registrar of Friendly Societies will register the society for £400.

The following organisations have model rules for co-operatives that have been approved by the Registrar of Friendly Societies for use by those wishing to form a co-operative. A reduced registration fee applies when the society's model rules are used, though a small fee for their use is also charged. Copies of the co-operative's rules, when approved by the Registrar, must be made available to members of the society at a cost not exceeding 5p. The organisations to which a society may become affiliated are:

- Co-operative Development Society Ltd. — 5 Fitzwilliam Place, Dublin 1, Tel: (01) 678 9660.

- Irish Co-operative Society Ltd. — Plunkett House, 84 Merrion Square, Dublin 2, Tel: (01) 676 4783/6.

- National Association of Building Co-operatives Ltd. — 84 Merrion Square, Dublin 2, Tel: (01) 661 2877 / 668 2241.

As soon as a society is registered, or before that date, it is advisable that a public auditor should be contacted for advice on the books that it will be necessary to keep for the society's records and accounts. A public auditor must be elected at each annual meeting of the society in accordance with the Acts.

Note: An individual shareholding in the society is limited by statute to £6,000, except for "agricultural" or "fishing" societies where the limit is £100,000. (A registered society being a member of another society may have a holding greater than these limits in that society.)

SEE ALSO: CENTRE FOR CO-OPERATIVE STUDIES
FÁS CO-OPERATIVE DEVELOPMENT UNIT
IRISH LEAGUE OF CREDIT UNIONS

REGISTRY OF BUSINESS NAMES

Lower Castle Yard, Dame Street, Dublin 2
Tel: (01) 661 4222 Ext. 4206, Fax: (01) 679 5254
Contact: Marian O'Connell

When starting in business, entrepreneurs have a choice of five main types of business entity through which to conduct their enterprise. The forms of application for the relevant business entities are:

- Sole trader — RBN1

- Partnership — RBN1A

- Limited company — RBN1B

- Unlimited company — RBN1C

- Co-operative.

Whichever option is chosen, entrepreneurs are obliged by law to register their company with the Registry of Business Names, or the relevant body in the case of co-operatives, if any individual or partnership or any body corporate carries on a business under a name other than their own names without any addition thereto. Specifically it is required of:

- An individual who uses a business name that differs in any way from their true surname

- A firm that uses a business name that differs in any way from the true names of all partners who are individuals and the corporate names of all partners that are bodies corporate

- A company that uses a business name that differs in any way from its full corporate name

- A person whose business is publishing a newspaper.

However, registration does not give protection against the duplication of the name. Nor does registration imply that the name will necessarily prove acceptable subsequently as a company name. Registration also does not authorise the use of the name if its use could be prohibited for other reasons. It should not for instance be taken as an indication that no rights (e.g. trade marks rights) exist in the name.

No comparison is made by the registrar with the Trade Marks Index or the Company Index or Business Names Register. It is advisable to investigate the possibility of others having rights in the name that it is proposed to use before incurring expenditure on business stationery, etc. (Enquiries regarding trade marks should be addressed to: Controller, Patents Office, 45 Merrion Square, Dublin 2, Tel: (01) 661 4144.)

Both the Company Index and the Business Names Register, containing, respectively, an alphabetic list of all registered companies and a list of all business names in the state, have been reproduced on microfiche. The fiche may be inspected at the Companies Office during office opening hours (10.00 a.m. – 4.30 p.m.). Staff are at lunch from 1.00 p.m. to 2.15 p.m. — the office is still open to the public during this time. Alternatively, the microfiche may be purchased.

REVENUE COMMISSIONERS

Dublin Castle, Dublin 2
Tel: (01) 679 2777, Fax: (01) 679 2035
Contact: Mary Casey

The Revenue Commissioners have a single Registration Form — Form TR1 for individuals and Form TR2 for companies — which is used to enable registration for Income Tax, Corporation Tax, VAT and Employers' PAYE/PRSI — in a single operation. In addition, the forms can be used to register an established enterprise for any of these taxes. The completed form must be returned to the local tax office or, in the case of Dublin and its surrounding counties (Meath, Kildare, Wicklow and parts of Louth, Westmeath and Offaly), to Taxes Central Registration Office (see below for address).

Registering for Corporation Tax

Every company is obliged to supply specified information to the Revenue Commissioners within 30 days of commencement of trading, whether or not it is requested to do so. This is a requirement of Section 141, Corporation Tax Act, 1976.

In practice, the Revenue Commissioners are notified by the Registrar of Companies that a new company has been incorporated. This means that the company will then be sent a Form 11FCRO with an accompanying explanatory letter. This Form must be completed and returned immediately to the local tax office or, in the case of Dublin and its surrounding counties, to Taxes Central Registration Office (see below for addresses). The Tax Registration Form TR2 can be used instead of the Form 11FCRO.

Obligations to File a Company Tax Return

Self-assessment legislation requires a company to file a tax return for its accounting period, whether or not requested to do so by the Inspector of Taxes. While the period covered by accounts may be longer than 12 months, an accounting period for tax purposes may not exceed 12 months. The tax on the company's profits is due six months after the end of the accounting period. The tax return must be filed within nine months of the end of the accounting period. Failure to file in time leads to the tax charge being increased by 10 per cent and/or certain reliefs being restricted by 50 per cent.

Registering for VAT

A business must be registered for VAT (which means that VAT must be charged on all sales, but a business may recover VAT charged to it) when its turnover exceeds, or is likely to exceed the following limits:

- Goods — £40,000

- Services — £20,000.

Tax Relief on Seed Capital

The Finance Act, 1993, introduced an innovative scheme, which will repay income tax previously paid to people leaving employment to start their own businesses. In the year of starting their business, qualifying individuals may claim back the tax paid in respect of up to £25,000 of income in each of the three of the previous five tax years. This means that up to £36,000 may be available. (Accountants and local tax offices can provide further details.)

A proposal was announced in the Budget on 8 February 1995 to increase the level of total investment that qualifies for relief from £75,000 to £125,000, allowing the investment to be made in 2 stages over three years.

OTHER REVENUE ADDRESSES

Taxes Central Registration Office (TCRO)
Árus Brugha, 9–15 Upper O'Connell Street, Dublin 2
Tel: (01) 874 6821, Fax: (01) 874 6078

Office of the Revenue Commissioners
VAT & Indirect Taxes Policy & Legislation Division
Castle House, South Great George's Street, Dublin 2
Tel: (01) 679 2777, Fax: (01) 671 8653

Office of the Accountant General and PAYE, Income Tax and
VAT (Unregistered Traders) Repayments,
Government Offices
Kilrush Road, Ennis, Co. Clare
Tel: (065) 41200/ (01) 677 4211, Fax: (065) 41366/40394

P35 Section
Revenue Office, Government Offices
Nenagh, Co. Tipperary.
Tel: (067) 33533 / (01) 677 4211, Fax: (067) 32371

Office of the Collector General and General Administration
St Martin's House, Waterloo Road, Dublin 4
Tel: (01) 668 8666, Fax: (01) 668 6039 / 668 7299

Other sections of the Collector-General's
VAT Collection and enquiries
4th Floor, 4–5 Harcourt Road, Dublin 2
Tel: (01) 478 4111, Fax: (01) 475 3751

VAT Repayments (Registered Traders)
Shelbourne House, Shelbourne Road, Dublin 4
Tel: (01) 660 6111, Fax: (01) 668 2188

Payments to the Collector-General
Apollo House, Tara Street, Dublin 2
Tel: (01) 671 6998 Fax: (01) 679 8224

Office of the Chief Inspector of Taxes
Setanta Centre, Nassau Street, Dublin 2
Tel: (01) 671 6777, Fax: (01) 671 6668

Dublin Tax District (Self-employed)
1 Lower Grand Canal Street, Dublin 2
Tel: (01) 661 6444, Fax: (01) 661 8956

Dublin Tax District (Corporation Tax)
Lansdowne House, Lansdowne Road, Dublin 4
Tel: (01) 668 9400, Fax: (01) 668 6512 / 668 5502

*The following sections of the Collector-General's office
are based at*
Sarsfield House
Francis Street, Limerick
Tel: (061) 310 310 / (01) 677 4211, Fax: (061) 312 500:

Annual Collection Section (PAYE/PRSI)
Employers' PAYE/PRSI Monthly Collection
Employers' PAYE/PRSI Instalments
Employers' PAYE/PRSI Solicitor/Sheriff Enforcement
Tax Clearance
Income Tax
Corporation Tax
Capital Gains Tax
Contractors' Withholding Tax (Relevant Contracts)
Sheriff/Solicitor Enforcement

SAINT PAUL'S AREA DEVELOPMENT ENTERPRISE LTD.

St Paul's, North King Street, Dublin 7
Tel: (01) 677 1026, Fax: (01) 677 1558
Contact: Ken Price

Saint Paul's Area Development Enterprise Ltd. (SPADE) opened in 1990 in the former St Paul's Church.

There are three floors with about 6,200 square feet of letting space. The average workshop unit ranges from 150 to 400 square feet. A tenant's licence fee (rent) and service charge includes access to in-house secretarial services, central reception facility, fire insurance on buildings, use of the conference room, off-street car parking, waste disposal etc.

Space is available on a monthly renewable licence. Current licence rates are £6.50 per square foot per annum for a standard unit and £8.50 for a food unit, plus VAT at 21 per cent in both cases.

Eight purpose-built food manufacturing units have also been constructed on an adjacent site. These consist of a 400-square-foot food-preparation area and a 100-square-foot dedicated store. This specification includes a double-bowl catering-style sink, extraction canopy, centre floor drain etc. These units, for which tenants have their own key, cost £500 per month plus VAT.

SHANNON DEVELOPMENT

Town Centre, Shannon, Co. Clare
Tel: (061) 361 555, Fax: (061) 361 903

Shannon Development is the Regional Development Agency responsible for the economic development of the Shannon Region. This region encompasses Counties Clare, Limerick, North Tipperary, West and Southwest Offaly, and North Kerry.

As a Regional Development Agency (the only one of its kind in Ireland), the company is engaged in the integrated development of industry and tourism throughout the region.

In carrying out its industrial development mandate, the company is responsible for the development of indigenous industry throughout the region, all industry operating within the Shannon Free Zone and aviation-related industry in the greater Shannon area.

It is also responsible for the development of Eurotechnopole — an initiative to encourage the smaller Japanese manufacturing companies to set up at the National Technological Park, Limerick. Through its subsidiary company, the National Technological Park Plassey Ltd., the company is responsible for the infrastructural development of the National Technological Park at Plassey — a 650-acre site, with the University of Limerick at its core.

The development of the Shannon Estuary is also the responsibility of Shannon Development and is promoted internationally by the company in conjunction with IDA Ireland.

Details of Support Services Available to Small Indigenous Companies and the Format for the Submission of Business Plans
Shannon Development provides incentives and support programmes for both new and established firms. Incentive programmes include:

- Feasibility-study grant

- Employment grant

- Capital investment grant

- Employee training grant

- Enterprise Development Programme
- Technology acquisition/Joint venture/Licensing grant
- Management development grant
- Research and development grant
- The Early-Start Technology Fund
- Mentor grant
- Rent subsidies.

Support programmes include:

- Advice
- Business/Workspace centres
- Various entrepreneurship programmes
- Start Programme
- Food Business Innovation Programme
- Enterprise Centres/Industrial Estate
- The Innovation Centre
- Limerick Food Centre
- Natural resources and organic-farming development programmes
- Project-development programmes
- European Information Centre.

Before making an application to Shannon Development, project promoters with either an industrial or a tourism project idea are advised to meet and discuss their business proposals with a Shannon Development Executive in the relevant area. Promoters must then submit a formal application for support, which must meet the approval of Shannon Development's Industrial Development Grants Committee. Grant payment or payment of the support package is then made to the project promoter.

Tourism Grants

The European Regional Development Fund (1994–1999) provides assistance to the private sector for investment in product-related, infrastructural work and also helps in the provision and development of amenities aimed at attracting additional tourism revenue to Ireland. Projects in the Shannon region are administered by Shannon Development.

Grants range from 10 per cent to 50 per cent of eligible expenditure on projects such as sailing, equestrian, cruising, angling, water, field and adventure sports, golf, language/traditional-craft learning, theme parks, leisure facilities, conference facilities, historic houses, castles, gardens and interpretative centres. Land and building acquisition costs are not eligible.

The Agri-Tourism Grants Programme

The Agri-Tourism Grants Programme is part of the Operational Programme for Agriculture, Rural Development and Forestry, promoted and administered in the Shannon region by Shannon Development on behalf of the Department of Agriculture, Food and Forestry.

The Grants Programme provides grant-aid towards the cost of providing facilities that will enhance the attractiveness of the area for tourists and meet clearly-identified tourist demand.

Grants to a maximum of 50 per cent towards leisure and accommodation facilities may be available to groups. A group may qualify for aid on investment, subject to a maximum investment ceiling of £250,000 per group during the lifetime of the scheme. Aid will be given only where at least 50 per cent of the investment undertaken is on-farm.

Grants to a maximum of 50 per cent towards leisure, and 20 per cent towards accommodation, are available, when such investment is part of a larger investment in tourist facilities. Investment must be on-farm. Farmers and rural dwellers are eligible for projects such as fishing, sailing, horse-riding, pony-trekking, walking, cycling, golfing amenities, farm museums, interpretative centres, visitor farms, theme farms and viewing facilities for traditional crafts.

The following grants are administered by Shannon Development in the Shannon region:

Employment Grants

Available to companies planning to start-up or to increase employment. Grants range between £4,000 (for projects with less than 15 employees) and £9,000 (for projects with more than 15 employees) per new job created, depending on the industrial sector involved. Half is paid on recruitment, the balance after six months' employment.

Feasibility Grants

To encourage companies to investigate new products or processes, grants of up to 50 per cent of eligible expenditure (for example, salaries, travel costs, development of product prototypes, consultants' fees, etc.) are available up to a maximum of £15,000 per study. The following feasibility studies qualify:

- Market research

- Negotiations with potential joint-venture partners

- Negotiation of manufacturing licences

- Assessment of suitable plant, equipment and building requirements

- Sourcing raw materials

- Preparation of costing and financial projections

- Assessment of manufacturing processes involved.

Applications must be made prior to commencing the feasibility study, while grants are paid on completion of the study.

Capital Grants

On plant and equipment, plus industrial rent reduction for up to 5 years. (Note: Projects may receive one grant type only — either employment grants or capital grants.)

Rent Subsidies

Typically in the range 25–40 per cent up to 5 years.

Interest Subsidies and/or Loan Guarantees

Available, in exceptional cases, in lieu of capital grants on new loans for fixed-asset investments.

Product and Process Development Grants

Jointly administered by Shannon Development and Forbairt, these grants are available to enable companies to acquire new technology and/or products. Grants of up to 50 per cent are available for new product research. Grants of up to 30 per cent are available for process research.

Management Development Programme

To assist firms in strengthening their management capabilities and structures, a modular series of management development programmes is available. The modules focus on:

- Record and management information systems (MIS)

- Business planning

- Strategic planning

- Strengthening the management team.

Training Grants

Grants of up to 100 per cent of the agreed cost are available for operatives in significant start-up projects, for small manufacturers planning to employ more than 15 people if they can demonstrate that they have the ambition and the opportunity to grow in terms of staff numbers.

Enterprise Development Programme

Offers the same range of incentives for new projects as already listed. The programme is aimed at experienced managers, academics and professionals who have the necessary experience and qualifications to establish and run a substantial successful new business. Promoters should be employed as professionals or at middle-to-senior-management levels in the public or private sectors. Other eligible people include Irish citizens working abroad and non-Irish residents in Ireland for at least two years. Projects should be internationally-traded and/or involve a substantial degree of import substitution.

In addition to the Capital Investment or Employment Grant Package, the Enterprise Development Programme offers loan interest subsidies and loan guarantees on working capital loans. Shannon Development may also invest in selected firms through equity participation. Participants in the Programme may undertake a significant amount of project development work at the Innovation Centre, located at the National Technological Park, Plassey, Castletroy, Limerick, or the Limerick Food Centre.

Mentor Programme

Links small businesses with experienced business people who are willing to act as mentors on a short-term basis, to assist the businesses in identifying and overcoming the problems and obstacles that limit their ability to grow. Mentors are not professional business consultants. They neither become actively involved in day-to-day management nor assume the role of an executive in the business. Mentors help to identify and solve problems in the following areas:

- General management

- Corporate organisation

- Strategic planning

- Financial structuring

- Production planning

- Marketing.

New Venture Briefings for Entrepreneurs

These are held over a couple of sessions to cover topics such as:

- Developing a saleable technology-based product

- The venture team approach to business success

- Licensing, technology transfer and intellectual property

- Business format franchising

- Focus on international service businesses.

Research and Development Grants

Grants of up to 50 per cent of eligible expenditure, subject to a maximum grant of £25,000 per project, are offered to cover the cost of salaries, travel expenses, overhead charges, technical consultancy fees, materials and prototype moulds and purchase, rent or lease of sites, premises and equipment, where relevant to research and development costs. The R&D project must involve a reasonable level of innovation relative to the firm's current level of technology. The product must be manufactured within the state and the majority of the R&D work must be undertaken within the Republic. In the case of second-round R&D applications from companies, the R&D support is generally only given in respect of the firm's incremental R&D, and the level of support may also be reduced accordingly.

START Programme

This is an evening programme run throughout the Shannon region by Shannon Development, to introduce people to the essential elements of business formation and development. Topics covered include:

- Sourcing business ideas

- Business planning

- Project development

- State supports available to new businesses.

Early-Start Technology Fund

This fund is the seed capital investment fund of Shannon Ventures Ltd. The company was established by a core group of leading business organisations and companies within the Shannon region. The Fund provides seed capital for investment in selected firms involved in the development of innovative, highly technological, protectable products or ideas, which are either at a research and development stage or are suitable to exploit identified growth markets. Preferably, such investment would take place during the early developmental stages.

International Services Programme

The main categories of internationally-traded services that will be considered for support under the programme are:

- Data processing

- Software development

- Technical and consultancy services

- Commercial laboratories

- Administrative headquarters

- Research and development

- Media recording

- Training services

- Publishing

- International financial services

- Healthcare.

To qualify, projects in the above selected areas must generate sales revenue from export markets. Qualifying promoters have the option of an employment or a capital Investment Grant Package. Also available are technology acquisition/joint-venture/licensing grant, research and development grant and access to the Innovation Centre and the Entrepreneurs' Programme.

The Entrepreneurs' Programme

The Programme is developed and managed by Shannon Development's Innovation Centre and is a complete training-based programme, lasting six months and including consultancy. It is oriented towards the formation of venture teams by participants for the purpose of the development and launch of new, technology-based, export-oriented, indigenous businesses.

Company Development Programme

Shannon Development operates the Company Development Programme by providing direct consultation between Shannon Development and the company's management. Workshops are also used to discuss issues arising from the consultations and to formulate strategies. Plans are initiated and implemented through this process.

Sectoral Development Programmes

By identifying the market opportunities/barriers/threats to business development for firms operating in the chosen sectors, Shannon Development aims to develop the selected firms through a managed approach. Shannon Development devises and organises promotions, seminars and workshops for a variety of industry sectors including:

- Engineering and electronics
- Fashion wear
- Food and drink
- Natural resources
- Wood and furniture.

Advice

Shannon Development has regional offices in Birr, Ennis, Nenagh, Limerick and Tralee. Each of these regional offices is staffed by Project

Management Executives who provide entrepreneurs with advice on matters relating to project establishment, management and development, and state incentive and support programmes designed to assist in the development and expansion of their firms.

Food Business Innovation Programme

The Food Business Innovation Programme is jointly promoted by FÁS and Shannon Development. Based at the Food Business Incubation Centre in the Limerick Food Centre, the Programme deals with the key training needs at business start-up stage. Topics covered include:

- Entrepreneurial skills development

- Market research

- Advice on food hygiene and quality requirements

- Development of a new food product

- Financial planning

- Preparation of a business plan.

A training allowance is paid to participants during the project-development stage, up to a maximum period of nine months. For the duration of the Programme, participants have the use of the units in the Food Business Incubation Centre and the facilities/services of the Limerick Food Centre.

Project Development Programme

The Programme is located at the FÁS Training Centre, Raheen, Limerick, and is jointly promoted by FÁS and Shannon Development. It is also assisted by the European Social Fund. The Programme provides:

- Production/service workspaces in which projects may be developed from concept stage to commercial reality

- Access to a range of in-house equipment for developing and testing prototypes

- Office accommodation with access to computer services, telephone and photocopying facilities

- Advice and support from technical and commercial advisors.

- Access to investment capital funds for selected innovative projects

- Training allowance and travel/accommodation allowance where applicable.

A series of training modules is offered, dealing with entrepreneurial-skills development, feasibility analysis, finance, market research, production and the preparation of business plans. Participants are involved in the practical development of their projects:

- General appraisal of the proposed venture

- Prototype development and testing

- Technical, financial and market feasibility analysis

- Test-marketing

- Preparation of a business development plan.

The Programme is designed for:

- Individual entrepreneurs or graduates with a business or technical background

- Small companies interested in developing or diversifying their product range

- Community groups.

Participants are admitted to the Programme for a minimum period of 10 weeks and a maximum of 36 weeks. Applicants must apply in writing, describing the programme of work they propose to undertake in order to develop their product ideas. The following information should be included:

- Research undertaken on the project to date

- The steps proposed to establish the product/service

- The finance needed to back the idea to the stage of start-up

- The applicant's own business/work experience.

Natural Resources and Organic Farming Development Programmes
The Natural Resources Development Programme focuses on the following areas:

- Natural stone

- Industrial minerals

- Floriculture

- Forestry

- Bog-land products

- Aquaculture.

The Organic Farming Development Programme focuses on the areas of:

- Organic vegetables

- Organic milk

- Organic lamb, beef and other meats

- Organic crops.

The Innovation Centre

The Centre offers a range of facilities, services and supports, including:

- Forty small workshops and project incubation units

- Secretarial services (word processing, fax, receptionist and photo-copying)

- Access to financial incentives

- Project-development assistance on-site

- International consultancy work

- Advice or assistance on licence/joint-venture negotiation

- Training/conference-room facilities, including catering

- Close links with University of Limerick and the National Micro-electronics Application Centre.

Limerick Food Centre

The Centre provides modern facilities and infrastructure for food processors. Constructed to stringent standards, it assists occupants in obtaining EU and US export licences for their products. The Centre offers:

- Product accommodation, which may be adapted to the specific needs of individual firms

- Food Business Incubation Centre — food product development units of about 300 square feet each, which may be used to develop and test new products

- A Food Development Laboratory

- Food and Natural Resources Information Bank

- A fully equipped processing hall in which clients may undertake pilot batch production of their proposed products

- Network of overseas food centres, with associate centres in Europe, the USA and Canada.

Serviced sites are also provided for clients interested in providing their own premises.

Business/Workspace Centres

A business/workspace centre provides space in the form of workshops or offices. Overheads normally associated with running any business are shared by the centre's occupants, thus significantly reducing the costs.

Shannon Development has a network of business/workspace centres located at:

Clare Business Centre
Francis Street, Ennis, Co. Clare
Tel: (065) 20165/20166

Shannon Business Centre
Town Centre, Shannon, Co. Clare
Tel: (061) 362 422

The Tait Business Centre
Dominic Street, Limerick
Tel: (061) 419 477

Workspaces are located in Limerick city and county at Michael Street, Limerick (Tel: (061) 416 800 / 416 923), and at Kilfinane, Newcastle and Abbeyfeale (may be contacted through Shannon Development's Limerick Office — Tel: (061) 410 777).

Other Workspace Centres are located in Nenagh, Roscrea and Thurles and may be contacted through Shannon Development's Nenagh Office (Tel: (067) 32100/32692).

These Business Centres offer a recognised business address, receptionist, secretariat, photocopying, and meeting-room facilities. Specially constructed project incubation units are available at the Limerick Food Centre and the Innovation Centre.

Enterprise Centres/Industrial Estates

The purpose of these Centres is to facilitate firms whose space requirements exceed that available at the network of business/workspace centres. The centres are available for rent, so that firms do not have to tie up capital in buying or building industrial workspace. (Details of current rents/service charges are available from Shannon Development on request.) Depending upon site locations, industrialists may also have the option of buying some of these premises.

Wood Technology Centre

The Centre is a joint venture between the University of Limerick and Shannon Development. It is located in the National Technological Park, Plassey, Castletroy, Limerick. The Centre aims to develop technology-led, wood and furniture businesses in the Shannon region. Its workshops have modern equipment including CAD/CAM, to design, prototype and test new products. Firms may also avail of the University's undergraduate and postgraduate wood-technology students to work on specific projects. Facilities provided by the centre include:

- New product design and prototyping

- Development and application of machining technology

- Access to the Centre's database

- Research of new products, materials and technologies

- Research and development of the potential usage of Irish-grown timber, intermediate products and glulam

- Furniture-testing to Irish and international standards

- Training programmes on business development

- Development of new and modification/adaptation of overseas technologies for specific client firms.

European Information Centre

The Centre is based at Shannon Development's offices at the Granary, Limerick. It offers to companies:

- A single reference point on EU affairs

- On-line computer link to EU data bases

- Access to EU publications on policies, programmes and decisions of the European Union of particular relevance to industry.

Case Studies

Fashion Business Development Unit

To strengthen further the firms within the Shannon region's fashion sector, and to enable them more profitably to exploit identified markets, Shannon Development has established, with grant assistance from the EU Perifra Programme, the Fashion Business Development Unit at the Tait Business Centre in Limerick.

The Unit offers to firms in the region's fashion sector a number of programmes dealing with market opportunity identification and exploitation, product design, manufacturing and business-management skills development and market/marketing development, including a joint promotional programme.

OTHER ADDRESSES

Fashion Business Development Unit
Shannon Development, Tait Business Centre
Dominic Street, Limerick
Tel: (061) 419 477, Fax: (061) 414 315

Shannon Development, The Innovation Centre
National Technological Park, Castletroy, Limerick
Tel: (061) 338 177, Fax: (061) 338 065

Shannon Development, Clare Business Centre
Francis Street, Ennis, Co. Clare
Tel: (065) 20165/20166, Fax: (065) 21234

Shannon Development
The Granary, Michael Street, Limerick
Tel: (061) 410 777, Fax: (061) 315 634

Shannon Development
Silverline Building, Connolly Street
Nenagh, Co. Tipperary
Tel: (067) 32100, Fax: (067) 33418

Shannon Development
Brendan Street, Birr, Co. Offaly
Tel: (0509) 20440, Fax: (0509) 20660

Shannon Development
Ashe Memorial Hall
Denny Street, Tralee, Co. Kerry
Tel: (066) 24988, Fax: (066) 24267

SEE ALSO: FORBAIRT
                 LIMERICK FOOD CENTRE

SIMPSON XAVIER

Chartered Accountants
20 Merchants' Quay, Dublin 8
Tel: (01) 679 0022, Fax: (01) 679 0111
Contact: Colm Nagle

Simpson Xavier is a firm of chartered accountants that provides a wide range of services including:

- Auditing and accounting

- Corporate finance

- Corporate taxation

- Examinerships

- Reconstruction and insolvency

- Litigation accounting

- Personal finance and taxation

- Viability studies.

In addition, the firm offers consultancy in the following areas:

- Entertainment industry

- Family business

- Franchising

- Information technology

- Leisure and tourism

- Management and organisation reviews

- Marketing

- Recruitment.

Simpson Xavier aims to provide cost-effective accounting services and advice using a commercial and entrepreneurial approach. As members of

Horwath International, the firm applies auditing and accounting techniques that have been tested internationally.

Corporate Finance

These services are designed to support clients in achieving corporate
objectives, whether investing in new projects, carrying out rationalisation or re-organisation programmes, or in making an acquisition.

Taxation Services

Simpson Xavier's taxation services cover corporate taxation, personal
finance and taxation planning.

SMALL FIRMS ASSOCIATION

Confederation House
84–86 Lower Baggot Street, Dublin 2
Tel: (01) 660 1011, Fax: (01) 660 1717
Contact: Brendan Butler

The Small Firms Association (SFA) is a representative voice for small and medium-sized firms in Ireland and, as such, is regularly consulted by the Government, government departments, public servants, European institutions, banks and state development agencies, on matters that have an impact on small firms. The SFA is a non-party-political body, financed entirely by IBEC.

The SFA's primary objective is to promote the profitable development of small business in both the manufacturing and services sectors. The SFA develops public awareness of the vital role of small business in national economic development, through press, radio, television and public meetings. The Association aims to improve the competitiveness of Irish industry *vis-à-vis* Ireland's trading competitors, by providing advice, assistance and information on developments that may affect its members at national, European and international levels.

The SFA works to combat bureaucratic interference, red tape, excessive taxation and the burden of regulation. It provides business, economic, personnel, regulatory, technical and trade information, access to a range of discount services that offer firms financial savings, and a forum for small businesses to extend contacts and share information and views. Specifically, the SFA provides its members with practical advice and assistance on a range of crucial issues:

- Liaison with government departments and state agencies

- Industrial development policy

- National legislation

- EU directives

- Taxation — local and national

- Company law

- Economics

- Roads and infrastructure

- Supply of materials and services

- Foreign trade

- Industrial grants and taxation incentives

- Patents, trade marks and licensing.

Advice and assistance are provided on personnel and industrial relations issues, such as contracts of employment, discipline and dismissal. The Association will also provide:

- Advice on health and safety at work, including the preparation of safety statements

- Access to specially designed training and development programmes aimed exclusively at small firms

- Access to support services from IBEC's five regional offices in Cork, Donegal, Galway, Limerick and Waterford.

The SFA has a range of discount services available to members including the SFA Group Insurance Scheme, which gives advice on how to save on annual premiums.

The Association holds regional Management Development Workshops for small and medium-sized firms on a regular basis. It has published a guide to employment and social obligations and procedures.

Entrepreneurs can avail of the above services by becoming members of the SFA. The membership fee is dependent upon the number of employees and ranges from £200 + 21 per cent VAT to £350 + 21 per cent VAT. The annual subscription is allowable for income tax purposes. SFA membership is open to firms employing fewer than 50 people.

SEE ALSO: IRISH BUSINESS & EMPLOYERS' CONFEDERATION

SMURFIT JOB CREATION ENTERPRISE FUND

94 St Stephen's Green, Dublin 2
Tel: (01) 478 4091, Fax: (01) 475 2362
Contact: John McInerney

The Smurfit Job Creation Enterprise Fund was launched in February 1993 by Dr Michael Smurfit of Jefferson Smurfit Group.

The aim of the Fund is to assist in the process of job creation in Ireland by providing venture capital and other assistance to businesses that meet certain criteria.

The investment by the Fund is essentially in the form of a minority equity investment, with a typical equity stake of 20–40 per cent.

Other assistance is primarily in the form of management expertise, which the Fund will provide to interested investee companies. This assistance will not only be in the form of Board appointments, but a pool of expert managers from the Smurfit Group's Irish operations will also be available to help and advise investee companies.

Investment Criteria

- The equity investment range is between IR£100,000 and IR£500,000.

- The investee company must create a minimum of 10 jobs within the first three years of receiving investment.

- The Fund will consider investments from a wide range of manu-facturing and traded service companies.

- The Fund will examine each proposal on its own merits. However, investments in start-up companies will only be made by exception.

- The Fund cannot invest in companies that are in direct competition with Jefferson Smurfit Group Plc or its major customers.

- The ideal candidate for investment will have been in existence for two or more years, will have grown to 10 or more employees and will be in need of an investment boost to take the company into its next stage of development.

- The fund has invested in 12 companies to date. The average investment was £242K and the average equity participation was 27 per
  cent, ranging from a minimum of 5 per cent to a maximum of 49 per
  cent.

- The Fund has invested in a wide range of sectors, including computer
  software, plastics, precision engineering, furniture and pharma-
  ceuticals.

Proposals

The Fund welcomes applications and enquiries from companies located
within Ireland that are seeking IR£100,000–IR£500,000 in equity investment and that may fit the Fund's criteria.

The first formal contact should be in writing, by sending a Business
Plan to the Fund, together with audited accounts for the past two years
(if available), the latest management accounts and CVs of the promoters.

SOCIETY OF SAINT VINCENT DE PAUL (SVP)

8 New Cabra Road, Dublin 7
Tel: (01) 838 4164, Fax: (01) 838 7355

Although the Society of Saint Vincent de Paul is not an organisation that springs to mind in connection with enterprise development, following a change in national policy, it is active in the area of community enterprise. One of the Saint Vincent de Paul's many programmes is the Enterprise Support Scheme, which provides seed capital and business advice through a conference (local SVP branch). A conference can be contacted through the enterprise centres it assists.

There are seven SVP enterprise centres operating in the Dublin area. They offer free counselling to people intending to start up small businesses, followed by administration assistance and the letting of premises. Funds are obtained from the Society.

SEE ALSO: ACTION TALLAGHT

SOUTHSIDE UNION OF CARING COMMUNITIES ENTERPRISE SOCIETY (SUCCES)

Dom Marmion House
Sandyford Road, Dundrum, Dublin 16
Tel: (01) 706 7483, Fax: (01) 706 7481
Contact: Paul McNulty

SUCCES can provide funds to help small businesses to expand, in the shape of an interest-free loan of up to £5,000, or as a loan-interest subsidy. The Society also offers advice free of charge in the areas of accountancy, management, marketing and technology.

The SUCCES scheme is restricted to postal areas Dublin 14 and 16, and businesses hoping to avail of services offered by the scheme must be locally based or have strong local connections. There is no one type of business that SUCCES is willing to help. In the past the scheme has supported businesses as diverse as entertainment and manufacturing.

Following submission of a completed application form, the entry will be considered by the Board of Directors. Applicants are usually asked to meet with a director for discussion, and a decision regarding the proposed business will be made by the Board within three months of application.

STRATEGIC PROGRAMME FOR INNOVATION AND TECHNOLOGY TRANSFER (SPRINT)

119 Avenue de la Faiencerie, L-1511 Luxembourg
Tel: (00) (352) 46 55 88, Fax: (00) (352) 46 55 50
Contact: Daniel Routier

The EU Strategic Programme for Innovation and Technology Transfer (SPRINT), which aimed to increase the competitiveness of European companies by improving their innovative capabilities and by promoting the transfer of new technologies to SMEs throughout the European Union, merged with the VALUE programme at the end of 1994. The new programme will probably be named in the coming months.

The present programme provides *selective continuity* to measures carried out under the Third Framework Programme and introduces a set of new measures taken over from activities that were outside the Framework Programme, mainly the SPRINT Programme, but also the Thermie Programme.

In the following, the activities are grouped according to their main relevance for one of three objectives. As these objectives are interdependent, a given activity can nevertheless be associated with more than one objective.

Activities

1. An Environment Favouring Innovation and the Absorption of Technologies

a) European Innovation Monitoring System

b) Creating a financial environment favouring the diffusion of the new technologies

c) Regional actions:

- Regional Technology Plans
- Regional Innovation and Technology Transfer strategies and infrastructures

d) Science parks

e) Promotion of innovation management techniques (Managing the Integration of New Technology (MINT), value analysis, etc.)

f) Increasing public awareness of R&DT.

2. Establishment of an Area for the Free Circulation of Technologies in the EU

a) Examination of the barriers and obstacles to the free movement of technologies

b) Relay Centres

c) Network of technology transfer and Innovation support services

d) OPET network

e) Technology Transfer projects

f) Mobility of people in Technology Transfer, diffusion and tacit knowledge.

3. Supply of Technologies

a) Community information base on national sources of technologies

b) CORDIS + dissemination service

c) Methodological aspects and services in the field of protection and exploitation

d) Promotional activities

e) Technology validation projects

f) Accompanying measures: stimulation of technology transfer to LFR.

SEE ALSO: EUROPEAN COMMISSION

TEAGASC

Agriculture Food and Development Authority
19 Sandymount Avenue, Ballsbridge, Dublin 4
Tel: (01) 668 8188, Fax: (01) 668 8023
Contact: PR Department

Teagasc provides research, training and advisory services to the agriculture and food industry. It helps food firms, processors, manufacturers, merchants and agri-business firms, both large and small, with quality product development and market research needs. The facilities and scientific expertise within Teagasc are available on consultancy.

Small Company Support

Through the National Food Centre (NFC) based at Castleknock in Dublin and the National Dairy Products Research Centre at Moorepark, Fermoy, Teagasc provides pilot plant and extensive services to small food companies. Services provided include:

- Food and rural enterprise development courses

- In-service training and advisory activities covering food technology, quality management, processing techniques and hygiene

- Acquisition of new technology through research and technical development. Areas of special attention include food safety, product quality and product/process/package development.

The facilities available at the Product Development Plant at the National Food Centre and at the new pilot scale processing plant at Moorepark, enable Teagasc to undertake projects for clients.

Advisory Support

The Teagasc advisory network promotes and supports small business developments, in the following areas:

- Alternative enterprise

- Rural tourism

- Crafts

- Home-produced food products

- Organic farming.

The service can also help agri-business companies by bringing their message on product quality or the sourcing of raw materials to farmers, and by providing training or technical briefings for staff.

SEE ALSO: THE NATIONAL FOOD CENTRE

TIPPERARY SOUTH RIDING COUNTY ENTERPRISE BOARD

c/o County Hall, Emmet Street, Clonmel, Co. Tipperary
Tel: (052) 25399, Fax: (052) 24355
Contact: C. O'Brien

The procedure regarding the criteria and range of schemes available under the Tipperary South Riding County Enterprise Board is the same as with other County Enterprise Boards (CEBs). Particulars include:

Feasibility-Study Grant
Eligible Costs may include:

- Wages/salaries (subject to certain exceptions)
- Expenses such as travel and subsistence, postage, telephone, etc.
- Expenditure on prototype development
- Consultancy fees.

Applications must be made prior to the commencement of the study. Promoters making such applications should outline in their submission relevant work experience. The Board will look for details of the project — including expenditure details — in the application form.

Before making an application for a grant from the County Enterprise Fund, applicants may be requested to compile a business plan. Some details needed for inclusion in the business plan are:

- Background information on promoters
- Background information on the project
- Project detail/cost
- Project funding
- Job potential
- Benefits to promoter

- Benefits to community
- Competition — uniqueness of the proposal
- Market research
- Marketing
- Financial projections
- Conclusion — summary on why the promoter feels this project should be grant-aided.

Where required, a business plan should be included with the grant application. Finally, in making an application, promoters will be requested to outline how they expect their project to be commercially viable and self-sustaining without the need for ongoing subsidy after initial grant aid.

The following is a listing of a schedule of conditions relating to the offer of a grant from the Tipperary SR County Enterprise Board:

- Qualifying Expenditure: applications must be approved before the project starts.

- Balance of Capital: arrangements to be made for balance of capital provision.

- Equipment and Plant: only approved expenditure, which has been listed in the application and purchased new, will qualify for grant assistance.

- Buildings: planning permission (if required) must be obtained before commencement of any building works.

- Time Limit: the grant offer is valid for a period of 12 months and will lapse if not drawn down within 12 months of the date of the Letter of Offer. A fully documented claim for payment of the grant approved must also be received before the aforementioned date.

- Payment of Grant: the grant is paid only in respect of approved expenditure, with original receipted invoices supplied to the CEB. Grant-aid will be calculated on the net invoice amount after deducting the appropriate VAT.

- Insurance: grant-aided equipment, buildings and plant must be kept insured by the promoter against loss or damage, and if there is loss or damage, the entire insurance compensation received must be used to restore the equipment, buildings and plant.

- Restrictions: the grant-aided equipment, buildings and plant must not be alienated, assigned, sold or otherwise disposed of within five years of payment of the grant, without the consent of the CEB.

- Revocation: the CEB may revoke, cancel or abate the grant if:

  1) A receiver is appointed.

  2) There should be a material change in the proposal for grant application.

  3) An order is made for the winding up of the business.

  4) Any of the foregoing conditions are not complied with.

  5) Without the consent of the CEB, the operations of the business should cease.

- Repayment: if the grant should be revoked under any of the preceding conditions, the promoter must repay all sums received in respect of the grant.

- Records and Accounts: the promoter must maintain proper records and accounts relating to the business and must furnish the CEB with such information on the progress of the business as may be requested.

- Tax Affairs: the payment of the grant is conditional on promoters being willing to quote their tax number and confirm that their tax affairs are in order, and if necessary produce a tax clearance certificate. Where promoters do not have a tax number, their application cannot be considered until they acquire a tax number.

SEE ALSO: COUNTY ENTERPRISE BOARDS
DUBLIN CITY ENTERPRISE BOARD
LOUTH COUNTY ENTERPRISE FUND
MONAGHAN COUNTY ENTERPRISE FUND
WATERFORD CITY ENTERPRISE BOARD

ÚDARÁS NA GAELTACHTA

Na Forbacha, Gaillimh
Tel: (091) 592 011, Fax: (091) 592 037
Contact: Pádraig Ó hAolain

Údarás aims to establish and develop job-creating industries in the Gaeltacht regions of Donegal, Mayo, Galway, Kerry, Cork, Waterford and Meath. Údarás has grant and incentive schemes to help small and medium-sized enterprises in the Gaeltacht areas. The following grants are available:

Employment Grants

Rates vary from £3,000 to £9,000, according to skill-level and industrial sector. Half of the employment grant is paid when the job is created; the balance is paid when the job has been in existence for six months.

Capital Grants

Capital Grants are paid in respect of new machinery, new buildings or the refurbishment of an existing building. The normal maximum rate of capital grant currently payable is 40 per cent. In the case of certain food/fish-processing or aquaculture projects, assistance from the European Union's Fisheries Fund may be obtained up to a level of 50 per cent investment in fish-processing and 40 per cent in aquaculture projects. In such cases, a capital grant of up to 25 per cent may be approved by Údarás in addition to amounts from the Fisheries Fund.

Interest Subsidy

This may be paid to small industry projects where the total grant-aid is less than £100,000. It applies to agreed-term loan borrowings of up to £20,000. Under this scheme, 100 per cent of interest is subsidised in the first year, 75 per cent in the second year, 50 per cent in the third year and 25 per cent in the fourth year.

Rent Subsidy

Up to 40 per cent (or 60 per cent in exceptional cases) may be paid in respect of an industrial premises for a period of up to 10 years. This subsidy may be applied either to a premises leased from Údarás, if such is available, or to a premises leased privately.

Feasibility-Study Grants

At a rate of up to 50 per cent (maximum grant £5,000), these grants are available in certain cases.

Research and Development Grants

These grants are payable in respect of approved projects relating to product or process development. Grants of 50 per cent of research costs, up to a maximum of £100,000 or 60 per cent of the total research outlay, may be provided on direct material and labour, consultants, overheads, research and development, and buildings and equipment.

Training Grants

Training Grants can cover up to 100 per cent of agreed training costs and be paid in conjunction with employment grants.

Technology Acquisition Grants

These are payable towards the cost of a licence, technical consultants, salaries, R&D costs, etc. The technology must be capable of being produced in the state and must be innovative in relation to the company's existing level of technology.

Údarás also provides non-financial incentives, such as advice and consultation in English and Irish on legal documentation. Entrepreneurs can meet with Údarás na Gaeltachta at its regional offices if the project is a small business idea, or at the main office in Galway if the business involves overseas trading. Following that meeting, a business plan or feasibility study may be recommended.

OTHER ADDRESSES

Údarás na Gaeltachta
Teach IPC, Shelbourne Road
Ballsbridge, Baile Átha Cliath 4
Tel: (01) 660 7888, Fax: (01) 668 6030

Údarás na Gaeltachta
Na Doirí Beaga, Co. Dhún na nGall
Tel: (075) 31200/31479, Fax: (075) 31319

Údarás na Gaeltachta
An Daingean, Co. Chiarraí
Tel: (066) 51658/51417, Fax: (066) 51788

Údarás na Gaeltachta
Sráid na mBearaice
Béal an Mhuirthead, Co. Mhaigh Eo
Tel: (097) 81418, Fax: (097) 82179

ULSTER BANK

Small Business Section
33 College Green, Dublin 2
Tel: (01) 677 7623, Fax: (01) 702 5875
Contact: Michael Bradley

There is a Small Business Adviser at each Ulster Bank branch to help the entrepreneur to plan, to direct the promoter to other sources of help, and to explain the range of funding available from Ulster Bank. The Ulster Bank Enterprise Loan Scheme may provide entrepreneurs with the financial requirements needed for start-up costs, working capital, etc. and may suit manufacturers, retailers or those in the service industry
Ulster Banks requirements from the promoter will typically be:

- Business Plan, concentrating particularly on the areas of management, market research, marketing, productions/operations and finance

- Cash-flow and Operating Budget projections

- Management information systems in place (or planned) so that regular management accounts can be produced.

Ulster Bank Enterprise Loan Scheme

The loan is designed to provide support for those starting a business or expanding an existing business. The main features of the Scheme are:

- Repayments spread over 10 years

- Standard Commercial Rates (AA)

- Repayment holidays where appropriate

- No personal guarantee or mortgage on the family home required.

Other initiatives include:

- Term Loans/Loans — to cover capital expenditure in a business. The interest rate is variable and the loan can be used for virtually any purpose.

- Business Development Loans — the interest rate is fixed for the duration of the loan when money is needed to expand a business.

- SME Loan Scheme — Loans from £20,000 to £150,000 at Prime Loan Rate, for start ups or expansion. Fifty per cent reduction on bank charges for 3 years for new business.

- Commercial Mortgages — to provide long-term finance for purchase or development of business property.

- Leasing — available through the Ulster Bank subsidiary, Lombard & Ulster Banking, for purchasing equipment including vans, lorries or machinery.

- Debtor Finance — available through the Ulster Bank subsidiary, Ulster Bank Commercial Services, releasing funds tied up in debtors for cash-flow/expansion.

- Business Reserve Account — a deposit account that provides investors with interest and instant access to their funds.

- Franchising — Ulster Bank Franchising Unit offers professional advice and a range of services to the franchisee.

Ulster Bank Small Business Start-up Guide is a free publication for those interested in setting up their own business. It emphasises the importance of planning and contains blank business plans and cash-flow forecasts, with guidance notes on their completion.

In Control is a free pack of guides and worksheets to assist the small-business owner/manager with financial planning.

Small Business Digest is a quarterly publication, distributed free of charge to 4,000 business advisers and small-business owners. It contains information on small-business practices and initiatives.

(For further information, contact any branch of Ulster Bank or its Small Business Section at the above address.)

Case Study

Beeline Healthcare Ltd.

Winner of RTE's "Up and Running" programme in 1993, Beeline Healthcare is an Irish-owned manufacturing, sales and marketing company in the healthcare sector. The company manufactures and markets a wide range of vitamin and dietary supplement products for the domestic market and other world markets.

With help from Ulster Bank through its Enterprise Loan Scheme, the company was founded in 1988 to manufacture and distribute vitamin and dietary supplements. It has succeeded in gaining a significant share in multinational companies. The Beeline branch has become firmly established on a nationwide basis with listings in all the leading multiple groups — Quinnsworth, Dunnes Stores, Roches Stores, Superquinn, Supervalu, L&N, Centra, Londis, Spar — as well as many independent stores, chemists and healthfood shops. Distinctive packaging, coupled with the quality Guaranteed Irish label has ensured that the market share of the company has increased consistently.

UNIVERSITY COLLEGE DUBLIN
MARKETING DEVELOPMENT PROGRAMME

Michael Smurfit Graduate School of Business
Blackrock, Co. Dublin
Tel: (01) 706 8910, Fax: (01) 288 6108
Contact: Frank J. O'Carroll, Programme Manager,
Sean Dorgan, Assistant Programme Manager

Aims and Objectives

The UCD Marketing Development Programme was established in 1982
by Professor A.C. Cunningham to assist the recently qualified business
graduate to learn and develop in a practical business environment, by
working on real problems for client companies.

In order to achieve this, the Programme assists SMEs (ranging from
start-up operations to well-established manufacturing concerns) and
entrepreneurs with business ideas, in solving their marketing-related
problems and in developing their businesses.

The Programme

The Programme has been successful, not only in improving the understanding and operation of marketing within Irish industry, but also in
developing a pool of broadly experienced marketing personnel, well-
equipped to meet the changing needs of Irish business in tomorrow's
world.

It operates as a marketing advisory service and remains a unique
university/industry co-operative venture, functioning from its own
offices within the Michael Smurfit Graduate School of Business.

Client Companies

Clients come from both the manufacturing and service sectors of Irish
industry. While some client companies are quite large and well-
established, many are small and are generally without a well-defined
marketing function.

In having its own offices (and not having to work in clients' offices), and numerous marketing resources available to it, as well as the time that clients sometimes cannot afford to set aside to address marketing-related problems, the *Programme* provides a valuable marketing-advisory service to companies that have a genuine need for this managerial function.

The Work Method

Potential products typically commence with an informal discussion between a member of the Programme Management Team, graduate marketing advisor(s) and the potential client.

This leads to the development of a proposal, which is completed by the graduate marketing advisor(s) and closely overseen by Programme Management. This document defines the parameters of the potential assignment, the methodology, timing and an outline of the costs that would be incurred during the project.

Upon agreement between the client and the Programme to the content of this proposal, an assignment briefing document is prepared through the Programme's offices, confirming the exact scope and timing of the assignment.

This is agreed and signed by both client and graduate marketing advisor(s). It typically involves the graduate marketing advisor(s) undertaking a thorough analysis of the client's industry sector. This is followed by a careful analysis of the client company itself, leading to the agreement of the objectives, structure, timing and requirements of the work to be undertaken and completed.

Throughout the assignment itself, the graduate marketing advisor(s) maintain(s) regular contact with the client, through to report findings and recommendations stage. The work is at all times closely overseen by an experienced Programme Management Team.

Confidentiality

The relationship between the Programme and its clients is treated on a strictly confidential basis, including the name of the client, and the objectives of the assignment, the final report and recommendations. No piece of work is discussed with a third party without the express permission of the client.

The Cost

Participating companies and individuals are required to make a payment for the service, which is agreed in detail in advance of commencement of assignments. This payment will depend on the volume of work to be completed, timing and resources required to complete the task, and the size of the company at hand.

Base of Graduate Marketing Advisors

Besides the experienced Programme Management Team and support structures that the Programme can call on, the graduates are selected from all third-level institutions in Ireland and from established institutions across Europe. The graduates undertake a postgraduate Diploma in Marketing Practice while they are on the Programme and typically complete five assignments during their nine-month activities.

For a confidential discussion, contact Frank J. O'Carroll or Sean Dorgan at the above address

WATERFORD CITY ENTERPRISE BOARD

7 Lombard Street, Waterford
Tel: (051) 73501 Fax: (051) 79124
Contact: Fergus Galvin

The Waterford City Enterprise Board, like other Enterprise Boards throughout the country, provides Feasibility-Study, Employment and Capital Grants to persons starting their own business or expanding an existing business. The amounts of grant assistance available fall into the following categories:

- Grants of up to 50 per cent (subject to a limit of £50,000) of cost of capital and other investments

- Grants of up to 75 per cent (subject to a limit of £5,000) of cost of preparing a feasibility study/business plan

- Employment Grants of up to £5,000 (subject to a limit of £50,000) per new job created.

Grant applications will be considered for small manufacturing and service industries.

Further information and application forms can be obtained by contacting the City Enterprise Board either by phone or in person.

SEE ALSO: COUNTY ENTERPRISE BOARDS
DUBLIN CITY ENTERPRISE BOARD
LOUTH COUNTY ENTERPRISE FUND
MONAGHAN COUNTY ENTERPRISE FUND
TIPPERARY SOUTH RIDING COUNTY
ENTERPRISE BOARD

WATERFORD REGIONAL TECHNICAL COLLEGE

Cork Road, Waterford
Tel: (051) 75934, Fax: (051) 78292
Contact: Dr Erik Lunde/Dr Venie Martin

National Certificate in Business Studies (Small Business Enterprise Development)

Over the past five years, the Continuing Education Department of Waterford Regional Technical College has offered a series of short courses as a service for owners or managers of small business enterprises. These courses have provided a good working knowledge and practical skills relevant to the setting up and running of a small business in modern Ireland.

This is a unique course in that it has been designed specifically for adult students and will be delivered and assessed in ways that are appropriate to adult needs. It is fully accredited by the National Council for Educational Awards — giving it recognition as a qualification both nationally and internationally.

The course is designed in modules, so that each person can attend one course or several courses appropriate to their needs at a specific time. Credits for the individual modules can be accumulated towards a National Certificate in Business Studies (Small Business Enterprise Development).

Insofar as possible, assessment will be part of the learning experience (projects, case studies etc.), avoiding written examinations.

Modules include:

- Setting up a Business Enterprise

- Managing People

- Book-keeping

- Financial Management

- Selling Goods and Services

- Business Law

- Administration for Small Businesses

- Marketing & PR

- IT for the Small Business.

These modules are also on offer at out-centres in the Southeast Region. (For details, enquire at the local VEC).

WERKSAÂM IRELAND LTD.
(WORK TOGETHER)

Coolock Development Centre
Bunratty Drive, Coolock, Dublin 17
Tel: (01) 867 0488, Fax: (01) 847 9525
Contact: Ron Immink, BSB

WerkSaâm Ireland is a sister company of WerkSaâm Holland, a
specialist company in enterprise development, targeting mostly long-
term unemployed. Based on 20 years' experience in enterprise
development in Holland, WerkSaâm has developed a very successful
working method, which focuses on preparation before starting a
business, high-quality business plans and developing entrepreneurial
skills. WerkSaâm Holland has a success rate of more than 90 per cent (3
years after start-up). The normal drop-out rate of Dutch start-ups is 50
per cent after 3 years.

Enterprise Training

WerkSaâm Ireland has been set up to provide training in the WerkSaâm
method, which can provide advisors in Ireland with a successful and
structured approach towards assisting clients in starting a business.

Enterprise Outplacement

Outplacement is used by companies that are making part of their
workforce redundant. WerkSaâm organises outplacement programmes,
assisting those employees in becoming successfully self-employed.

Business Planning

WerkSaâm also helps clients to prepare high-quality business plans.
Based on their successful method, and in co-operation with Oak Tree
Press, WerkSaâm has published *Planning for Success, a Business Plan
Workbook for Start-ups* (Oak Tree Press, £7.99, May 1995, ISBN 1-
872853-89-7). This model helps individual clients to take all the
necessary steps *before* starting a business. The workbook can also be
used by financiers to judge the viability of a business idea.

WESTERN MANAGEMENT CENTRE

IDA Business Park, Newcastle, Galway
Tel: (091) 28777, Fax: (091) 28649
Contact: Berni Ferris

The Western Management Centre (WMC) offers a range of training and development programmes geared towards the needs of business owners and entrepreneurs. The subject areas covered include:

- Management Development

- Production Management

- World Class Manufacturing

- Marketing and Selling

- Financial Planning

- Business Planning

- People Management and Team Building

- Health and Safety Management

- Time Management.

Since the WMC was established in 1984, it has amassed a diverse range of tutoring staff with practical experience from a number of business sectors. The majority of the Centre's work is in-company assignments, focusing on the development and implementation of new production systems, materials and capacity-requirements planning, world class manufacturing, etc. Prior to the commencement of each project, specific objectives and targets are identified and agreed. The WMC team then works alongside the company to achieve the desired results. This service is equally valuable for new businesses, as many costly mistakes can be avoided at the start-up stage.

The WMC staff are happy to answer any questions about the range of services offered and to give a detailed break-down of the content and cost of each programme. A brochure is available, outlining the schedule of public training programmes and a profile of services.

WEXFORD ORGANISATION FOR RURAL DEVELOPMENT (WORD)

Redmondstown, Johnstown, Co. Wexford
Tel: (053) 46453, Fax: (053) 46456
Contact: Ronnie Melbourne

Wexford Organisation for Rural Development (WORD) is a voluntary partnership organisation whose members are representative of statutory agencies, agri-business, farming and local community associations operating in County Wexford. Its mission is to promote the long-term development of Wexford, in accordance with the wishes and aspirations of local people, and to mobilise individual and community resources in creating and assisting economic, social and environmental initiatives aimed at such development. It has already had over two years of success in promoting these aims under the EU LEADER programme.

Individual projects likely to be supported by WORD during LEADER II will exhibit innovative features and will be expected to contribute to product diversification or the attraction of customers from new markets.

The priority sectors most likely to attract support are:

- Agriculture

- Marine Products and Services

- Tourism

- Enterprise.

Case Study

The Taste of Wexcellence

"The Taste of Wexcellence" is a promotion that is being jointly organised and co-ordinated by WORD, together with a group of small food producers. The initiative aims to increase awareness and consumption of natural Wexford foods, and is being supported by retailers and food service outlets throughout the country. In addition to lifting

consumer support, The Taste of Wexcellence hopes to raise product standards and quality awareness among food producers.

Approximately £30,000 had been budgeted for the promotion, which was provided by participating producers and WORD. Leaflets, advertising, public relations, point of sale displays, in-store promotions and product labelling, carried The Taste of Wexcellence logo so that consumers were able to identify and purchase these products.

WOMEN'S LOCAL EMPLOYMENT INITIATIVES (LEI)

LEI Network Expert — Ireland
Contact International Limited
Equity House, 16–17 Upper Ormond Quay, Dublin 7
Tel: (01) 873 0711, Fax: (01) 873 0474
Contact: Patricia Brand (LEI Network Expert) /Jo-Anna Brand

The Women's Local Employment Initiatives Programme (LEI) is an initiative of the European Commission. It aims to promote female entrepreneurship, and thus combat women's unemployment in the community. Since 1987, over 1,000 women's initiatives across the European Community have been financed, and many times that number have received technical assistance.

The Women's Local Employment Programme is aimed at women in business, before start-up or in the first two years of business trading. Awards range from approximately 2000 ECUs to 10,000 ECUs, but it should be pointed out that there is a limited amount of funding available for the LEI award.

Eligible initiatives must demonstrate particularly innovative or creative characteristics. Projects in retailing, beauty care and liberal professions are excluded unless they demonstrate clearly innovative aspects. Two types of award are available, each supporting different stages of the business life cycle:

- Awards for the development of a business idea and compilation of a business plan for enterprise creation. To be eligible, the following two conditions must be fulfilled:

  1) The project must be innovative, (in terms of the product or services envisaged, the method of organisation of the activity, use of particular resources).

  2) The applicant must demonstrate that she has taken concrete steps to develop the idea (e.g. an initial market study, development of a prototype and/or support from local/regional structures for business start-up etc.)

- Awards to help young enterprises in the early stages of their development — this award is open to women, alone or in partnership, who have set up their own business, co-operative or local employment initiative, where management positions and the majority of jobs (or the equivalent in part-time posts) are for women. The employees' contracts and conditions of employment and the situation of the woman/women who created the business must comply with national law (in particular, registration with social security). Application must be made within 24 months of the official registration of the business. People can apply by contacting the above office. They will be informed of the necessary procedures and requirements.

In general, awards are restricted to enterprises that demonstrate viability and innovative characteristics, in specific fields such as:

1) Initiatives in developing sectors (e.g. new technology, environment, culture and leisure)

2) Initiatives in male-dominated fields

3) Rural initiatives providing a new product or service

4) Initiatives meeting the needs of disadvantaged localities or particular social groups

5) Transnational initiatives (e.g. joint ventures, import–export, international business services, etc.).

The LEI Network provides technical assistance to women setting up and developing their own enterprises, through:

- Information on sources of support available locally, regionally, nationally and at European level

- Advice in the development of business ideas and in business planning

- Assistance in completing applications for financial awards

- A network between women's enterprises across Europe, to promote the exchange of experience and business co-operation.

- Training and technical support programmes for women's enterprise, through transnational partnerships with enterprise and training and development organisations (there are equivalent organisations in other European countries to encourage links between organisations)

- Practical guides and materials as outlined below to strengthen the competitiveness of women's enterprise on a European dimension.

Publications/Materials

The LEI Network produces a series of specialised publications. These information materials and training tools aim to spread best practice, and support women in the creation and development of competitive enterprises, on an international dimension. Regular publications of the LEI Network currently include:

- *Guide to Better Business*. Produced annually, the *Guide* is a practical handbook to assist women in setting up and running their own business. *Guide to Export* (1992) and *The Generation of Business Ideas* (1993) are two other issues in the series.

- *Dossier*. Produced biannually, the *Dossier* is a practical tool to disseminate information, spread best practice and promote partnerships and business co-operation, in the field of women's enterprise.

It should be noted that there is a limited amount of funding available for the LEI grant.

Case Study

Maidensteel

Recent LEI Award Winners are Nemara Hennigan and Fiona Egan, two young workers in metal, trading under the name "Maidensteel". Both graduated from the University of Ulster four years ago, Fiona with a degree in furniture design, and Nemara with a degree in art and design.

Maidensteel was born in the garage of Fiona's flat. With just basic equipment, they began to produce zig-zag candlesticks and steel-and-fibreglass wall-torches. They got their first break when a Galway restaurant ordered 10 wall-torches. Shortly afterwards, they moved into a bigger workshop in Stoneybatter, and since then have extended their range considerably. Their products have proven very popular at the annual Mansion House Craft Fair.

SEE ALSO: FÁS CO-OPERATIVE DEVELOPMENT UNIT
NEW OPPORTUNITIES FOR WOMEN (NOW)
WOMEN'S BUSINESS DEVELOPMENT CENTRE